PRAISE FOR
JOURNEY INTO MOTHERHOOD

WHAT A WONDERFUL BOOK! It's about time someone told the other side of the story — that giving birth can be a time of peace, joy and beautiful memories. This collection of inspirational stories, along with the practical information that follows each one, is a "must have" for any expectant parent.

> — LINDA ACREDOLO, PH.D.
> AUTHOR, *BABY SIGNS AND BABY MINDS*

Every mother remembers her birth experience in vivid detail for the rest of her life. You'll delight in these glimpses into the heart and soul of birth. We share their convictions and praise their persistence in having the births that they desire for their children. *Journey* is a guide for women as they prepare for motherhood, and for providers to see what natural birth looks and sounds like. Thank you for sharing these powerful stories of natural birth and women's inner wisdom.

> — BARBARA HARPER, RN, DIRECTOR OF WATERBIRTH INTERNATIONAL
> AUTHOR, *GENTLE BIRTH CHOICES* (BOOK AND DVD)

Journey Into Motherhood will take its place beside *Ina May's Guide to Childbirth* as a book that should be read by every pregnant woman.

— DEEDEE LAFAYETTE, EXECUTIVE DIRECTOR OF
THE ASSOCIATION OF LABOR ASSISTANTS AND CHILDBIRTH EDUCATORS

Journey Into Motherhood is an anthology of pregnancy and childbirth stories that emphasizes the positive. In today's culture of fear surrounding childbirth, *Journey Into Motherhood* offers a much-needed alternative vantage…. The 48 heartwarming tales are sure to kindle the spirit with the knowledge that childbirth is indeed an experience to look forward to, and offers suggestions toward creating an optimum birth to suit the mother's desires and needs. Highly recommended supplementary reading for expectant mothers.

— MIDWEST BOOK REVIEW

With *Journey Into Motherhood*, Sheri Menelli has given us a wonderful collection of positive natural birth stories. "Ordinary" women, giving birth in a variety of settings, share their stories of challenge and transformation, empowerment and love, illustrating both the real possibilities and the immeasurable values of giving birth as nature intended. Read these stories and be inspired! Highly recommended!

— SUSAN HODGES, PRESIDENT OF CITIZENS FOR MIDWIFERY

The fact that we hardly ever hear an inspiring natural birth story fills the whole process with fear for many first time mothers. If we can just trade that fear for education and preparedness, I believe many more women would opt for a more natural birth experience. Menelli has provided women with a book that is both educational and inspirational. By reading these stories while preparing for birth, mothers can feel empowered by their decisions and know that others have gone before them and had a beautiful, natural birth.

— C.J. WONG, M.S., M.L.I.S.
EDITOR, *ORGANIC FAMILY MAGAZINE*

I first heard of *Journey Into Motherhood* at one of my last prenatal appointments. I asked my midwife if she had any additional advice for me to overcome some of the lingering fears and apprehension I had about the upcoming birth. She gave me the book to read, and it helped me tremendously. Each time I found my mind wandering in a fearful direction, I read a couple of the testimonies. The stories encouraged me and empowered me. I'm passionate about natural birth — it is the best way!

— JESSICA J. DASSOW

I can't recommend this book highly enough! It is truly amazing and reminds all women that we have power over our bodies, and that birth is a natural and wonderful process. This book is filled with amazing, joyful birth experiences, not the usual birth "horror" stories. I am about two months away from delivering my first child, and after reading this book, I feel truly empowered to make choices regarding the birth process. I know I have nothing to fear.

— KELLY A. HADSELL

This book is tremendous! The stories are heartfelt and awe inspiring. I recommend this to all of my patients who are preparing to have a baby or are needing a book to lift their spirit about womankind. It is beautifully arranged and the editor's notes are helpful for expectant moms. I relish my time with this book, looking forward to reading a few more stories every night. I can't wait for Sheri Menelli's next book. This is a treasure every woman should receive.

— KRISTEN BURRIS, ACUPUNCTURIST, M.S., HERBALIST

Inspirational stories, indeed!! Whether you are already planning a natural birth, or would like to but aren't sure you can do it —READ THIS BOOK. You'll then know, without a doubt, that not only is it possible to birth naturally, but that it can be an ecstatic experience.

— CAROLYN MADRID-BRAMLETT, CERTIFIED HYPNOBIRTHING EDUCATOR

I read *Journey Into Motherhood* and now long to have another child so I can experience a wonderful birth. I wish I read the book before delivering my first two children. There is no other book like this one. The stories are inspiring and give so much valuable information about the choices mothers have while giving birth.

— HOLLY PIERSON, TEACHER

I've read it all... and this is my favorite! I could not put this book down! I tried to save a story to read each night during my pregnancy, but I always read more! EVERY pregnant woman should read this book. It minimizes fear of childbirth and will actually get you excited about this amazing rite of passage into womanhood. There are so many ways for babies to come into this world. If you're pregnant, don't even think of not reading this book!

— LISA DRUXMAN, CEO OF STROLLER STRIDES

As a labor doula, *Journey Into Motherhood* is now on my list of required reading for all of my clients. Please join me in encouraging all pregnant families to have this book on their night table. Not just as women, but as an entire society, we need to stop scaring the daylights out of women who are venturing into this beautiful journey of motherhood. My hope is that every pregnant woman reads this fantastic book. It will prepare a woman for a fantastic birth, whether she chooses medication or not.

— DAWN THOMPSON, CERTIFIED DOULA

This book does need to be in the hands of every pregnant woman — more so than any other book on the market. It is women talking to other women — no agenda, no specific technique to sell. I have been recommending this book at all of my childbirth classes, and now I'm recommending it at the doula training workshop and the Hypno-Birthing educator workshops I have recently been teaching around the country.

— JENNY WEST, MIDWIFE, CHILDBIRTH EDUCATOR AND CERTIFIED DOULA

Journey Into Motherhood

Inspirational Stories of Natural Birth

Sheri L. Menelli

Carlsbad, California

White Heart Publishing
P.O. Box 235705
Encintas, CA 92023-5705
www.WhiteHeartPublishing.com

Menelli, Sheri.
    Journey into motherhood : inspirational stories of
natural birth / by Sheri Menelli. -- 1st ed.
    p. cm.
    Includes bibliographical references.
    LCCN 2004 105622
    ISBN 0-9747853-2-6

    1. Natural childbirth. 2. Motherhood. I. Title

    RG661.M46 2005   618.4'S
                                        QBI33-2103

DEDICATION

I DEDICATE THIS BOOK to this generation as well as future generations. May you never again have to hear another birthing horror story.

I also dedicate this book to my husband Ron, and our beautiful daughters Allison, Caitlin, and Lauren. Without the four of you, I never would have found the inspiration and courage to give birth to this book.

ACKNOWLEDGEMENTS

THANK YOU to all of the wonderful moms (and a few dads) who chose to share these beautiful stories. Your wisdom and words are shaping our generation, as well as future generations. I feel so blessed that I was able to be a part of your birth through writing and compiling this book.

My thanks also goes to Carolyn Madrid-Bramlett, Kim Wildner, Dee Nipper, Chantel Sicle-Kira, Darlene D'Angelo, Elien Alexander, Rendy DuRay, Dan Poynter, Holly Pierson, Barb Steffes and Challis Farley. And thanks to the members of the Pub-Forum newsgroup for all of your help and advice.

Thanks to Michele DeFilippo and the team at 1106 Design in Phoenix for the great cover design and typography.

With deep appreciation, I thank Monique Evers, Davis Ehrler, and KC Kohler for your continued inspiration and belief in me. Your tremendous support has meant more than you know.

Most of all, thank you Adriane Smith, my editor. Adriane, your elegant touch and professional expertise have done amazing things with the stories in this book, and your guidance has been indispensable. Thank you for turning a good book into a future best-seller. I'm overwhelmed with gratitude, so very thankful the Universe sent you.

Visit our Website!
www.JourneyIntoMotherhood.com

I RECEIVED SO MANY birth story contributions for this book—we couldn't possibly include them all in the printed version. But I couldn't bear to just cast them aside; they're all so special! So please visit the website for more inspiring stories of natural birth, including the story of a teenage mother and one from the Australian outback!

You'll also find pictures—lot of them!—of the births and families you read about in the book. Be a part of their births through the intimate images they captured on film, and share their most tender moments in a whole new way.

In addition to more stories and pictures of the families, the website connects you with a wealth of resources and information for the expectant mother. You'll find:

- Articles for expectant and new moms, including:
  The Top 10 Secrets for a Better Birth
  Breastfeeding tips
  Natural childbirth advocacy information

- An online community, where you can:
  Chat with other moms in a discussion forum
  Be a part of discussions with the authors of the stories
  Vote for your favorite story
  Subscribe to a newsletter
  Shop for pregnancy and birth-related resources, books,
    DVDs and CDs that were mentioned in the book
  Sign up for free gifts, booklets and bonus material

The website is also the place to send your friends and family when they're ready to submit their own story for our next book!

CONTENTS

INTRODUCTION

THERE WAS A TIME when I thought that I never wanted to get pregnant. It wasn't that I didn't want a baby; I was just plain scared of giving birth. At that time I had never heard a birth story that didn't inspire horror and tell of unbearable pain.

In my late twenties, after taking a few hypnosis classes, I discovered that it was possible to use hypnosis to achieve a painless birth. I was so excited! Now that I knew it was possible, I felt compelled to explore that option. Just a year later, I had experienced a nearly painless birth and was teaching that method to others. I haven't been able to contain my enthusiasm! I want to share my knowledge… I want to do everything I can to help women defeat the fear that has pervaded the subject of birth for as long as any of us can remember.

I have taught childbirth classes to hundreds of couples over the years and I have been continuously frustrated for my students. Every television show about childbirth seems to focus on and encourage that horror, pain and fear. Most pregnant women encounter random strangers who share unsolicited horror stories. Even on the Internet, when I go looking for stories of positive birth experiences, I am repeatedly horrified by what I read. Most women don't even realize that they are contributing to the fear and pain of others by retelling tales of difficult births.

More and more women are shunning the horror stories, actively seeking inspiration and evidence of wonderful, natural birth experiences. Women dramatically increase their chances of having a satisfying birth experience when they take responsibility for educating themselves, and creating a supportive team and environment before labor begins.

In support of this, I searched for stories of women who were committed to creating the best experience they could; stories of women who were really challenged as well as those who seemed to sail right through labor; stories that instill confidence and dispel fear, and strengthen the connection to our innate feminine wisdom. Birth can be an ecstatic experience of unparalleled joy; a gateway to the next chapter of womanhood; an experiential lesson in personal power and trust in the divine.

Each story in this book is told in the authentic voice of a mother, a woman who has completed the Journey and lived to appreciate it. These stories chronicle some of the most vivid days of a woman's life. Following each chapter you will find notes from the author, titled *A Mother's Guidance*, on the resources and practices she found most helpful as she prepared for and moved through her Journey into Motherhood.

Whether you choose a medicated or natural birth, this book is for you. These women will empower and inspire you, offering a deeper understanding of what the female body is capable of, and where the feminine psyche turns in moments of intense emotion and vulnerability.

The intention of this book is not to dictate how you should give birth; rather just the opposite—it was created to empower you to make your own decisions, even in the face of popular dissent. The decisions a woman makes about birthing her child are inherently, intensely personal, and what is right for one woman would not fit for many others. The book is designed to reveal the myriad of options, techniques and tools available to pregnant and birthing women, many of which you may not have heard of, so that you can have the kind of birth that YOU want.

Accept the words of these women as guidance, and take only what resonates with you. As many of them directly implore you, listen to your own inner voice on what is right for you and your baby.

Each person must make her own decisions, in collaboration with her healthcare provider and parenting partner. Some people may disagree with the decisions that some of the authors made, but each story offers a contribution to a larger understanding of the birthing process. Through these stories you will come to realize that it is only the birthing mom who can do the mental, physical and spiritual work required to bring a child out of her body and into her arms. Even when women are surrounded by the world's best doctors, midwives, nurses, doulas, spouses, friends and family members, each birth is, at some level, unassisted.

My dream is to see women demanding better care, and retelling beautiful birth stories instead of horror stories. I hope that in subsequent birth story books, I can include stories from women who read this book, were positively influenced by it and go on to have their own beautiful births.

So, Happy Birthing! May you have the birth of your dreams.

LIKE THUNDER RUMBLING THROUGH

BY KELLY CAMDEN

BEING PREGNANT brought me renewed vitality, but as every mother knows, there comes a time when you have had enough of being pregnant. Maybe it's your body's way of preparing for the separation that is about to occur. In addition to your own anticipation, there are the questions, the phone calls, and people dropping by with hopes of seeing you in labor. Your hormones are shifting and everyone wants to know, "HAVE YOU HAD THE BABY YET?" Maybe these social annoyances are nature's way of conditioning us for the patience we will need as parents.

It was August and hot, of course. I was pitting the forty pounds of cherries that I had picked from my favorite orchard. I needed a project to pass the time, because I was nine-and-a-half months pregnant. As I finished laying the fruit in the dryers, I began early labor. I had the typical stream of emotions. Mostly I felt excitement: *it's finally happening!* I had prepared our living room for the birth a month before with a birth kit, birth stool, and a variety of other things we would need.

Home birth is a common occurrence in rural areas of Colorado and many women hire a licensed midwife. My midwives, Suzanne and Jeanette, gave me such special care and attention throughout my pregnancy; I knew I could rely on them during my birth. In the last weeks, we had been in contact every day, either by phone or by home visits. When I called to tell them the good news, they assured me that they were prepared to come at any time.

Since everything was ready for the birth, I decided to go out to dinner. I was hungry and I figured this was my last chance to just sit and eat. Besides, my baby's grandparents had just pulled into town and I wanted to visit with them. It was sort of nice, but my meal and conversation were continuously interrupted. I would be in the middle of a sentence and suddenly trail off… losing my train of thought; another contraction. I was surprised that they kept coming so regularly. The grandparents, seasoned in childbirth, understood my incoherence, but I felt awkward when I couldn't carry on a conversation.

After dinner I walked home, and put everything and everyone else aside. I labored through the night, sweating, moaning and even vomiting at times. During my pregnancy I had read every book on childbirth that I could find, watched lots of videos and talked with nearly every mother in town. I understood the physiology of childbirth, and part of my coping mechanism was to rationalize each sensation I felt. When there was immense pressure in my lower back, I told myself, "OK, the baby is against my back and I can counteract this pressure." Luckily, the baby shifted positions after a few contractions, so that feeling didn't last long.

My midwife came over and spent the night with us. Although her presence was comforting, I knew that I was the only person who could give birth. I retreated to the deepest parts of my mind, reviewing scenes from my childhood like an old film. Every spoken word, whether or not it was directed to me, became a distraction. I wanted silence. I just sat there, letting my body do its work. I didn't want to move or be touched, just to be still. Contractions came and went, and in between I would drift off, resting without sleeping.

Unlike the hospital setting, where a classroom-sized clock is staring at you from across the bed, I had a tiny clock placed strategically behind me. But in the childbirth time warp, the hours, minutes and seconds didn't hold any meaning. Soon the sunlight was shining softly into the room. My labor was changing. I felt the baby moving, like thunder rumbling through me, and I had to surrender. I pulled together every bit of strength I had left. Suddenly I was re-energized, as if I had slept through the night. For every bit of pushing, I had to do just as much letting go. I could not hold on to the fact that I was totally naked in front of a room full of people, or consider the sounds I would hear coming from my mouth. I understood why they call it the "urge to push"—I remember asking Suzanne, "Do I have to wait for another contraction?"

Finally, at 9:03 on a Monday morning, my son was born. The midwife immediately put him in my arms. I was stunned—the sight and sensation of holding your own child for the first time is not truly conceivable before it happens. He did not cry or breathe right away, and it seemed everything was in slow motion. I was speechless and holding my own breath. My midwife said, "Talk to your baby!" as she suctioned his airways and he began to breathe.

I felt as if we were calling his soul into his body. My words were probably a jumble, but in my heart I said, "I'm so glad that you're here!" I watched him fill with oxygen and a rosy color spread through him. He was aware, but silent, and we watched each other closely. I felt that I was looking at a stranger, and gazing into the eyes of an old friend. Maybe, as he gazed back with a slightly wrinkled brow, he felt the same way. I barely noticed when our physical tie, a purple and shockingly rope-like cord, was severed. We had completed the journey and evolved into two individuals. With some practice I was able to nurse him, and we reconnected. Afterwards I began to cry. I was sobbing, not only tears of joy, but also relief and gratefulness. I realized the fullness of my being. Every muscle, every hormone and every action of my body was nature. I had experienced the completion of one cycle, and the beginning of another.

A Mother's Guidance: I did not take any birth classes. Instead, I read midwifery books and spoke with women who had faith in the birth process. Some of the books that

I read were *Spiritual Midwifery* by Ina May Gaskin, *Heart & Hands: A Midwife's Guide to Pregnancy & Birth* by Elizabeth Davis, *Birth without Violence* by Fredrick Leboyer, and *Immaculate Deception* and *Seasons of Change*, both by Suzanne Arms. I read everything that my midwife had in her office, and anything in the library that supported normal birth.

The secret to having a great birth is... hire a midwife! Finding a midwife for your hospital or home birth is the best thing that you can do for yourself and your baby! The midwifery model of care encourages freedom of movement, use of water during labor, and no separation of mother and baby. Midwifery care is very respectful of the process that mother and baby are experiencing.

Additional Thoughts: Kelly mentions that she strategically placed her clock behind her. You will find that it is much easier to labor if you are not concentrating on how long it's taking. If you are giving birth at a hospital, drape a towel over the clock or take it off the wall.

Kelly Camden is the mother of two boys, both born at home. She has worked with families as a labor support and postpartum doula since 1999. Kelly facilitated the creation of the Albuquerque Birth Network (www.abqbirthnet.org), an organization that educates the community about options for healthy pregnancy and birth, and advocates for evidence-based care.

$\mathcal{A}$ LOVE LETTER

BY ANNA STEWART

LISTEN, MY CHILD, I have a story to tell you. On the day you were born, my whole body smiled.

The morning of your birth day, I got up about 8 a.m., had a bowl of shredded wheat and orange juice for breakfast, and read the newspaper. My friend Sue called at 9:30. I told her I was tired of waiting for you to be born.

I hung up and tried to sit down on the couch again, but I was too uncomfortable. I was feeling cramping and pressure low in my pelvis. So I walked around the house, feeling restless. The cramping got more intense in just a matter of minutes. I called your dad at 9:50. "I think I'm in labor," I told him, "but I'm not sure. I'm going to take a bath so why don't you finish up whatever you're doing and come home." I sounded calm but then I started to cry. I felt strange—lightheaded, flushed. Dad was home in 10 minutes. He found me leaning against the shower wall, the hot water massaging my back.

Before Dad got home, I talked to you. I said, "OK Kyle, this is it. We're going to birth you now. You tell me if there's anything I need to know. We'll do this together, gently, easily. I love you so much. I can't wait to meet you and hold you in my arms." I know you heard me. Do you remember?

My uterus was squeezing you down into the birth canal, hugging you tightly, pushing you down firmly and softly. My contractions were two minutes apart, each lasting about 30 seconds. Dad changed his clothes and called our birth assistant, Alice, between contractions. I wanted him close to me during them. I got out of the shower and walked around the house between contractions. It was hard work but I felt exhilarated, energized, excited.

Alice got to our house at about 11 a.m. and watched me through a few contractions. I was focusing on relaxing and keeping my voice low. Alice asked me if I was nauseous. I was. She said, "I think you're in transition. We had better go to the hospital." It hadn't occurred to me that I would have to go anywhere. I was fully concentrating on our belly hugs.

Dad drove to the hospital in a hurry, arriving in six minutes. I was trying to hang on in the back seat as he changed lanes. I didn't want to sit down. At the corner of Broadway and Arapahoe, I cried out, "I feel his head. I think he's coming." You were moving down the birth canal, gently and easily, just like we'd talked about. Dad was worried you'd be born in the car!

Dad stopped in the emergency entrance. I closed the car door and tried to walk to the maternity wing, but I only got about 20 feet before another contraction took over. I leaned on the pay phones in the lobby and moaned loudly. Heads popped out of doorways all down the hall. A nurse nudged me into a wheelchair and rushed me to the maternity ward.

When I was ready, the nurse checked my cervix. I was completely dilated. She wanted me to start pushing you out, but it wasn't time yet. Dad put on the CD I had been listening to at home, *Ocean Dreams*. You and I had listened to it many times as we rested and prepared for this moment.

At one point when I was pushing hard, working with you, squeezing Dad's hands, I noticed Dad was crying. "What is it?" I asked him. He could barely speak. I kissed him. "We're about to have a baby. Our baby," he whispered. That was the moment he fell in love with you. He hadn't seen you yet but he knew he loved you as much as anyone can love someone.

Slowly, the top of your head emerged. Dad could see your black hair. My body stretched big enough so your head could pass through. You were born at 12:54 p.m. on Friday, October 7th. You started breathing right away and making little noises. Finally, I got to hold you in my arms. I was so happy… my whole body smiled. I whispered in your open, curving ear, "Welcome Kyle. Welcome to the world. Welcome to your family. We are so glad you're here."

A Mother's Guidance: Practice surrendering by breathing and relaxing to music, especially in the last few weeks of pregnancy when the reality of impending birth is coursing through you. I took an independent/alternative birth class and read tons of books, especially other women's birth stories. At that time, one of my favorite books was *A Good Birth, A Safe Birth* by Diane Korte and Roberta Scaer. I also like Penny Simkin's book, *The Birth Partner*. Having a doula made a huge difference, both prenatally, because I could talk more about my feelings than I could with my OB, and during the birth. A doula reinforced the belief that birth is natural, and helped me stay centered and not get lost in the hospital environment. I also "daydreamed" a lot by meditating to the same ocean sound track that I used in my birth.

Additional Thoughts: Before your child is born, write out your vision for an ideal birth. Writing down your intentions will help your mind and body to manifest that. Then let go of that plan, so you are holding no expectations. If you can think of your contractions as belly hugs or bear hugs, you will perceive those sensations as something more pleasant.

Doulas are a wonderful addition to your birth team; they provide great emotional support, and so much more. There are two large organizations that certify doulas: Association of Labor Assistants & Childbirth Educators (www.alace.org) and Doulas of

North America (www.dona.org). Interview at least three doulas, and choose the one that both you and your parenting partner feel most comfortable with.

Anna Stewart reads this story to her first-born on his birthday every year. They live in Colorado, along with her husband and two other children. She has published over 250 articles, essays, columns and reviews, and is currently marketing two books for publication. She can be reached through www.motherhands.com.

CHERISHING EVERY SENSATION

BY SUSAN McCLUTCHEY

FROM THE MOMENT David and I discovered our pregnancy, we were awash in blissful excitement... tainted only by my fear of childbirth. After a lifetime of hearing birth horror stories, I was worried about how I would handle it. But at the same time, I didn't understand why it should hurt. After all, pain is usually a way for our bodies to tell us something is wrong, yet pregnancy is a natural and healthy process. If Mother Nature provided us with only one way to (naturally) complete a pregnancy, why would She make that one method painful?

With that question in mind, I began earnestly researching childbirth... and I soon found answers. The more I read, the more I realized that childbirth is not inherently painful. It is, however, extremely intense and can be overwhelming without proper preparation and support through labor. When a woman is unprepared for that intensity, she is likely to tense up and resist the process, which leads to pain.

Armed with a new understanding of childbirth, I found a course called HypnoBirthing that taught relaxation through self-hypnosis. My husband and I enjoyed the classes, but when they were over we still felt unprepared. Fortunately, we found supplemental resources on www.hypnobabies.com. Armed with these

wonderful techniques, we settled confidently into a routine of practicing our relaxation, and waited for the big day with eager anticipation instead of fear.

We didn't have long to wait! Four days before our due date,
our sweet little man came into the world and completely stole
our hearts.

I first began to suspect that labor was close when I noticed a
little bloody show late one Friday night. The show was still present the next morning, and I was having easy little surges (that's
hypno-speak for contractions) every seven to ten minutes for the
first several hours after I awoke. I was so excited to know labor was
starting, but I tried to remain calm, knowing it could take awhile.
I wandered downstairs, had some breakfast and made brownies
for the labor-and-delivery staff. By 9:30 a.m. the surges were four to
five minutes apart, but still gentle. I knew I wasn't making dramatic progress, so I just napped and relaxed, enjoying time with
my husband.

When the surges intensified, David called our doula and she
joined us by noon. We were all happy and a little giggly with excitement. In the midst of our mirth, David pulled out the video camera
to get some funny footage of me struggling to put socks on feet I
hadn't seen in months. He turned the camera on our doula and
asked her to tell the audience who she was and why she was there.
Her dazed response: "Dude, I don't know anything about babies…
I just brought the pizza!" The jovial atmosphere helped to keep
me relaxed, despite my excitement, and for the next few hours we
just hung out, chatting and laughing, while I used the birthing ball
and listened to my relaxation tapes.

To this point, I had been concentrating on staying relaxed and
visualizing my cervix opening easily. In the beginning, I worked on
using deep, relaxing breathing, but soon it just became second
nature. I spent quite a lot of time on my birth ball (which was really
a large exercise ball). When I felt a surge beginning, I would place
my hands palm-up on my knees and try to release all tension from
them. I found that if I kept my hands loose and free of tension, I

would automatically relax my shoulders, and the rest of my body followed the trend. After doing this a few times I could feel a tingling sensation in my fingers, and would picture all the tension in my body flowing out of my fingertips. It wasn't something that I practiced prior to labor, I just found myself doing it.

We continued to relax and joke and have a wonderful time while we waited for me to feel that I was making progress. My surges grew more frequent, about two to three minutes apart, and lasted well over a minute, sometimes peaking twice. The double peaks concerned my doula, making her wonder if the baby might be posterior. But thanks to my relaxation, the surges were still comfortable, despite the fact I was experiencing back labor. I knew I wasn't very dilated, but with my strange pattern of surges and the fact that they were well under five minutes apart, I decided to go to the hospital and make sure that the baby was well. When I felt ready, I had a light snack and we headed to the hospital, elated with the prospect of finally meeting our first-born child and finding out if we would have a son or a daughter!

When we arrived at the hospital, we found that we had a full moon working against us. With occupants in every Labor-and-Delivery room, we found ourselves sequestered in a tiny triage cubicle. Monitoring confirmed the healthy, happy state of the baby, but despite strong and frequent surges, I had only dilated three centimeters. My bag of waters was protruding down the birth canal and was so taut that the baby couldn't make any downward progress. This was the reason my dilation stalled at three centimeters, and it was causing the back labor. The bag of waters had the baby pressed against my spine, unable to descend. This awkward situation caused a lot of pressure on my urethra, which inhibited urination, but the relaxation techniques kept me from agony. Using self-hypnosis, I was able to relax and stay comfortable.

We tried walking around to see if we could encourage my membranes to rupture. Occasionally we would have to stop so I could lean on the wall while the doula and David pushed on my hips during surges (what relief!), but the nurses kept coming over and trying to have conversations with me while I was concentrating. This was so distracting that we decided to forgo the benefits of walking and head back to triage.

It sounds weird, but while I didn't actually feel any pain, I was well aware of its existence. It seemed like my relaxation acted as a wall between me and the painful sensations that some women experience during childbirth. If anything started to shake my concentration, I would feel a dark shadow looming over me, and I worried that it was the pain about to come crashing over me like a huge wave. Luckily, that thought always made me come up with another way to relax, and the shadow never reached me.

While in the triage area, we heard three women deliver in cubicles around us, but I was determined to hold out for a room! So we just continued the relaxation, concentrated on visualizations of my cervix softening and expanding, and endured the holding pattern. David rubbed my back and shoulders when I needed it and I continued listening to relaxation tapes. By this time my surges were continuous, with no down time in between, and I knew I wasn't progressing. But David and our doula kept me calm and comfortable, and took turns pestering the staff for a room.

I continued using the birthing ball and taking walks to the bathroom. I guess I was being overly optimistic by going to the restroom all the time—I still couldn't urinate. Eventually I reached the point where I needed to remain on my side with my eyes closed to stay relaxed. I hadn't had a break between surges in a few hours, and it took all my concentration to stay calm. At some level I knew that I had every right to be frustrated by not having a room, but I just kept telling myself that I would be holding my baby very soon, so a few hours didn't really matter. I found myself thinking about getting angry, then realizing the harm it would do, and consciously deciding to be patient.

Finally, around 10 p.m. we got a birthing room! Once we were settled in and had the lights turned down to a comfortable level, I knew my body needed my water to break in order to progress. I discussed the situation with my doctor and we decided to intervene. It was the right thing to do, according to what my body was telling me. She broke my water just after 11:00 p.m. I remember being surprised by how warm the liquid felt when it came out, and somehow that warmth helped me relax even further. I was dilated to five centimeters, but after my water was broken I actually regressed to four centimeters. Again, I had the fleeting thought that I should be frustrated by my lack of progress, but decided such thoughts were not helpful and remained patient.

Having my water broken was a huge relief to my body, and I was lucky to experience a rest period when my surges were only occurring every five to seven minutes. I took that time to go into deeper relaxation, and I napped. With the membranes having released, the baby could finally move down. The pressure on my cervix really got things moving. When I awoke, I was in transition and things became more intense. I was having trouble staying calm, but David and the doula were miracle workers. They helped me regain control by telling me how well I was handling the surges, and reminding me that I was not going to experience anything more difficult than what I had already handled. (They also kicked out the rude anesthesiologist, who laughed at us when we declined an epidural and said to let him know when we needed him.)

By 12:30 a.m. I was dilated eight or nine centimeters. Only a few minutes later, I began feeling my body push with the surges and asked for the doctor. When she arrived, she confirmed that I was completely dilated and told me to push when I was ready. I was relieved to hear that—my body had already begun pushing without my consent!

When I shifted from my side into a sitting/reclined position, the surges stopped almost completely. I was in absolutely no discomfort and felt no surges, but since so many people were standing there watching me expectantly, I still put on a show of pushing from time to time. I felt like a stage actress who made a grand entrance in front of a full house and promptly forgot all her lines! Everyone was so fixated on me, and absolutely nothing was happening! It sounds silly now, but I was so embarrassed about not having any surges after asking for the doctor. I tried to discreetly use the technique of breathing the baby down when I wasn't actively pushing. Despite my being ridiculous and trying to do it without anyone noticing, it worked! The baby was nearly crowning, but I wasn't working with my body anymore. I was annoyed that I had to do all the work, since I wasn't having surges to help things along. I finally asked to roll onto my side again, and instantly relaxed into a wonderful surge that brought the baby to crowning without any work on my part.

I rolled right back and started pushing with gusto. I loved this stage! Prior to the birth, I had done perineal massage while using relaxation techniques, and visualized crushed ice coming down before the baby's head, cooling and soothing everything before it stretched around him. As a result, the pushing felt wonderful and the smooth warmth of my son's face and body emerging from me felt like a massaging caress. I could feel every magical little detail of him as he moved through and out of me. I marveled at the sweet warmth of his skin against my birth canal and cherished every sensation. It seemed as though the entire world came to an expectant halt and nothing existed except those of us in the room. Everyone responded to the sacred but joyful feel of those moments by using hushed tones to give me quiet encouragement and exclaim over the beauty of the event.

Our beautiful son Luke emerged peacefully into the dimly lit room and was passed immediately into my hands, where he lay while my husband checked to see his gender. The cord was very short, so he stayed on my stomach for several minutes until it stopped pulsating and we cut it. His brow was furrowed as he peered back and forth from my face to David's with a look of both concern and interest. He had no interest in anyone else in the room, and the three of us just gazed at each other in awe as David and I told him how happy we were to meet him. From that moment we were so utterly in love with him that we could barely breathe as the weight of that devotion settled into our hearts. I will never forget the feeling of his warm little body in my hands and my surprise at how clean and soft he felt. I had braced myself for him to be slimy and bloody, but he was soft and clean and perfect.

Despite 19 hours of labor, I felt ready to run a marathon. Before I even delivered the placenta, I told David that I was looking forward to giving birth again—our doctor nearly fell over with shock! Both my doctor and doula said they had never seen a more serene and beautiful birth. Nurses from throughout the ward came by to discuss the hypnosis techniques we used. Apparently we were the talk of Labor & Delivery all weekend, and I like to think that hypnosis for birthing will be taken more seriously there in the future.

I had no soreness or aching whatsoever after the birth, never needing so much as an aspirin. I loved my pregnancy, but the joy of those 40 weeks pales in comparison to the exhilaration of Luke's birth!

A Mother's Guidance: We worked hard to create a wonderful birth experience. The HypnoBirthing classes, supplemented by tapes from the Hypnobabies website, were invaluable tools for us. Since our first pregnancy, we have made it our mission to let the pregnant women we meet know that they have options—that birth doesn't have to be a painful, drugged and medically-controlled experience. We are currently expecting our second child and are using the Hypnobabies course exclusively this time.

Additional Thoughts: It really is possible—a pain-free labor with an orgasmic pushing stage. *Ina May's Guide to Childbirth* by Ina May Gaskin can provide additional information on releasing the fear of pushing.

Susan McClutchey is a chemical engineer and her husband is currently a stay-at-home father. He also acts and does development work for local theaters and charity organizations.

ROM DENIAL
TO ECSTASY

BY MICHELE ZECK

YOU COULD SET A CLOCK by my menstrual cycle. But when I was four days late, I focused on all of the physical signs indicating my period was on the way. I bought an Early Pregnancy Test on my way to work, just to put my mind to rest—I knew I was not pregnant.

I went to the restroom the second I arrived. That stick couldn't have turned positive any quicker than it did… I was horrified! At 32, I had just gotten engaged to Rich, and did not want kids at all. In a state of shock and hysteria, I tried to tell a couple of my co-workers. I was incoherent, carrying on and pointing to the stick, so distraught that I had to leave work. I headed straight to Rich to tell him the news. I could not have asked for a more sympathetic man as I sat in his office blubbering about the situation.

That night we talked over our options. Do we keep the baby or do we give the baby up for adoption? I cried and prayed until I finally fell asleep that night. The next day I had an overwhelming feeling of peace about the pregnancy. It was a go. We accepted our unexpected gift.

As we talked about the kind of birth we wanted—a hospital or home birth—I made it clear that I am against any kind of pain medication or anything that interferes with the natural birthing process. I don't understand why people would take care of themselves during their pregnancy but allow drugs to enter their body, and the baby's, during labor. Our bodies are made for birthing. Labor pain won't last forever, and there is such a bright light at the end of the tunnel. Although it can seem unbearable at times, I see labor as such a small window of time compared to the bigger picture of growing and birthing a child.

We were aware of the problems that could arise if we chose a hospital birth, but I didn't know anyone who had given birth at home. We talked with friends about our dilemma, and they knew of a midwife who had been in practice for over 20 years and delivered over 1,000 babies. Encouraged by this sign, we contacted her to set up an interview. She answered all of our questions and talked with us about our philosophy on birthing. She advised us to not make a decision right away, to think about our conversation for a week or so.

We figured it would be smart to talk with my Ob/Gyn about home birth. So we made an appointment, but before we could see the doctor we had to fill out a stack of paperwork. Oh, brother! Then the nurse proceeded to go through her routine, or as I call it, "pushing us through like a herd of cows." She gave us the "pregnant packet" full of propaganda, which annoyed Rich and I to no end. We just wanted to TALK to the doctor, that's it. Finally, we were led to an examination room and I was told to get into a gown. I said, "I'm sorry, but I'm here strictly to talk to the doctor. No examination is going to take place." Thank goodness Rich was there, or I wouldn't have felt brave enough to stand up for what I believed should happen during that visit.

My doctor, a woman I really liked and had been to for five years, came in a few minutes later. We talked about the possibility of working with a midwife and having a home birth. While she was open to a midwife, she objected to a home birth because of the fact I had herpes. (Herpes can be passed from mother to baby during birth, but only if the mother is experiencing a breakout.) I was so grateful that I had already discussed this with my midwife. She had put my concerns to rest right away, educating me on foods and immune-boosting supplements that would suppress breakouts. She had safely delivered many babies with moms who had herpes. To hear my doctor try to scare me with the herpes angle did not make me happy. She said she respected our feelings about whether or not to vaccinate our baby, and other choices we wanted to make, which made me feel better. However, she couldn't guarantee she would be on call when I went into labor, and she warned me that the other delivery doctors wouldn't be as open-minded. That was all I needed to hear. I wasn't going to give birth under such uncertain circumstances.

After we were done with the question-and-answer session the doctor said, "I see you didn't want an exam." I confirmed that we were just there to talk, so the office charged us for a consultation, which our insurance does not cover. That was the cherry on top of the whole unpleasant experience.

The next day we called the midwife, Yolanda, and told her we were ready to work with her. We met the following week to fill out some paperwork and exchange expectations, and just to talk. She told us that she did not conduct vaginal exams until the home visit, which is two weeks before your due date. She had a 0% infection rate. She does not offer any drugs for pain and will only do episiotomies if absolutely necessary. During the birth she uses oil and massage to help stretch the perineum and make it more elastic. Yolanda also advised me to use ginger for morning sickness… those ginger tablets were my best friends for months. Peppermint oil was also helpful for my tummy. Our next appointment was in two months, which would put me at 13 weeks along.

Our first real appointment with a midwife was astonishing. The wealth of information she had blew me away. My husband has children from a previous marriage and even he was flabbergasted. He told her that no doctor had ever taken the time to include him in the prenatal discussions, or teach him how to help prepare a woman's body for the birthing process.

In my second trimester I was feeling so much better, now that the nausea had left. But that is also when the fear set in... I was so scared of the pain of labor. Some days that's all I thought about, and I knew I had to take control of my mindset. I told Yolanda about my low tolerance for pain, and asked what I could do to cope with my fears. She encouraged me to read *Birthing from Within* by Pam England and Rob Horowitz, an excellent book. It was key to helping me manage the pain issue, but also so much more. It is perfect for women planning a home birth, or a hospital birth.

I needed to hear the baby's heartbeat, and we finally did for the first time at about the 17th week. Until that day, a part of me was still in denial about being pregnant. I didn't want to get my hopes up in case something went wrong during my first trimester. Once I heard that little heart beat I was overwhelmed with happiness. I really was pregnant! There really was a little person growing inside me. The reality of having a baby finally set in.

The more I read my book, *Birthing from Within*, the more thrilled I was and the more confident I became that I could have a perfectly wonderful home birth. Birthing at home can be a very daunting thing for most people. My mom and friends resisted the idea at first. All I heard was, "What if, what if, what if... hospitals are safer and better equipped to handle emergencies...." I told them to educate themselves about home births and hospital births before making a judgment call. As I shared more and more information with them, they gradually opened up to the idea.

Two weeks before my due date, our midwife came for a home visit. She examined me and confirmed that all was well with the baby and me. She checked our birthing supplies to make sure we had everything we would need. Rich and I were so ready to have a baby... we were just waiting for the baby to be ready to join us.

And then, the day came. It was about 3 a.m. when I started feeling uncomfortable so I went downstairs to lay on the couch. By 4 a.m. I was sitting at the table, reading a chart in a book, trying to determine if those sensations were fake contractions or true contractions. I honestly didn't know. According to the book, I was having some of each. I timed them, but there was no consistency. By 5 a.m. I knew they were true contractions, coming about one minute apart. An hour later I yelled upstairs, telling my husband to call our midwife.

I lay over the side of the bed, breathing and talking to Yolanda. She asked me questions, trying to discern if I was in true labor. She was just finishing up with another birth and was about 30 minutes away, but said she was on her way. Rich called my mom to tell her I was in labor and asked her to pray for us.

Yolanda arrived at the house at 7:30 a.m., bringing with her an energy of calmness. I was safe and at peace with her there. I felt the safest in our bedroom, so that is where we stayed (along with our dog and cat). I can't remember much of what she said to me but I remember that Yolanda's voice was very soothing. Rich was at my side the whole time. Whether I was in the bathtub or on the toilet wanting to throw up, he was there. He was my rock.

My midwife would not let me stay in any one position for too long. She believes that different birthing positions encourage the baby to move into the birth canal. She was right. By 8:30 a.m. I was dilated to eight centimeters. My water still had not broken; it never really did, it just leaked a little at a time. By 10 a.m. I was fully dilated and ready to push. My husband was a great coach, and I clung to him like never before. I needed him, and he came through like a knight in shining armor!

Yolanda listened to the baby's heartbeat one more time before I started pushing. Believe it or not, I asked her if she could tell what sex the baby was by the heartbeat, and she said yes.

With each contraction I pushed deeply... I wanted the baby out and I wanted it out now! For the first 20 minutes of pushing I was on the bed, and then I moved to a birthing stool. That was perfect. As our baby was crowning, she told me she could see the baby's head and that it had lots of hair. She lowered a mirror so I could see, and then I put my hand down to feel the hair. How incredible that moment was! To feel part of the baby before it entered this world was just magical. Yolanda gave me specific instructions, telling me to stop pushing. She was preparing the baby's opening with oil, massaging it to stretch with the baby so there would be no tearing. I started pushing again, but had to stop—as much as I didn't want to, I knew what the consequences would be if I didn't. With one final push, the baby emerged face up. Yolanda told me to grab my baby girl and pull her out. What a glorious experience, to pull your child out of your body and welcome her into the world!

Shea Kiley lay on my chest with the cord still attached for 10 or 15 minutes before Rich cut it. I was helped up onto the bed and started nursing my precious angel. God was good to me. Everything went exactly the way it should have—perfect.

A Mother's Guidance: Having a home birth with a midwife was my key to a great birth. Birthing is difficult, that's just reality, but to give birth in the comfort of your home can make it an awesome experience. Choose a midwife who explains everything to you and lets you know how your pregnancy and labor are progressing. She will reassure you that you are doing a great job, and you won't be stuck in bed or have monitors hooked up to you. (That idea scared me, and felt like we would be anticipating problems.) What a story you get to share with your child—that they were born in their home!

Additional Thoughts: One of the most important things you can do at the beginning of your pregnancy is to carefully interview doctors or midwives. If you do not feel comfortable with them at the beginning of your pregnancy, you probably won't feel any different when you are giving birth. You can find a great list of interviewing questions in the appendix of this book.

Michele Zeck is a stay-at-home mom to one daughter. Her husband Rich has managed a chiropractor's office for the last four years.

IN HER OWN TIME

BY CATHERINE AMADOR-LOCHER

I ONLY PUSHED twice before Lola shot into the world. After a long couple of weeks with less-than-enthusiastic contractions, my daughter suddenly decided she was in a hurry, and my active labor was quick. She didn't come out slowly, like most babies: first the head and then the shoulders, and finally the tiny body. She came into the world all at once. It was as if she wasn't going to let anything stop her. Not even her own cord could get in her way.

I gave birth to my first child, Jonathon, when I was in my early twenties. Throughout my first pregnancy I was scared and overwhelmed, but very excited. While Jonathon's birth was one of the most intense and thrilling experiences of my life, laboring in the hospital was less than satisfactory. My doctor broke my water; they hooked me up to an internal fetal monitor, making it impossible for me to walk around. Fourteen hours and a routine episiotomy later, I delivered my son. Jonathon's father cut the cord and then there he was—in my arms, my beautiful boy. I was thrilled with my new baby, but couldn't help wondering if I'd missed out on something....

I hadn't been emotionally comfortable in a hospital setting, and I knew there had to be a better way. Over the next few years I researched labor and delivery, reading every book I could get my hands on. I studied everything from routine hospital births to unassisted ocean births. It was when I began reading *Mothering* magazine that I decided to give birth at home with my next baby. I didn't know at the time that it wouldn't happen for another 16 years.

Jumping ahead to a new life and new marriage, I was 36 when I tried to conceive my second child. I was having ovulation problems, and had undergone fertility treatments for almost a year when my husband Jason and I decided we needed a break from the emotional roller coaster. We were both getting nervous about long-term consequences of the continuous Clomid doses, and we were both tired of being disappointed month after month. We took a breather to find our balance. We were happy raising Jonathon, and knew we were blessed even if another child wasn't meant to be. We didn't stop trying; we just stopped thinking about trying. Well, to be totally honest, I have to admit that I never really gave up thinking about getting pregnant; I just stopped obsessing over it and gave my emotions a break. It was nice to let go and get back to "us" for a while.

After about three months, we were mentally and emotionally prepared to begin treatments again. This time we would have my husband tested as well. I knew he was uncomfortable with the idea, but I also knew that having a baby was just as important to him as it was to me. He was willing to do whatever was needed to get some answers.

I don't know if it was luck or relaxation... I like to believe it's because we finally grounded ourselves, and that a precious little soul decided it was time. The day before Jason went to his doctor's appointment, two lines on a home pregnancy test confirmed what we had barely dared to suspect—we were pregnant! We were thrilled with the news, and in shock that we actually did it. No drugs, no monitoring, just two people and a lot of love. I kept thanking the baby over and over for choosing us. I called everyone I knew and announced that there was finally going to be a baby! Our dream was coming true.

Because of my research, we knew we wanted a home birth. I had worked in the local health food store the year before, and one of my best friends from there was able to guide us to a wonderful midwife, April. I couldn't believe the difference it made to have her come to our home for my prenatal visits, as opposed to going to the doctor's office. She took her time and would stay for a couple hours, talking with us about any concerns, hopes, dreams or fears we had. She gently poked and prodded my growing belly, checking both the baby and me. She carefully showed my husband and me just where our baby's head, shoulders and butt were at each visit. After my appointments I would feel radiant with confidence that both the baby and I were doing well. I fully trusted my midwife's assessments.

In contrast, the doctor I was seeing at the same time would come into the exam room, listen to baby's heart, check my blood pressure and tell me he'd see me again in a few weeks. The whole thing would last ten minutes, at most. I was never reassured or comfortable. We were only seeing him because of my age, and we wanted to get the appropriate tests to make sure everything was going OK. It was a huge waste of our time.

Everyone has their own comfort levels, and every decision is personal and should be honored; but for us it was such a relief to finally separate ourselves from the doctor and rely solely on my midwife and her wisdom. My family and I formed a very close friendship with her, and we trusted her explicitly. She became family. I realized that we were in the best of hands and that it was OK to let go of my age-related concerns. I had a great pregnancy, and it was only the last couple of weeks that I felt uncomfortable.

Every day throughout the last few weeks, I experienced contractions off and on, some Braxton-Hicks and some more painful contractions, but nothing that was leading into true labor. After a night of being sure it was time, only to have the contractions stop at four centimeters dilation, I was getting really frustrated. Despite all the time it took to get pregnant, these last couple of weeks seemed the longest part of our journey. I knew this was normal, but I didn't care; I was sure I was the most pregnant woman ever... and I wasn't even past my due date yet! I was ready to see my baby.

We had decided on a water birth, so the birthing tub sat in our home, empty, waiting. My mom and sister had flown in to support us through the birth, and April was standing by offering words of encouragement and patience, but Lola wasn't quite ready for her debut. My poor husband never knew if he should stay home from work or not. I was trying to be patient and to have faith in my body, but some days were harder than others.

The day after my due date, April came over to conduct a blessing ceremony and foot wash with me. The ceremony was simple; she shared a few words of blessings and washed my feet, thanking me for allowing her to participate in this sacred event and assuring me she would be there to help guide my baby into the world. It was very moving, and when she proceeded to dry my feet with her long hair, my tears started to flow. The love I was receiving from her and everyone else in the room pulled me into such a serene space, at peace with my body and our baby. I was able to let go of any impatience and discomfort, and finally find balance. I released any concept of a due date and decided to enjoy the last few days I'd have my daughter all to myself. So with this new attitude in place, I didn't think much about it when the contractions started again—I was certain it was more false labor.

It was March 23rd, two days past my due date, and the Academy Awards were on. We had just sat down with some burritos when I started to feel crampy again. Peter O'Toole was awarded an honorary Oscar. My mom told us that the night she and my dad saw his Academy Award winning performance in *Lawrence of Arabia* was the night she'd gone into labor with me. She said maybe it was a good sign. We all laughed and carried on with the evening as usual. I didn't say anything about the cramps I was having; they were like the others I'd had all week, so I didn't want to get everyone excited. At about 11:00 p.m. we decided to go to bed.

My husband immediately fell asleep, but I wasn't feeling too great. I got up to use the bathroom, sure that the burritos were the cause of my discomfort. The cramps were getting stronger, so I decided to take a shower and try to relax. I let the hot water massage my lower back, knowing that if it was false labor the water would relax me enough to slow down the contractions. It felt good, and afterwards I laid down again but the cramps kept coming.

I still wouldn't allow myself to believe this was it, so I got up and took another shower. While the water once again felt good, it wasn't helping the discomfort as much as the first shower had. I started to get more excited. I lay down again and felt a definite change with the next contraction… it took my breath away! I reached out and squeezed Jason's arm, unable to talk through the pain. Realizing what was happening, he got up and helped me walk through the next several contractions. He was my rock and my balance. I would wrap my arms around his neck and he would hold me up, gently stroking my back. Finally I told him we should call the midwife. By now it was almost 1:00 a.m.

While I woke up my mom and sister to tell them that April was on her way, Jason began filling the tub. Everyone was excited. The contractions were coming every 30 seconds, and getting stronger. My midwife arrived about 1:45 a.m. and checked me. I was dilated to five centimeters and fully effaced! Yay!

I was given the go ahead to get into the tub… I practically ran to it. It felt incredible to sink down into that warm water. I had been moaning throughout my contractions, and now April reminded me to visualize my cervix opening up. As my "oh's" became a chant of "open… open…" I began thinking how relatively calm I was still feeling. I never "checked out" or got at all dreamy with my contractions. I was handling them vocally, even singing through a couple of them. I'm not saying it didn't hurt, because it did! But they were not overwhelming me.

I was thankful to be in the water, as it was helping me handle the contractions. I was feeling very balanced, and I waited for the desperate feeling of the transition stage to hit. Since it hadn't come yet, I figured I still had a lot of time before baby was ready to make her entrance. Almost immediately after this thought, my contractions became more demanding… within seconds I was feeling the urge to push. The time was 2:35 a.m.; I'd been in the tub for about half an hour. I asked my mom to go wake up my son so he could be present. I was happy that she and my sister could be there with us, and I was feeling so much love for everyone in the room.

The pressure was building and I told my midwife that I couldn't hold back, so she checked me and said that any time I was ready I could go ahead and bear down. But I already was! My body was working just like it should. My midwife saw my unbroken bag of waters bulging and said that Lola's head was right there too. The only thing going through my mind right then was that I had to get this baby out. So with my next push, I gave it all I had. I felt the rush of water as my bag broke and said, "Here comes the water!" At the same time, April swooped Lola up out of the tub and said, "No, here is your baby!" She came out all at once, like a bullet. The time was 2:37. The membrane from the water sac was still covering her body; she was born en caul.

Jason had been saying throughout our pregnancy that she would be born in her bag of water, and he was right! I looked down and saw her big eyes looking around from inside the sac, and noticed a bubble around her nose and mouth. The midwife pulled the membrane away from her face and there was my beautiful little girl, just looking up at me. She was breathing fine and already turning pink. I looked up at my husband and saw his face covered in tears. A feeling of serenity filled me. She was finally here, and she was perfect.

I was marveling at the beauty of my new daughter, oblivious to what was going on around me, when suddenly the midwife asked, "Where's your cord?" I laughed and said I didn't know, but then I saw real concern on her face. About four inches of umbilical cord was hanging from my daughter, and the other end was coming out of me. The tub had a lot of blood in the water.

Apparently our new daughter was in such a hurry to get out that she broke her own cord! April immediately clamped Lola's end and said I needed to get out of the tub. I asked her if Lola was OK and she reassured me that the baby was perfect; it was me she was concerned about. I felt very calm and allowed myself to be guided to the bedroom. There was no way to be sure that all the blood was from the cord, and she wanted to get me in bed to check for tears and hemorrhaging. She also wanted to get the placenta out to make sure it hadn't pulled away from my uterus when the cord broke.

Once they got me settled the midwife clamped the cord and went to work, checking my yoni for tears and making sure I wasn't losing any more blood. I had the smallest of nicks and we delivered a healthy placenta within 15 minutes. She concluded that the blood had in fact come from the pulsating cord and that I was in perfect health. When she measured the cord, adding the few inches from Lola's end of it, she figured it to be around 16-18 inches in length. Although she didn't talk to me about it at the time, she thought that if it had been extremely short, that would explain why it had snapped. Since it wasn't too short, she could only guess at what caused it to break. She was just thankful that it didn't pull off from Lola's navel, or snap before she was through the birth canal, thereby cutting off her oxygen supply. In 20 years as a midwife, she had never had anything like this happen. I'm sure we caused her a few new gray hairs that night!

Through all of this I was feeling great and kept reassuring everyone that I was fine. I even exclaimed, "Let's do this again!" causing everyone in the room to laugh. (The next day she asked me if I remembered saying that, and if I really wanted to go through it again. I told her, of course! She said that is usually not one of the first things she hears from a mom who's just gone through labor, and she laughed again.) The adrenaline was surging through my system. I was thrilled with our gorgeous girl, and very happy that we were able to realize our dream of delivering at home, in water. I was so thankful that we were both healthy and happy. Most of all I was grateful that we had decided to trust our midwife so much. If we had given birth in the hospital, I'm sure labor would have lasted longer, and upon discovering the broken cord they would have taken Lola away while they assessed the situation. As it was, Lola never left my arms and no one panicked. April handled it with a wonderful calmness that kept everyone at ease. We will be forever grateful to her for being there with us and guiding our daughter into the world with such love and peace.

Lola weighed in at a healthy seven pounds, eight ounces, and was very alert. She knew exactly what to do when I put her on my breast, and she ate with gusto. We all felt very blessed that early morning. After a couple hours, April went home to research anything she could find on umbilical cords breaking at birth. She heard from one midwife who said she'd experienced something similar several years before, but no one else had ever gone thorough something quite like this. Thankfully there were no ramifications from it.

The balance I achieved right before giving birth is still strong, and I love every minute of being a new mom again. Lola and I went through an incredible journey together, but it was only the beginning. I love watching her learn and feeling her love. Her smiles light up a room and I realize once again that the most important things in the world are right there in that smile. Even with all this goodness, I can't help but wonder if the details of her birth are mere hints to what we have in store as she gets older. How many cords will she snap on the road to growing up? How much symbolic blood will I lose as I guide her to adulthood? No matter what, I'm going to be there, patiently helping her through each process, experiencing all her joys as well as her sorrows, and learning some valuable lessons on staying balanced along the way.

A Mother's Guidance: My strongest advice for an expectant mom is to make sure that she is completely comfortable with her surroundings, and to maintain control of her environment. Sometimes hospital personnel or family members can be intimidating, but I believe that if the mother (or her primary support person) remains in charge of the situation, it will help her relax more during labor.

Fear is probably the biggest barrier to overcome in labor. It can be especially difficult with first babies, because you don't really know what to expect. You can read everything, but until you go through it you never really know. But trust your body. During Lola's birth I was very aware that my body was working the way it was supposed to. I would whisper to my belly, "It's OK Lola, we are doing this together."

Finally, make sure you have 100% trust in whoever you have chosen to be with you in the birthing room. This includes any and all doctors, family members and friends. If you don't like your doctor while you are pregnant, it will be that much more difficult to deliver. A woman has every right to change practitioners, and should never be made to feel guilty or intimidated into staying with someone she doesn't completely trust. The same goes for family and friends who want to be with her. If she just wants her partner, then she needs to be able to say that. My sister just had her first baby, and during labor she had her husband's entire family in the labor room with them. She wasn't progressing, and she finally looked around and realized that she couldn't relax because of everyone in the room. So they kicked everyone out, and an hour later had a beautiful little boy. I was comfortable having my mother, sister and son with us, but I had also set down some guidelines on what my needs were and how each one could help them be met. It was a wonderful and empowering experience.

I did not take any classes to prepare for this birth. Although I learned Lamaze techniques before my son's birth, I found that the breathing wasn't really helpful for me. With my second pregnancy I did a lot of meditation, and found Robert Bradley's book *Husband Coached Childbirth* to be very helpful. The relaxation techniques were great; I especially liked the suggestion that if you relax your face, the rest of you will follow. I also read *Birthing from Within* by Pam England and Rob Horowitz, and *The Birth Book* by William and Martha Sears. I would highly recommend both of these books.

Spiritual Midwifery by Ina May Gaskin was also a very good resource for me.

I also stayed active during my pregnancy. The last month I was still swimming three times a week with my husband on his lunch breaks.

My midwife taught me that by opening my mouth and chanting or moaning, I would help my cervix open. During the last phase, when the contractions were almost on top of each other, I would focus on a picture we have hanging on the wall and chant, "Open, open..." while imagining my cervix opening up. That was the biggest help of all in handling the pain.

Additional Thoughts: The blessing ceremony, which has gained tremendous popularity, is a non-denominational tradition that nurtures, honors and celebrates a woman's transition into motherhood as a rite of passage. Friends and family come together to give love, wisdom and support that will empower the mother to face the labor and birth ahead. It is a positive and powerful ritual, and sets the tone for a wonderful birth experience.

Another great tool that Catherine used is a warm shower. Warm water on the breasts and stomach can really get labor going, as well as relax the mom. Visualizing the cervix opening is also very helpful, and the image of rose or lotus flower opening is often used. Visualizing the opening of the hips, as well as the cervix, can also help labor progress, as tension and fear tends to accumulate in that area.

It is rare for a baby to be born "en caul," meaning in the amniotic sac. In some cultures, a baby born this way is believed to have psychic gifts.

Catherine Amador-Locher is a stay-at-home mom who loves art, writing, music and her family. She is currently studying to become a certified doula. Her husband Jason is an architectural draftsman at a small architectural firm that designs custom homes. Both Jason and Catherine attended Humboldt State University in Arcata, California. They currently live in Kailua Kona, Hawaii, with their son Jonathon, daughter Lola, dog Rita, and their two cats, Elvis and Alobar.

A SECRET HOME BIRTH

BY GINA KENNEDY

MY HUSBAND ROB and I have three children, all born naturally. During our first pregnancy, we knew we wanted to have our baby naturally, but we had no one to turn to for support or advice. My mom could barely remember giving birth in the 1960s. She said she had been so drugged, she hardly knew her own name! In the 1980s, my older sister had a C-section because her baby was breech. She went on to have two VBACs (vaginal birth after cesarean), but not without anesthesia. In speaking to other parents that we knew, we had not come across anyone who had a natural birth. It was frightening for me to realize that I was attempting to do something that had not been done by anyone familiar to me.

I began to read everything I could about natural childbirth. It may sound extreme, but in 1995, choosing to have a natural birth was a bit of a battle. My husband and I found that there was not much of a support system in place for women who wanted to give birth naturally; you had to work hard for it. We had to listen to our elders say, "Just take the drugs, why put yourself through all that pain?" They honestly believed that the drugs were harmless.

Today, a few clicks on the Internet will teach you that the drug in an epidural may be just a few molecules away from crack cocaine! We had to deal with many ignorant people who would ask us, "What is a midwife?" In the next sentence, they would be lecturing us on why we really should use a doctor to have a baby, when they didn't even know that most midwives have more hours and training in birth than obstetricians.

Our first two children were born at a birth center in Pennsylvania, where the staff included midwives with an obstetrician on call who could assist if circumstances led you to deliver at the hospital across the street. It was a great facility, with four bedroom suites decorated much like a home. In the corner of each suite was a large tub for anyone who wanted to labor in warm water. In the lobby area, there was a nice living room with a full kitchen, a play area for children, and plenty of room for siblings and grandparents to be together while waiting for the arrival of their newest family member. They even had great flags that announced "It's a Girl!" or "It's a Boy!" for the proud siblings to display on a special pole outside the building. It was the perfect setting for us to birth our babies.

When it came time to have our third baby, we had just moved to New Jersey and found that there were no birth centers in the state at that time. We did our research and found a nearby practice of midwives who delivered at a local hospital. While living in Pennsylvania, we had not considered a home birth because the birth center was just perfect, and we were concerned that our home was too far away from the nearest hospital, should complications arise. While I always held the idea of a home birth in the back of my mind, Rob was uncomfortable with the idea. I never really pushed the issue, until we toured the hospital I was to give birth in.

During the hospital tour for expectant parents, I watched him raising his hand to ask questions about every detail of the tour. People were beginning to make faces. It seemed that Rob was perplexed by every other sentence that came out of the tour guide's mouth! For example, he wanted to know why the babies were separated from the mother between the delivery room and recovery room. He was told it was a safety matter. The babies needed the heat of an incubator to stay warm while being transported from one room to another. Our first two babies stayed warm on my chest after they were born. They nursed and cuddled and never left my side. When my husband explained this and questioned their reasoning, they said that it was an insurance matter, and it would be unsafe for the baby to be held in the mother's arms while they were transported from one room to another. Then came the question, why were we moving so much from room to room? Nothing made sense, and we sadly seemed to be the only ones on the tour who felt that way. We left the hospital tour disgusted. After our experiences at a birth center, we knew we could not possibly give birth there. At this point it didn't take much to convince my husband that maybe we should reconsider a home birth, so I made an appointment with a local midwifery practice.

We met with two midwives, Gee Gee and Linda, to discuss whether we could be candidates for a home birth. By this time I was in my seventh month, so we needed to meet with the back-up obstetrician and have my medical records sent from the other midwifery practice. I was healthy and having a good pregnancy, and with two previous natural deliveries, it didn't take much to deem me a suitable candidate for a home birth. We were very happy about our decision. It seemed as if a weight had been lifted. There were no more uneasy feelings and fears about whether the hospital staff would allow us the type of birth we wanted. We knew that the home birth would be the best for everyone in our family.

Unfortunately, we could not tell our parents about our home birth plans—they had been questioning our decision to use midwives since our first pregnancy. We were lectured constantly. "Shouldn't you have a real doctor there?" Talk about not having support! Not only was there no one we could call on for advice about natural childbirth, everywhere we turned we found ourselves defending and explaining our choices. So we kept the big secret. We pretended that we were still using the midwifery practice that delivered at the hospital, and we privately prepared our young children for the home birth.

My husband didn't care who knew we were having a home birth, but I could not bear the thought of all the difficult conversations that I would inevitably find myself in. I just didn't have the energy or attention to satisfy other people's curiosity, or deal with their insecurity and lack of faith in nature. I much preferred to concentrate on preparing my two young children for the day they would witness a miracle. Our son was five years old, our daughter two and a half. Our midwives offered a library full of videos and books that we could take home and share with the children to help them prepare for the birth. *Birth in the Squatting Position* was by far their favorite video... they liked to see the placenta hit the floor! They kept asking me to rewind it, watching it over and over in amazement. It was one big science project for them.

We chose to have a water birth in our sunroom. This was also a big hit with our children, because the birthing tub looked just like a kiddy pool. Our midwife dropped it off at the house a few weeks before my due date, and from that point on we got many requests from the children to set up the pool. They were ready!

When the baby was ready, the contractions began on a weekday morning. I went about my usual business, taking my children to school and their other activities. By the afternoon, I was in labor. My husband came home to set up the tub. It came with a sterile liner that needed to be attached to the inside of the tub prior to filling it. I tried to relax on the hammock in my yard while Rob prepared our sunroom. When he came outside to check on me, something made me ask if he remembered to put in the sterile liner. He smiled and quickly headed back inside to empty the tub and start over.

A few weeks before this day, we had made the decision to let my older sister Michele in on the big secret so that she could be there to support us. We knew we could count on her, even though she had not experienced natural childbirth herself. She was someone who sincerely wished that she had, and was not the type of person who would question our decision. She arrived and helped bake a birthday cake (organic carrot!) with the children while I labored. I preferred to labor in the warm water of the tub, but got out a few times to let gravity help things along. It was a perfect labor. I used the buoyancy and warmth of the water to manage my pain, and I walked around a bit to help the labor progress.

My support team was amazing! The midwives used a Doppler to listen to the baby's heartbeat, but they allowed me to labor naturally, without internal exams that could introduce or increase the chance of infection. My doula, Denise, held firm pressure on a point between my thumb and hand, and helped administer homeopathic remedies for labor that had been prescribed by our family homeopath. Even my five-year-old son, Robbie, held my hand during parts of the labor.

I remember telling myself during each contraction, "You won't remember this pain." That mantra had worked well for me during my previous labor, and it was true—I didn't remember the pain. I kept thinking about holding my new baby. After a few hours, I felt a change in my contractions, a feeling similar to having to poop. Suddenly I was unaware of my surroundings. I was unaware that Denise had begun to take incredible photos of the birth. I was on my knees, leaning on the edge of the tub with my arms folded. GeeGee had placed a mirror on the bottom of the tub so that she could see what was going on without disturbing my comfortable position. Denise's camera caught the reflection in the mirror, and you could see a dark shadow protruding... my baby's head making its way out. I concentrated on keeping my breathing deep and slow. I remember Linda saying, "Keep it low," which helped me moan through the pain in a productive way. Anytime my voice got high, it broke my concentration and my breathing became erratic.

It was dark outside, and the room was softly lit. My water broke during my first push, and my baby was born slowly through the next three contractions. I was not aware of whether or not my children were in the room, until I heard my daughter Erin's sweet voice say, "Baby." She was at the edge of the tub, watching as his head came out; then a pause; then his shoulders and waist came out; another pause.... He was floating with his arms out; then his legs followed, and with a hand from his dad, he floated up into my arms. Denise's photos captured the entire sequence, as if it had been shot as a movie and then edited into freeze frames. It was such a gentle birth. The whole time, Robbie was at the edge of the tub taking pictures with his camera. Since Denise was also taking pictures, the back of Robbie's head is in many of her photos. It is really funny to see the Mickey Mouse instamatic sticking out from the side of his head as he clicked away. He wanted to be the one to identify the sex, and when he took a look, he squealed, "A peepee, it's a boy!"

I got out of the tub so that Molly could draw the cord blood for storage. Molly was a CNM associate who had asked to come along for the experience of drawing the cord blood. Stem cell storage was still so new at that time, and many midwives were not experienced with the practice.

My baby nursed immediately and then rested on my chest while we collected the cord blood. My children got impatient with me, asking, "Where's the placenta?" The midwives laughed at how eager they were to see the placenta. The children took turns trying to cut the cord, and my husband helped their tiny hands manage the scissors. After I delivered the placenta, Linda took the children to the kitchen table for a "placenta show." She taught them everything they could possibly want to know about it. Robbie took a whole roll of film of the placenta spread out in the middle of my kitchen table. We still have the pictures, all 36 of them.

After the newborn exam, we had our birthday party. Our children opened up their big brother and big sister gifts, and presented the baby with the gifts they had selected for him. We had birthday cake, took some more pictures, made some phone calls and went to bed. The next day my children went to school with Polaroid snapshots of themselves holding their new baby brother. At a parent-teacher conference a few months later, my son's kindergarten teacher commented about the birth, wondering if his description had been a tall tale or not. It was not every day that a five year old came into her classroom announcing, "Mommy had a baby in the sunroom last night."

Our children still love to talk about that night, and our little baby Liam, who is now three years old, loves to look at the photos and hear the story of his birth. We hope that through the photos and the telling of Liam's birth story, our children will have a good foundation when it comes time for them to have their own children.

A Mother's Guidance: You have to seek out the people who think like you. If you don't have friends or relatives who have experienced natural childbirth, you will need to be very proactive to get the information and support you need. Some general advice: shop or browse at your local health-food store. You are likely to run into other pregnant women there. Start conversations. Ask other customers or the staff for recommendations for a good midwife or prenatal massage therapist. Seek out the information and support you need. Go to prenatal yoga classes. Make sure your childbirth preparation class is really geared towards natural birth. (We were surprised to find that the most famous course was not!) Go anywhere that you may find childbearing people who think like you! A natural birth is the healthiest thing you can do for yourself and your baby. It is something that requires dedication, faith in yourself, and a heartfelt desire to stay in tune with nature.

I came across a book called *The American Way of Birth* by Jessica Mitford. It was a compelling, historical overview of how birth had changed over the years in our country. I was amazed by how nothing in modern obstetrics seemed to support a natural birth. Many people our own age told us how they had to have a C-section because there was fetal distress or the cord was wrapped around the baby's neck, and thank God for the doctor. We wanted to say, "Well, lying on your back can decrease oxygen to the baby, and that will cause some distress...." But we bit our tongues, seeing how inappropriate it would be to tell someone what they should have done. In fact, it would have been just as inappropriate as what they were doing to us, sharing their horror stories!

Know in your heart and mind that you can have the type of birth you want. Remember that women have been giving birth for years and years. If painkillers and interventions were always necessary, humankind would not exist! I recommend the following publications: *Mind over Labor* by Carl Jones, *Gentle Birth Choices* by Barbara Harper, and *Mothering* magazine.

> ***Additional Thoughts:*** If you are committed to attending a natural childbirth class, you may have to find one that is not associated with a hospital—an independent class. Hospital-affiliated educators are often not allowed to advocate for natural childbirth.

Gina Kennedy and her husband Rob live in Spring Lake, New Jersey, with their three children, Robbie, Erin and Liam. They run an indoor instructional basketball facility called Rebounds in Neptune, New Jersey. They spend summers in the Pocono Mountains of Pennsylvania, where they own a basketball camp that has been run by the Kennedy family for more than 40 years.

BORNFREE!

BY LAURA KAPLAN SHANLEY

IT'S A WARM NOVEMBER MORNING in Colorado. I haven't slept well and I'm irritable. My husband David and I have been fighting and I'm nine months pregnant. I've been feeling contractions for the past 24 hours.

David says he is going to the library. Good, I think to myself. I need peace and quiet. The minute he leaves, my contractions change and I know birth is imminent. Four-year-old John and two-year-old Willie are sleeping. I think about calling my friend, Laurie, but decide not to. This time I am giving birth alone. John had been born into David's hands in our bedroom, and Willie had been born into mine, with David and John standing nearby. I know I can do this one myself. This is my challenge. This is my mountain to climb. I know I can do it.

I take a shower. The contractions are intense—more intense than they were with previous labors, but this time I am alone, and I know I am afraid. The water soothes me. I cry. "I am not afraid," I say aloud. "I CAN DO THIS!"

I get out of the shower and take out my little baby bathtub so I can stand over it and catch my baby. The phone rings, and for some reason I answer it. It's a secretary at the university wanting to order donuts—I run a donut delivery service out of my home. I tell her I'm in labor and to call me back later. She panics and says, "But who am I going to give this donut order to?" I hang up the phone and laugh.

I return to the bathtub and straddle it. I am not pushing. This baby is coming out on her own. I look down and see a face covered by a thin film. The baby is still in the water bag. It breaks as she slides into my hands. She looks into my eyes as her body emerges… I am elated. There is no one else in the world, only she and I. She is the most beautiful gift I have ever received. I hold her close and cry. I have climbed the mountain. I have reached the top and been rewarded beyond my wildest dreams!

Within minutes the placenta slips out as I squat over the bathtub. I tie and cut her cord and put her in a baby seat. Suddenly, I'm exhausted. I lie down on the couch and begin to hear strange, lovely sounds—ocean waves gently crashing on the shore, and wind chimes—but we are a thousand miles from the sea and there is no wind today. I am in ecstasy.

The boys wake up, kiss their sister, and make me a glass of chocolate milk. I drink it down and ask for more. An hour later I get up and take a shower. I feel wonderful. As with my second birth, there are no after pains. We all get dressed and put our new baby in a white wicker doll carriage. Down the street we go, off to find David. I am floating on air. I am high.

We find David. He kisses me. He kisses our new baby. All is right with the world.

A Mother's Guidance: Remember not to do too much. The same loving, intelligent consciousness that knows how to grow an egg and a sperm into a human being, knows how to get it out. Nature, God, is efficient. It completes the process—if we let it. Our job is simply to relax and allow our bodies to work the way they were designed.

Childbirth without Fear by Grantly Dick-Read was my favorite book during my first pregnancy. I also liked *Spiritual Midwifery* by Ina May Gaskin, but no longer feel good about recommending it as I find it too limiting. These days there are several wonderful birth books on the market that do a much better job of reassuring women that giving birth can be a safe, empowering, ecstatic experience—*The Power of Pleasurable Childbirth* by Laurie Morgan, *Unassisted Homebirth* by Lynn Griesemer, *Prenatal Yoga and Natural Childbirth* by Jeannine Parvati Baker, and my own book, *Unassisted Childbirth*. My favorite birth magazines are *The Mother Magazine*, *The Compleat Mother* and *Pandora's Box*.

Additional Thoughts: According to the author of this story, Laura Shanley, less than 0.33% of births are unassisted, and the numbers are rising. Of those, there are no statistics on how many were planned unassisted or unplanned unassisted. There are about 20 to 30 unassisted childbirth newsgroups online, with one of the largest composed of over 900 members.

Laura Shanley is a writer, speaker, poet, and author of the book Unassisted Childbirth. She and her family live in Boulder, Colorado, where Laura runs an online bookstore and a nanny referral service. More information on Laura and her books can be found at www.unassistedchildbirth.com.

HEAVENLY SCENT

BY LEANNE MITCHELL

I HAVE BEEN OFFERING labor support and postpartum doula services, as well as specializing in pregnancy massage, for five years; so planning and conceiving my first child was an exciting step for me, both personally as a woman and professionally. It was finally time to step beyond the informational books, trainings and professional experiences, and turn inwards to apply them to my own life. Conception marked the beginning of an amazing journey and course in self-realization, one that carried all the way through the birth of my son, Jahsiah.

For years I had anticipated a home birth. But that dream was shattered when I discovered that I carry two genetic blood disorders. One trait, called Protein S deficiency, I inherited from my father; Factor V Leiden came from my mother. Carrying both disorders meant my pregnancy was classified as "high risk," and a home birth was discouraged. I was heartbroken.

I was closely monitored for blood clotting by the perinatology department. My doctors insisted I begin anticoagulant medication immediately, continuing through six weeks postpartum, when the risk of blood clotting would be at its highest. I thoroughly researched the clotting disorders and challenged the doctors, requesting that they consider my research and allow me to proceed with a non-medicated pregnancy. The perinatolgists made several comments about how impressed they were with my research and proactive stance. They ultimately "agreed to disagree" with me and allowed me to take my own chances, under two conditions: they would monitor me closely throughout the pregnancy; and I had to agree to take anticoagulants, starting at 36 weeks and continuing through six weeks postpartum. I was satisfied with this compromise and agreed. It was a frustrating process at times… the close monitoring, ultrasounds, Doppler scans of my veins, and non-stress tests twice a week for the last month. Deep down inside I knew everything was OK, and that feeling never left me, not once.

For 40 weeks my husband and I had awaited the estimated due date of April 13th. As that day approached, I anticipated any and every change that my body could go through to show me signs of labor. On a day of reflection, as I looked back over the entire pregnancy with amazement, I sat and talked with my baby about how we would be meeting any time now. I imagined my labor and birth, and talked to my son about how very important it would be to work together through the labor, and that we needed to communicate with each other to help his birth move as smoothly as possible. I told him that there could be some discomfort, but promised that it would be short lived in comparison to the enduring, immense love that I would give to him for the rest of his life. The day ended with no signs of labor, but I felt a deep sense that it would be starting soon.

Anticipation grew throughout the week until finally, on the morning of April 19th, I awoke with mild cramping, very similar to menstrual cramps. My family was in town, so I wanted to keep everything between my husband and I to avoid too much focus on me. My experience as a labor doula had taught me about the problems that a laboring woman could experience when under the well-meaning but intense scrutiny of family members and friends. So much attention from others can be very distracting, and often keeps a woman from completely surrendering to her labor.

It's as if the birth becomes an event, instead of the truly intimate and serious process that it is between father, mother and child.

As the day proceeded, the cramping stayed very consistent and then I developed some spotting. I called my labor support midwives, Michelle and Gerri, to let them know what I was experiencing; we agreed to keep in contact throughout the day. I had planned on doing a lot of walking around in labor, and I did… to the bathroom! I wanted to see if I was still spotting, which reassured me that this was the real thing, and I knew that the more frequently I emptied my bladder the more room the baby would have to move down. Little did I know, my sister was keeping a mental note of how often I was using the bathroom, and the amount of attention I was giving to my cramping. I thought I was being so sneaky. At 1:30 p.m., during lunch at a local restaurant, I told my husband it was time to go home. Labor was definitely picking up to the point where I needed to get comfortable in my home environment. By then the entire family had figured out that I was in labor, and our excitement danced throughout the conversations.

Once we were home, we lit some nice candles, turned on relaxing music, and moved into the active stage of labor. I had a good idea of what I needed to do and which positions would be most effective, so I managed to flow with the rhythm of labor.

My plan to keep my family involved during my labor did not go as well as I had hoped. My husband and I had made arrangements for my mother and sister to stay at a local hotel while I was in labor, but when we asked them to go they got very angry and aggressive, giving ultimatums and threatening to leave town. No laboring woman should have to deal with family politics between contractions—I needed to focus. To minimize the stress, I decided to just go with the flow and allow them to stay present, but told them they either had to help or stay out of the way completely.

Around 5:30 p.m. my wonderful midwife/doula arrived and a very strong sense of confidence came over me. I believe it was because I felt so safe and well taken care of. I labored in the bathtub, in the shower, on my knees with a birthing ball, sitting on the birthing ball, hanging on to my husband, and leaning on the back of the sofa… we moved around a lot! Between contractions I rested deeply, almost asleep, taking advantage of the well deserved breaks. I listened closely to my body as it labored, staying active and hydrated to avoid exhaustion. I had to take it one contraction at a time, and allow the experience to be whatever it needed to be —to let go of the need to control the situation.

I learned along the way to relax everything in my body, including my excitement, and let my mind stay steady with thoughts of the baby moving down. I was actively visualizing his birth, over and over, and over again. I kept the mental and physical relaxation steady through deep breathing and moaning with each contraction. Moaning allowed me to take long breaths, and to follow my voice instead of my thoughts. I know that these coping strategies, as well as my confidence in the people surrounding me, contributed to a relatively short active labor of 11 hours.

My midwife checked my dilation and the position of the baby around 9:00 p.m. —I was five centimeters dilated and the baby was very low. We decided it was time to go to the hospital, based on my steady progression and the need for time to adjust to a hospital environment. Shifting into a "managed" environment, I really didn't know what to expect. I knew anything could happen and I reminded myself to stay strong, informed and focused.

We arrived at the hospital by 10:00 p.m., and as we walked through the hospital, I did not rush. I continued to hold my "meditation," not letting the new environment disrupt my progress. During the admittance process, if I was asked a question during a contraction, I let them know I would answer in a moment, and I paced myself the entire way through the emergency entrance to my laboring room. Once in my room, everyone worked together to keep me comfortable and recreate the environment we had at home. The nurse did a vaginal exam and let me know that I was at seven centimeters.

I utilized every space available in my laboring room, including the birthing ball. Two hours later, another exam confirmed that I was nine to nine-and-a-half centimeters dilated. Almost there! I followed the cues of my labor support midwife to do some light pushing in a squat position, and all of a sudden, I felt my son's head do an unforgettable slide down and under my pelvic bones. The doctor on call was not nearby, so my midwife grabbed her gloves and guided my husband's hands into position, in case birth was moments away. At that point I was asked if I would like a mirror to see my son. I declined, focusing intently to keep my thoughts away from any discomfort... the sight may have just been too real for me. The doctor arrived, suctioned my son's nose and mouth, and with one more gentle push my son was born into his father's hands at 12:42 a.m.

My first sight of my son will never leave my memory. As I write this, tears are welling up in my eyes. Only at that moment did I really unconditionally love. I had never known the feeling in my life. His beauty radiated within my husband's heart and mine. His first cry was like a psalm, and his scent was just as heavenly. He settled quickly to my voice and looked at me with the most loving stare, and then closed his eyes and rested peacefully. I would labor and birth a million times over just to see my son for the first time again. It was incredible! I have entered into a part of my life that only the hearts of other mothers know, and it is unexplainable.

Notes from Michelle, the Midwife

I accompanied Leanne to her first perinatologist consultation; she asserted herself intelligently and was received by the doctor as such. They interacted well and the doctor became empathetic to her concerns, leading to mutually respectful negotiations. They worked together on a plan that satisfied the doctor's concern for the mom and baby, while keeping intervention to a minimum. In my spirit I knew she would have a perfect birth and that she would not have a problem from her inherited blood traits, but we all agreed that we must put the mother's safety first and yield to caution. As a result, she had the perfect hospital birth. It was the most amazing, peaceful, nurturing, respectful hospital birth that I have experienced in my twenty years of attending births.

A Mother's Guidance: At the end of my pregnancy, I read the book *Active Birth: The New Approach to Giving Birth Naturally* by Janet Balaskas. It gave me the confidence that I could do this. This birth experience showed me strength, courage, faith, love and confidence. It was an education in the value of a good relationship with your caregivers, and being able to express to them all that you want and don't want, even if you have to meet in the middle.

Leanne Mitchell and her husband Patrick live in Vista, California, with their son Jahsiah. Leanne is a massage therapist as well as a labor and postpartum doula. Patrick owns Quashi Surfboards.

A PIVOTAL MOMENT

BY NANCY M^cINERNEY

LIFE IS FULL OF PROGRESSIONS, and wonderfully exciting moments that will shape who you are. If you pay close attention, and listen to the small voice within, you'll find transformation hiding behind your decisions.

I had wanted to experience natural childbirth with my first child. Unfortunately, I was surrounded by people who had never even considered a drug-free, vaginal birth. I myself was a C-section baby, and my sister had only C-sections; both my mother and sister told me that I couldn't have a baby "normally."

I gave birth to my first child in the hospital with drugs and an epidural, and the experience was far from perfect. I was so caught up in my excitement about having my son and being a new mom that I let other people have too much influence in my decisions about how to do things. I only breastfed a short while, as all my family and friends at that time discouraged it, telling me it was too hard, that I would never get enough sleep. I listened because I was afraid and unsure of myself. I also had my son circumcised, which I instinctively knew not to do, but did anyway. It was not until years later that I was able to face the pain of how I was treated in the hospital, and how I had let others tell me what to do. I had a lot of disappointment and guilt to overcome before I could move on to having another child.

By the time I was ready to give birth again, I had grown considerably in my ability to trust myself and do what I needed to do. I had studied herbal medicine, which took me on a journey of healing both my body and my spiritual self. That phase of my life took me up to upstate New York, where I attended an herb symposium that introduced me to Jeannine Parvati Baker, a shamanic midwife. She birthed all six of her children at home, home-schooled her children, and is an amazing mother. I instantly felt a connection and realized I needed to empower myself. I decided right then that I would not birth my next child in a hospital.

I was living in Brooklyn, New York, and believe it or not, there were only three home birth midwives in all of New York City. The one I chose happened to live three blocks away. However, right after I became pregnant, I lost my job in a domestic violence shelter. My husband was just starting a new job and I had no insurance... a scary place for a pregnant woman to be. I had to find a job fast, and find insurance. I went on prenatal Medicaid, which doesn't cover home births, and hoped it would all work out. To apply for Medicaid, I had to go to a hospital and have all the routine tests done, including ultrasound. Nothing was working out as I had planned; I was stressed, to say the least.

When I went to have my ultrasound done, the nurse brought in a female doctor to tell me that I had placenta previa, and there was no way I could have a normal, vaginal birth. "Doing so could kill you and your baby," she said. I was horrified, and asked her to explain again. She seemed annoyed and probably assumed I was uneducated because I had Medicaid. I was only four months pregnant, and knew you could not decisively diagnose placenta previa that early. (**Editor's Note:** Placenta previa is a condition where the placenta is positioned very low in the uterus, and threatens to or even does cover the cervix. If the cervix opens while the placenta is covering it, the woman will hemorrhage and the baby's oxygen supply is cut off. An important thing to remember about a diagnosis of placenta previa: As the uterus grows with the baby, the position of the placenta shifts. Someone who is diagnosed with this condition early in her pregnancy should be checked again as the pregnancy progresses. It is often a self-correcting condition.)

I never went back to the hospital. I was committed to trusting my body and myself. I knew that if I did have placenta previa, I would probably experience some bleeding around the seventh month. I didn't have any bleeding, and proceeded to go into my ninth month without any complications. The hospital's diagnosis was incorrect.

I eventually found a job and had the insurance I needed, but it was a very stressful time for all of us. Through it all, I continued to say, "I will have this baby at home."

On the morning of July 21st, I awoke at 2:00 a.m. I was having some bloody show and bad cramping. I felt sure it was time. I called my best friend, Holly, and she came right away to help me and to watch my oldest son while I labored.

I was very calm, but very afraid as well—I still did not have total trust in myself. Through the early part of my labor, I walked outside with Holly, snacking and drinking herbal teas. I felt alive and excited. Then after about 10 hours of fairly easy labor, it all changed. I became very afraid and wondered if I had lost my mind. I wasn't at all sure that I still wanted to have a home birth. *What the hell was I thinking? Oh my God, I cannot do this.*

I sat in my bathtub with my husband, and he helped me so much by just being there. I then went to my bed, where I immediately felt safer. My bed, my wonderful bed! It was a pivotal moment—the safety of my bed relaxed me enough to calm me. I imagined myself as a flower opening, getting wider and wider, and I opened my legs as wide as they would go. I allowed the pain to just be, instead of fighting it. I was very quiet, and everyone else sensed the need to be quiet, even my four-year-old son. I needed the quietness to help me. I didn't even know who was in the room. I went into myself and began facing it all. I began to realize that this was a defining moment in my life.

At the same time, I was very afraid of pushing. When the time finally came, I panicked. This was the most difficult time for me. I had not been able to push with my first child; the epidural had made me too numb, and the doctor resorted to forceps. The memories of someone else pulling my baby out of me were still in my mind, and at some level I believed that I just couldn't do this by myself. I wasn't sure what I should do, but the midwife kept saying, "You will know."

There is a moment in labor when the woman realizes that there is no turning back. On the threshold of a new chapter of her life, she literally pushes her way through thoughts of, "I am having a baby and I am not quite sure I am ready for it, but it's happening." I most definitely needed to hear positive remarks from everyone around me at this time, and they were amazing in sensing that need in me. I remember hearing, "You can do this," and I believed all of them when they said it.

I continued to feel very afraid of the pain. It was quite intense, but also very different from earlier contractions. I was able to push my son out in thirty minutes. I felt like I was tearing, but I wasn't. I remembered reading that the first response to vaginal pain is for a woman to close her legs, so I just kept opening as wide as I could and it really eased the pain for me. I went with it, and just allowed my body to feel all that I could. We have the inner knowledge that is necessary to get us through anything.

When my son finally came to me, I was just so unbelievably happy that I had given birth, and done so without one drug or intervention. It was the most empowered I ever felt. I just felt so high and amazed at myself, it was truly a surge of power.

I am still high from that day. On a weekly basis, I draw upon the strength that I found in birth. When I start to doubt myself and my abilities as a mother, or as a person trying to get through life, I look at the videos of both of my children's births. They call me within myself, and remind me that I can do anything!

A Mother's Guidance: Don't believe everything you hear, especially in a hospital. I have worked in hospitals throughout most of my career as a social worker. You have to understand that it is someone's workplace. They aren't always interested in your highest path; they may be tired, or sick of their job, or wishing you would just hurry up and have that baby. Continue working on trusting yourself throughout your pregnancy and entire life. Write down your fears and worries in a journal—it helps to get them out of your head and onto paper. Write letters to your baby and explain how you feel. It helps you keep in touch with all that is happening. Trust in yourself, and have only people around you that you feel safe with. Don't be afraid to say what you want, and remember to open your legs wide. Allow the pain to be a part of you.

I love *Mothering* magazine. I read every issue and owe them a lot. Anything written by William and Martha Sears is good, and I loved Ina May Gaskin's *Spiritual Midwifery*. I also adore Jeannine Parvati Baker and her words of wisdom.

I did take Lamaze classes with my first pregnancy. I think childbirth classes are great and would recommend them only if the person teaching them is really in support of natural childbirth; otherwise you may get a lot of scary propaganda.

Nancy McInerney and her husband Tim live in upstate New York. Nancy works in a hospital as a case manager. She is planning on going to nursing school to get her RN license, and then moving on to midwifery. Tim is a fourth-grade school teacher. Finn is in kindergarten, and is quite shy but a comedian at heart. Kieran is in fifth grade and still remembers the birth of his brother.

WATER BIRTH UNDER THE STARS

BY GAYLA MAY BURDEN

THE MORNING OF APRIL 22nd was the first day of my 38th week, and I felt different. As I rolled out of bed I felt a tiny bit of water dribble down my leg. But just a tiny bit. I wasn't sure if this was a sign or not, so I went about my day... but stayed at home. About 1:30 p.m. I felt some mild cramping. Again, I didn't think much of it, and when I talked to my husband, who was at work, I told him not to bother coming home early. He reminded me that when I went into labor, he would need time to fill the hot tub, where we planned to birth the baby. So I thought twice and told him to come home.

I called my midwife, Yelena, and told her how I felt. She said to keep in contact with her, that this was most likely it. Well, it was. By the time my husband came home, I needed his help in timing the contractions. I kept walking around through each one. I felt like my body was starting to transform. Change was happening fast.

At 7 p.m. I phoned my midwife again, and as we were speaking my water gushed onto the carpet like a broken water balloon. This was the beginning of a new stage, and the contractions were coming on strong and fast. I stayed on my feet, rocking back and forth to ride them out. Circling my hips really helped. My midwife had said to phone her when I needed her, and suddenly, I did. Our baby was coming soon.

When my midwife arrived I felt like it was just in time. The contractions were starting to overwhelm me. She suggested a shower, which was very calming, but I was just itching to get into the hot tub. I had read every story on www.waterbirthinfo.com— twice. I think I had them memorized, and those memories were pushing me to the hot tub. When my midwife checked me and found that I was already at five centimeters, I was elated. She gave me the go-ahead to get into the tub, so at 8:45, in I went. The water felt so wonderful. It was a warm spring evening, and night had just begun to set in.

My husband and I had done many test runs to gauge how long it took the hot tub to fill and heat up, and it was a good five hours. My labor was moving fast, and it had only been four hours since we filled it so the temperature was only up to 83 degrees. Once I got into the water the contractions slowed down a little. So my wonderful husband connected a garden hose to the hot water heater inside the house and started pumping it in. The water circled around my body like a warm blanket.

The transition stage came on fast. I remember looking up at the stars and letting out a scream that felt animalistic. I moaned and moaned as I felt the baby's head making its way down. My husband gently rubbed my back, and the midwives took the baby's heart rate a couple of times.

When I was ready to push, they asked me to get out of the tub. The midwives were concerned that the water wasn't hot enough for the baby. Well I thought it was damn close enough! Nothing was getting me out. It wasn't 98 degrees yet, maybe only 92, but I wasn't moving. I panted, "Babies have been born in the Baltic Sea in Russia, I'm not getting out." They looked at each other and said, "OK." I knew my baby would be just fine; something deep inside told me. I trusted my instincts.

The pushing stage went fast. As the head started coming down I gave some really strong pushes. I remembered reading that many women enjoyed reaching down to feel the head emerging, so I did. Then I grabbed my husband's hand and had him feel it too.

Our baby's head was covered in hair. Touching our child for the first time gave me a lot of encouragement to push the head out. We had the hot tub light on low so we could see, and when his head came out he had his eyes wide open. I looked down and there he was, staring back at me. I rested for a moment, then pushed the rest of his beautiful little body out. My husband put his hands underneath him and gently brought him up to the surface.

The cord was kind of short, so I couldn't nurse him right away. My husband and I just held him for a few minutes in the water. It was amazing to see this new person emerge into the world. In a matter of seconds, we had shifted from a family of two to a family of three.

We got out of the tub and walked inside. Our family room was quiet and warm, with soft music in the background. It was just like a dream. We sat on the couch and got acquainted for a while. After several minutes with the lights very low, my husband said, "So, what is the sex of our baby?" (We hadn't had any ultrasound tests, so we didn't know ahead of time.) I had been so caught up in birthing that I hadn't even thought to check. It had been so dark outside, and the lights were so low inside, we hadn't noticed. I said, "I feel little balls, I'm pretty sure it's a boy." And it was. Logan James had been born.

My husband cut the cord, and about 25 minutes later I was ready to release the placenta. I got on my hands and knees and gave a huge push; out it popped, right onto the floor. It was big and beautiful, and completely intact.

The birth was more wonderful than I ever could have imagined. It happened so fast. From the time I got into the hot tub to the time he was born was about an hour. The entire labor lasted about four to five hours, and I know it was so short because of the water. I think water birth is a miracle; it makes birth wonderful and enjoyable.

The process was perfect, without interruptions and distractions—just like I wanted it to be. I didn't want a circus of people around me. I love my family very much, but I felt that it was important to have very few people there. I believe people birth naturally, just like animals, when we are left alone. Our bodies know how to take over. I'd do it again right now, and again tomorrow. I look back on the experience and get excited to do it again soon.

A Mother's Guidance: Research made such a difference in my understanding of birthing. With that wonderful website out there and with the help of many books, I have come full circle. I used to believe that I would have a hospital birth, with drugs, and maybe not nurse my child. Yet I had a home birth (naturally), and am a proud member of La Leche League. Thank the heavens for the Internet. It literally changed my life... and Logan's! He is stronger and healthier than most babies his age; even his doctor agrees. And he loves the water!

I am so thankful for the water birth. It has been a dream, not to mention an empowering experience as a woman. It has made me realize that I am strong, and capable of anything.

Your surroundings play a huge role in the birth experience; studies have shown that the very minute you walk through that hospital door, your pulse rises. I believe we need to be left alone, to birth like the mammals we are, doing what comes naturally in your own environment. At my birth I had my husband, my best friend and two midwives. I told them to leave me alone for most of the time, and for me, that was what I knew I needed; to be alone, to know help was there, but not to have people hovering over me or talking around me. I believe my birth was fast because of that. I was totally relaxed and moving at my own pace; no one told me to push, I did it myself.

Logan's birth changed my life. Having a gentle birth, and having things my way, on my terms, gave me a confidence and womanly power I never had before. Birthing naturally makes you realize there's nothing in life you can't conquer.

I decided not to take childbirth classes. I do not agree with the Lamaze or Bradley approach. However my midwife gave a short class and incorporated some *Birthing from Within* techniques that I liked. I also found the following books helpful: *Water Birth:*

A Midwife's Perspective by Susanna Napierala and *Immaculate Deception II: Myth, Magic and Birth* by Suzanne Arms.

Gayla May Burden and her husband Justin live in San Jose, California, and have one son, Logan James Burden. Gayla is a full-time stay-at-home mom. Justin works as a glazier with architectural metal and glass.

MY LITTLE FLOWER

BY TRICIA KRUSE

As I sit watching my child pick dandelions and rinse them off in a bucket, I am reminded of how my little "flower" came to be. My birth story begins on a beautiful day in September....

At nine months pregnant, I had been sleeping on the couch for quite sometime. The couch was so firm, and when I lay on my side my big belly fit perfectly into the crook between the two cushions. It was about 5:30 a.m. when I rolled from my living room oasis and stood up to go to the bathroom, and a little trickle went down my leg. I have often heard of women who mistake their water breaking for accidental urine leakage, and I always wondered how that could be, but for a split second it happened to me too. Then I realized what was happening! As I made a beeline for the bathroom I grabbed the phone. I called my mom (who, fortunately, is an early riser) and said, "Mom?" to which she responded, "Yes?" in a voice about two octaves higher than normal, elevated with anticipation of news. "I think my water broke," I said, starting to explain what had happened. As I sat on the toilet and talked, a huge rush of water suddenly flowed out.

I got cleaned up and went upstairs to change. When I opened my drawer it woke my husband up. I told him everything was

OK, so he went back to sleep. (I figured it would be nice to let him sleep as long as possible since I was pretty sure it was going to be a long day.) I quietly moved back down stairs and began making travel arrangements with my mom, who regrettably lives 1000 miles away. I hung up and tried calling our travel agent, but of course it was too early. I called my mom back and told her to get ready, although I knew her birth bag was packed even before mine was! I promised to call her back once our travel agent was in the office. The next call I made was to my office to say I wouldn't be in today—or ever again.

I proceeded back upstairs, and this time Ron knew something was up (or coming down, which ever way you want to look at it). I told him my water had broken, and his demeanor instantly went from sleepy and relaxed to "Oh my God!" panic—he jumped up right away. While he was in the shower I called his parents to ask if they felt like becoming grandparents today.

My one fear about labor was that I would have to go to the hospital unshowered, with hairy legs, so I headed for the shower. Ron told me we didn't have time for that, but there was no stopping me. My contractions were coming regularly, but they were certainly bearable. So, being the hormonally-challenged prego lady that I was, I quickly put him in his place, got showered, and tried to dress as fast as I could. It must have been quite a sight to see a wet, full-term pregnant lady in labor hurrying to get dressed. Ron was so distracted by the sight that he nicked himself shaving, which proceeded to bleed for the rest of the day.

By 6:30 we had packed the car with the birth bag, CD player and my belly, and headed off to the hospital. I remember taking one of those surreal mental snapshots on the way, looking at the clock in the car while we were at a stoplight next to a Taco Bell and thinking, *it is 6:36 and I am in labor*. To this day whenever I pass the Taco Bell I am reminded of the big day!

By the time we reached the hospital 20 minutes later, my contractions were much stronger—strong enough to make me stop walking down the hall. Eventually we made it to the triage room, and while I was changing into a gown, the nurse tended to Ron's bleeding face! I was anxious to find out how far along I was, because three weeks earlier my doctor had told me I was already three centimeters dilated. Imagine our surprise when the nurse said joyfully, "You're already at five centimeters!" Half way there! Shortly thereafter we moved to the labor-and-delivery room, which was very pleasant.

With our baby on its way, we still had to deal with my mom's flight. I managed to call the travel agent, but had to hand the phone over to Ron as the contractions became more intense. They arranged for a flight that would arrive at 12:30 p.m. God had worked one miracle and was getting ready to work another! I was really looking forward to having my mother present for the birth. Having gone through four births naturally, I knew she would be a great support.

I spent the next hour walking the halls, but when I had an especially strong contraction I panicked. I was afraid I had wandered too far from my room, and would become a spectacle by being the first person to give birth in the hallway of the maternity ward. We made our way back to the room and I tried to rest by lying on the bed—a big mistake. The contractions were amplified when I was in a horizontal position. I made several visits to the bathroom, utterly convinced that I had to go, but ultimately producing nothing.

Eventually we (the baby, my husband and I) found a groove. I discovered that if I draped my arms over Ron's shoulders, swayed with each contraction and controlled my breathing, I could focus and remain positive. After each contraction we would sit on the bed together and I would just lean on Ron as I rested. During the resting phase I focused on the sounds of my favorite musical CD.

For the next two hours we held this same pattern. We were so focused and in sync that I don't even know who came and went from the room, although at some point I was aware that Ron's parents had arrived and were there to support us.

I was totally focused on each contraction and the growing anticipation of discovering if we would have a boy or girl. Keeping the sex of the baby a surprise until the end gave me a big incentive to make it through the laboring process. At some point my husband said they did another check and I had progressed to eight centimeters. You would think I would remember a pelvic exam, but I guess labor does have some benefits. At last the nurse asked if I thought it was time to push. I remember replying "yes" but then thinking, "Oh no, I don't really know if it's time to push or not. I've never been through this before!" But by the time I was in position, it was obviously time to push. As someone went to find the doctor, my nurse began to massage my perineum in hopes of stretching it out enough to avoid an episiotomy.

As I started pushing I felt a sharp pain in my lower left side, and I immediately thought the worst—I told the doctor I couldn't push through the pain. She very calmly asked the labor-and-delivery nurse to come to my left side to apply counter pressure. "Perhaps," she said, "the baby was on a nerve." After the nurse held pressure on my side I was able to push with no problem. Although I had prearranged for a mirror so I could watch the birth, I found it broke my concentration so I ended up not using it.

At one point during the 45 minutes of pushing, I felt frustrated because I thought I wasn't making good progress, and I knew I was losing my concentration. I'll never forget the boost my nurse gave me. I was truly grateful when she said, "Honey, you have made it further now without medication than 90% of the women I see. You can do this, and you are doing this. Relax, and on the next contraction, get your focus and go. This is it, and you know you can do it." I felt an instant bond with her at that point, and felt so much support that I knew I could do it. As the contraction subsided, I felt myself completely relax into the bed.

Then I asked my husband how he was doing. The doctor laughed, and said she doesn't often hear women asking the men how they are doing during labor. But Ron and I are a good team. I knew that the whole laboring process was just as challenging to him, but in different ways. Afterwards he told me it was very difficult to see me like that and not be able to do anything to help.

After the nurse's words of encouragement, I was able to push the baby out with the next contraction... and it was a girl! Jenna was born at 12:26 p.m. She arrived in Pensacola just four minutes before my mother. By the time my mom arrived at the hospital, Jenna was securely latched on and going to town! My mom's disappointment in missing the birth was quickly replaced by the joy of holding her first grandchild.

A Mother's Guidance: You've got to know and trust your body, your natural instincts. Accept people's advice and suggestions graciously—they are just trying to help—but in the end it comes down to only you and your body. Women's bodies are made for giving birth. They know what to do, and if we let our mind connect with what the body knows it paves the way for a successful birth. Many women tend to overthink labor, leading the mind to work against the body rather than accept the natural process of labor. Fears and worries about birth can create so much tension that we lose touch with what our body is telling us. All of the medications that are available take away our power to work with our bodies. Relax. Accept that your body is going to experience intense feelings, and know that it is natural—there is nothing to fear.

Early on in the pregnancy I knew that I wanted to try Hypno-Birthing to help with the delivery, but because there are no certified therapists in the area I decided to purchase a kit online. Although I had purchased the HypnoBirthing information, my husband could never coach me through one full session without laughing. So in the end, I didn't use the actual HypnoBirthing strategies, but I found another piece of the program tremendously helpful. Throughout my last two trimesters, I religiously played the "Affirmations" tape each morning as I got ready for work. The tape offers simple statements, set to calming music, that build your confidence. They suggest that as a woman you are naturally ready to have a baby... your body knows exactly what to do.

I can't wait to go through the miracle of birth again! I will never forget Jenna's birth, and I revel in the fact that through the help of the HypnoBirthing tapes, I was able to stay focused and calm through the natural process of birthing my child.

Additional Thoughts: The power of your support people cannot be overstated. It was the right words, at the right moment, that gave Tricia the inspiration and focus to conquer that last contraction. Sometimes during labor a woman loses concentration, and needs someone to reassure her and remind her to concentrate on just that one contraction, not on the ones in the future.

Tricia Kruse and her husband Ron met 13 years ago when they were 19 and 17 years old. After a long-distance relationship they married in October 1991. They spent the next 10 years working through college and finally got the "baby bug" in 2000. They have one daughter and are trying for another child.

MOTIVATED BY A NAP

BY MAISHA KHALFANI

SAFIYA IFE was born on Sunday, August 30th. Mild contractions came on Friday afternoon, and they got slightly stronger as the evening came, but I didn't give it much thought. I got very little sleep that Friday night because the contractions became so uncomfortable, and when my water broke that night, I thought, "This is it!" My husband called the midwife on duty at the birth center and told her how I was progressing. Since I wasn't out of breath and able to carry on a conversation, they told us that I didn't need to come in. I decided to do some laundry on Saturday and go for a walk, hoping it would help the baby come. I was so anxious to meet the baby inside me, and even more anxious to have my body back!

All day Saturday I had contractions. By Saturday night they were STRONG. Thank God for the Bradley classes we had taken! I was able to deal with the pain in a relatively easy way. It wasn't as bad as I thought it would be. Around 4 a.m. we called the midwife again, and this time I couldn't hold a decent conversation. It was time to go.

My husband called a cab (we didn't have a car at the time), and my stepdaughter, husband and I headed to the birth center. I think we got there a little after 5 a.m. on Sunday morning. (Your brain gets so fuzzy while you're in labor.)

I was seven centimeters dilated and quite effaced. I was led into the bedroom that I had previously chosen and I immediately changed my clothes. I didn't know how long this was going to take, but I wanted to be comfortable. You know, the funny thing is that I wasn't scared or nervous at all during labor. I was concentrating on my body, just like I had been taught in the Bradley classes. My goal was to relax and allow my body to do its job. I didn't want to interfere too much.

By Sunday afternoon I had been in hard labor for quite some time. I'm so thankful that I was at a birthing center and with midwives. They nurtured me and took the worry away from my husband. I felt calm and relaxed the whole time. I was even cracking jokes! I don't know if this sounds odd, but the labor almost seemed fun. Mind you, it was hard work, but it felt good. I don't know how else to explain it.

At 7:30 p.m. there was still no sign of Safiya. One of the midwives did some acupuncture around my ankles and all of a sudden, these deep, heavy-duty contractions began! Suddenly, my body was ready to deliver this baby. My husband held one leg, a midwife held the other, and they told me to push. And PUSH I did, with every fiber in my body. I remember wanting to take a nap during the pushing. My husband told me I couldn't do that yet, but I could take a nap once Safiya was out. The idea of a nap was so motivating, so I pushed again. And her head was out! I was invigorated, so energized that I felt as if I had slept for a good six hours. The experience was so amazing. There was a body coming out of me! I gave another good, hard push to get those shoulders going, and Safiya slid out, right into my husband's hands. I was amazed. I was shaking. I had just given birth. I had endured the labor. I had let my body do its job.

I was excited and exhausted all at the same time. My husband handed her to me and I laid her on my chest. I couldn't believe it. In my arms was the same child that had been in my body for the past 39 and a half weeks. I was so in love with her, and with the experience of her birth.

♡ *A Mother's Guidance:* Make sure you have a supportive partner with you while you're in labor. Relax and enjoy the experience; your body knows exactly what it's doing. And be sure everyone involved gets a copy of your birth plan.

Maisha Khalfani is the home-schooling mom of five-year-old Safiya, four-year-old Dakari and one-year-old Khalid, and help-mate to Jabari. She is also the stepmother to 14-year-old Rohana. Maisha is the founder of the Capital Area Home-schooling Community, as well as an active member of Mocha Moms, Inc. (www.mochamoms.org), which is a support group for stay-at-home mothers of color. All three of Maisha's births were unmedicated, either at home or at a birthing center.

HIGH ON BIRTH

BY DONNA SCHRADER

AFTER A DISAPPOINTING birth experience with my first son, Colin, I was determined that my second time around would be different. I spent three years reading, researching, and seeking out other families who had positive birth experiences. My husband Dave and I attended HypnoBirthing classes to learn relaxation techniques and to build my confidence in my body's birthing capability. We practiced fairly regularly, but I still had some fears up until I went into labor. I secretly harbored lingering doubts that I'd be able to give birth as easily as the HypnoBirth class suggested, or even as "bravely" as the other veteran moms I'd talked to at the birth center.

My due date, March 3rd, came and went with no sign of labor. On March 4th I decided to give up worrying. What would happen, would happen, and I couldn't do a whole lot about it. Colin and I went to the mall and walked around. We threw coins in all the fountains, wishing for the baby to come soon. When we got home, I felt much better. I was aware of a lot of pressure down low, but it had been there throughout the last trimester. That evening, the baby was moving a lot (constantly, actually) and much more strongly than I'd felt recently. In retrospect, I now believe I was in early labor, but it didn't register with me because, despite the HypnoBirth classes, I was expecting labor to be painful.

I awoke a little after 3 a.m. on March 5th. The pressure had intensified but I had no thought whatsoever that this was IT—that labor had started. I drifted in and out of sleep, and by 3:30 I knew that I needed to get into a warm tub. This was not unusual, as it had been my habit to do so throughout my pregnancy whenever I had insomnia or leg cramps. By about 3:45 a.m., I called for Dave. I still maintained that I was not in labor. I was having waves of intense pressure, but only down low, not at all in my back or abdomen as I had anticipated. I felt very calm.

I got through what I now know were surges/contractions by rhythmically sounding out EE...EE...EE, or OO...OO...OO, or LA...LA...LA, and sort of "conducting" with my arms in the air. Anything rhythmic during the contractions helped me get through them. This is the part that is hard to explain: as long as I vocalized, I got through them just fine. I wasn't really hurting, just feeling like I was in an altered state. My body had taken control of the rest of me and I was just along for the ride. I was moving and twisting in the tub as my body directed. It was all a bit surreal. Describing it here does it little justice.

Eventually Dave insisted we start timing, and after a while he said, "Well, whatever it is, it's happening every three to four minutes." At about 5 a.m. he called the birth center. Our midwife talked to us and we decided we'd better come in. I was starting to feel a little more certain that this was indeed labor. I wasn't fearful, but very serious and very focused on what was happening in my body.

Contractions were getting intense at this point and I didn't want Dave to talk to me or touch me, but I did want him right there with me. This was a problem, as he needed to load the car with our birth supplies. Meanwhile, I got out of the tub and threw on a nightgown, underwear, sweatpants, and slippers of all things!

Dave's mom arrived to stay with Colin. They loaded the car, and even managed to set boxes out onto the doorstep for the Cancer Society, which was coming to pick up our donation that morning! Between contractions I got myself downstairs and put my coat on.

It was the coldest night of the year, but I didn't even notice. Once I climbed into the car at about 6:15 a.m., everything seemed easier. It felt good to be sitting up. There was a lot of traffic, and I started to get a little nervous as I recognized the urge to push. I had fleeting thoughts that the baby would come in the car. I remember looking at the guy in the lane next to us thinking, "If he only knew." By the car's clock I noted that contractions were coming about every two minutes.

When we finally pulled into the birth center at about 6:45 a.m., I was so relieved. I walked in the door and had a contraction right away. My midwife was there and she guided me to the exam room so she could check me. She said I was nine centimeters dilated, and I was so glad.

When my water broke, I realized that I hadn't even thought about it until that point. I felt relief after it broke; the pressure was far less. I also realized my mouth was as dry as a desert, so the apprentice midwife brought me ice chips. My midwife said I wouldn't make it upstairs to the room that I had chosen earlier; would I mind going into the downstairs room? By that point, I would have given birth in the middle of the street if it had been the closest place!

I got into the room and onto the bed and again felt the urge to push. I remember feeling so good between contractions— completely normal and clear-headed. I pushed for a while, kind of on my back with two midwives and their assistant all guiding me, but I sensed the baby wasn't coming down like I wanted him to. The midwives were all encouraging me and just letting me do my thing. When I lost focus, they redirected me and guided me back. I never once thought, "I wish I had drugs," or "I wish I was at the hospital." I was just going along with it all. I do remember saying, "I want it out," but not in a panicked way, just that my body was ready. I wanted to try the birthing ball, but again, I was just going where my body led me, and it wasn't leading me there. I eventually got up at the head of the bed, turned on my back, and immediately felt the baby was coming. After less than 20 minutes of pushing, I gave one final push and out came the head. A few more pushes and my new baby boy was born at 7:28 a.m.—less than four and a half hours after I felt that very first little twinge!

My husband proudly announced, "We have another boy!" I was completely ecstatic. The best part was that I got to hold Denny right away. Because Colin had passed meconium, he was swept away from me and I didn't get to hold him for 45 minutes. Denny was on me instantly, and I loved it.

We were all surprised by how big he was (eight pounds, fourteen and a half ounces) and I was surprised that he was a boy, but really happy about it! He was so beautiful, with big fat cheeks and legs, blue eyes and a clump of black hair. The placenta came out with no difficulty about 15 minutes later. I was freezing and shivering, so a midwife brought blankets and tea, which helped warm me pretty quickly.

Denny nursed and then I got up and showered, whistling and singing the whole time. I was ready to go home after a few hours. I was so high and I didn't come down for days. I kept reliving it over and over in my mind.

It was only after I delivered that I realized that we'd done it all without tubes, needles, monitors or drugs of any kind—not even a Tylenol. It was 100 times easier than my epidural birth with Colin! I was more proud of myself than I'd ever been in my whole life. I thought about all the people who thought natural birth was crazy and that I wouldn't be able to do it. I couldn't wait to tell them all about it! At that minute I wanted to have a million babies. Suddenly, I understood what it was all about in a way that I never did with Colin's birth. This birth was everything I could have ever hoped for.

Denny is so calm and relaxed, a very easy baby. I am more calm and relaxed as well, so that probably helps. I'm already feeling sad that Denny is growing up so fast. I wish I could keep him like this forever, but I know how much joy awaits him (and me) as he grows up.

This birth experience healed wounds from Colin's birth. I am now an evangelist for the birth center and the natural childbirth experience. It is my sincere hope that someday births like Denny's will become a matter of course, and hospitals will be reserved for high-risk mothers or babies. I wish every child could come into the world as beautifully as my Denny did, and that every mother could know the pride and fulfillment that I feel now.

A Mother's Guidance: Surround yourself with positive people and influences. No watching *Maternity Ward* on TV, no listening to moms tell birth horror stories! (I would literally stop someone in the middle of their birth story if it was turning worrisome, and I told them I couldn't listen.) But most importantly, know that your body is designed to give birth! Childbirth needn't be a scary or painful experience... quite the contrary! Learn to trust yourself and believe in your body's amazing ability to give birth. Don't let other people dictate how your birth should progress. The process of childbirth is important, and women should be able to experience it the way it was meant to be.

Taking the HypnoBirthing class was a big help. Also, I read *The Thinking Woman's Guide to a Better Birth* by Henci Goer, which I think should be required reading for all expectant parents.

Donna Schrader is a 35-year-old stay-at-home mama, and also serves as a breast-feeding peer counselor through Nursing Mothers, Inc. Donna's family includes her husband, Dave Harkins, and their little boys, Colin Harkins, six, and Denny Harkins, two.

HAPPY BIRTHDAY, LITTLE MERMAN

BY MARIA BROCK KUNDARGI

MY HUSBAND DARRELL and I were very blessed to conceive our baby the first time we tried. I had a healthy pregnancy, and experienced very little morning sickness or other symptoms. I just got big. I mean really big. Let's just say that by the last four weeks I had figured out how Creator shifts a woman from being scared and anxious about giving birth and being a mother to, "I'm so OVER being pregnant, LET'S GO!"

When we got pregnant, we decided to move from San Francisco to my hometown of Albuquerque, New Mexico, to be closer to my family, and so my husband could begin graduate school. New Mexico is a state where home birth and natural birth is really embraced, and we were truly blessed to have the most wonderful midwives. We planned to have a home birth from the beginning and were so happy with our midwives, who provided excellent care for us as a family as well as invaluable input, advice and encouragement.

The day our son was born was a very warm and sunny June 3rd, but our adventure began the day before. I woke up with cramping pains and light bleeding around 4 a.m. on Monday, June 2nd. I couldn't sleep, so I got up, went outside and prayed to Creator that all would go well, as I knew it wouldn't be long before we would be meeting our child. Then I was able to go back to sleep. In the morning Darrell went to the grocery store to stock up on food, and then he went to work. He called me every hour or so to check on me.

My mom took me to a lunch of Vietnamese noodle soup, and all the while I was having light contractions at the restaurant. I remember taking a good nap that afternoon before Darrell came home from work. I made eggplant and tofu stir fry for supper, and we watched *Austin Powers* on TV and laughed a lot. I was ready for bed by 11 p.m., but Darrell decided he'd better get the birthing tub (a large inflatable kiddy pool) ready, so he went to the gas station to blow it up and got home around midnight. I was asleep, but not for long. My belly was very big and I had a hard time getting comfortable. Then around 2 a.m. the contractions became much stronger. I could not stay in bed any longer... there was a dirty stove to be cleaned and dishes to do!

The contractions were getting stronger so I decided to dance to them in hopes of helping to wiggle the baby out. I swayed my hips back and forth and around while holding onto the kitchen counter. After each contraction was over, I'd go back to doing dishes. Around 3:30 or 4:00 a.m. I woke up Darrell because I didn't want to be alone anymore; I knew that this was IT. He was so excited, and he started nesting too. I think he cleaned the whole house. At least I know he finished cleaning the stove for me, because I could no longer concentrate on chores. I was too busy working and focusing on our baby.

Around 7 a.m. we lay down to get some rest, but I was constantly woken up by contractions and I had to make noises like "OOOOOHHHHHH" to help them pass. Around 8 a.m. I called the midwife, and she told me she would be over soon. I also called my mom, who wanted to help and be there to welcome her grandson into the world.

After they both arrived, my labor got stronger and at around 11:00 a.m. the midwife said I was past the half-way point (dilated to six centimeters). I was very happy to hear this and felt so encouraged by my own body. I knew I could do it. Darrell really helped me so much; he rubbed my back when I would have contractions, and Mom was always there to wipe my forehead or get me a cool drink. My favorite thing to drink was cold herbal tea, and I snacked on raw almonds. I mostly walked in our bedroom, and held onto the end of the bed while sitting on the birthing ball.

On top of our dresser is a wooden, carved Ashanti that we received as a gift for our wedding. When we conceived our son, we knew it was going to be special because we were joking around and Darrell waved the Ashanti over my belly, "to make sure things took." Since then, she has been our guardian and I knew she would watch over all of us as our son was born. The house was dark; all the shades were drawn and it was very quiet... well, except for me. I was really moaning. I knew if I opened up my throat, it would open me up so he could be born easier. I also imagined how a mama elephant would sound while laboring. Elephants are special to me, and they are very good mothers.

I decided to go to the birthing pool. It was very warm, about body temperature, and the water seemed to make the labor more difficult at first. I got out of the tub and labored on the birthing ball some more, but by this time labor was so strong. I was in "laborland," meaning my endorphins were helping me by creating an altered state.

I went back to the pool to help the labor along, and at this point I had decided that I wanted to birth in the water so he would be born in a gentle way. In the birthing tub the labor got even stronger, and at around 3 p.m. I wanted to push. It felt natural. When the midwife told me it was OK to push, I kneeled down in the water and squeezed my hands so tight around my husband's fingers. I thought I was hurting him, but I wasn't. My mom kept encouraging me and wiping my face with a cool cloth. Another midwife arrived to assist.

The first pushes were very unproductive, so the midwife checked and said I still had a "lip" left, and not to push during the next few contractions, which was really hard to do. But within three or four contractions, the lip opened up and I could push again. I was so tired that I would have a contraction and then fall asleep, literally, and then jerk awake with another contraction. Everyone was very quiet and observant, and gave me gentle encouragement now and then. I pushed and pushed so hard, and when my waters broke, I decided to turn onto my back. This is when our baby started to emerge.

Darrell moved around the pool so he could catch the baby. When the head was being born Darrell was so overjoyed and overwhelmed he started to cry; my mom cried too. As his head was born, I reached down and it was the softest thing I have ever felt. I was overwhelmed with the sweetest feeling in my heart. I was consciously trying to birth him slowly so I wouldn't tear, and with a few more pushes the rest of him was born. Darrell lifted him gently and slowly out of the water. Our midwife saw the baby was about to take his first breath and swiftly picked him up and put him on my chest. The first thing I said to our son was, "We love you so much." Then I felt something on the hand that was supporting his bottom, looked down and said, "It's a boy!" I was so happy. Darrell was behind us, hugging me. It was so beautiful, even the midwife cried!

After the placenta was born, we went to our bedroom and just relaxed for about an hour. We were so amazed by our baby, so overjoyed and proud. We just kissed him, and he smelled so good. He had very wrinkled hands and feet, very long fingers and toes, and long fingernails. He had brown hair and pink skin, and he was very alert; he was looking at us too! He made a lot of puppy noises, and we figured he was telling us all about his experience.

Anand was born under water, so I call him Little Merman. To this day I sing, "Who's the little merman born in the sea," every time I bathe him. He weighed seven pounds even, and was born at exactly 4:00 p.m. Afterwards, I was so hungry that my mom went out to get us red chili hamburgers and fries, and veggie burritos for the midwives. We spent that whole night staring at our son and falling in love with him. We are so grateful we were chosen to be his parents, and that he was born in a really gentle and beautiful way.

When he was in my womb, I used to talk to him and ask if we could be a team in birth, helping each other, and that's exactly what happened. Darrell also helped so much, telling me how good I was doing and how much he loved me. After the birth, and even still, we joked about how the three of us worked together at the birth: "Team Kundargi."

I am not anti-hospital birth, but for me and my family, home birth was definitely our first choice. Those around me allowed the process to happen, and created a safe space for me to let the process happen. I cried at some points because of the pain, but my midwife encouraged me to let that go. By opening my hands and myself to the experience, I was born too. Having my mother there was so profound. Even now, I can barely express in words how this has deepened my connection to her. She was unsure about home birth, but I showed her many videos and she attended an appointment with my midwife to get to know her. Their courage to let me be in pain, to be the most "myself" I have ever been, was essential. My husband held the space of our home as a welcoming, peaceful and safe nest, but more importantly he held (and holds) the nest of our hearts, the internal space we inhabit now as a family.

Feeling very safe and comfortable in my own home facilitated my ability to really let myself get into the experience (i.e. moaning, being naked in front of my mom, etc.). Being in the birthing tub was also good, as I believe it kept me from having any perineal tears. I do wish we had taken more photos. Before the birth I felt it would be too invasive, but now I know that I was so out of it, I really wouldn't have cared, and I would love to have more pictures to give my son of his birth.

A Mother's Guidance: We took a *Birthing from Within* class, however my husband and I are of two minds about that class. Using art as a way of expressing one's thoughts and feelings about birth was fabulous, and I still meet regularly with many of the moms from the class for playgroup. But the book and the class were very "white wolf spirit," our code word for New

Age. We both come from traditions that have meaningful rituals, and the made-up ones in *Birthing from Within* seemed contrived and sometimes stolen from other cultures.

The class that helped me the most was a three-hour Yoga for Pregnancy and Childbirth class. I used the poses during labor, and they were so effective. I wish I had taken a breastfeeding class or gone to a breastfeeding support group, as that turned out to be the most difficult part of birthing for me.

After the Baby's Birth: A Woman's Way to Wellness: A Complete Guide for Postpartum Women by Robin Lim offered good birth stories, and *Mothering* magazine was helpful in my mental and emotional preparations for labor and birth. Please throw out all copies of *What to Expect When You're Expecting and What to Expect the First Year*, both by Heidi Murkoff. If an expectant mom is not anxious, she certainly will be after reading these books.

I think the secret to having a great birth is to feel as safe about the experience as you can physically, mentally, emotionally and spiritually. When we feel safe we can really let go and allow the process to unfold naturally. Surrender to the birth. Consider where you feel safest, with whom you feel safest. Most importantly, know that birth is the fruition of love. It is a sacred event, not just a medical procedure with "symptoms."

I encourage all first-time mothers and their partners to sit down and discuss their intentions for the birth, so there are no surprises in the heat of the moment, and to serve as a guidepost they can always return to throughout the journey of childbirth (and parenting).

Maria T. Brock Kundargi is a 32-year-old Native American (Laguna Pueblo/Santa Clara Pueblo/German/Czech) woman living with her family in Albuquerque, New Mexico. She is a clinical social worker, with a Masters in Social Welfare from University of California, Berkeley, and has dedicated her practice to healing violence against women and children, particularly in the urban Native American community. She is currently working full-time as a therapist serving children and families with abuse and neglect issues. She and her husband Darrell are committed to attachment parenting their son, Anand.

AMAZING AND WONDERFUL

BY ISABELLE SCINTO

I GREW UP THINKING that to give birth, you had to go to the hospital, lie on a bed, suffer and scream a lot, beg for an epidural and then have a baby. Watching movies or TV shows, I thought that's just how it happens. Little did I know....

When I decided to have a baby, my curious, "always searching for different options" nature kicked into high gear. I found myself drawn to midwifery websites and information on natural birth. On the Internet I learned so many things I never even knew existed... *hey—I could have a natural delivery and it could be wonderful!* I figured that if I had a healthy body and an uncomplicated pregnancy, then giving birth would be a naturally unfolding process. After all, women and female animals have been doing it since the beginning of time. I also learned about all the risks of using drugs during labor, which really concerned me. I decided to do everything I possibly could to have a natural delivery. Doing this was hard work, though. I had to research a lot; I just couldn't settle for the opinion or experience of one person, one book or one doctor.

Part of my research included a wonderful weekend workshop at the Omega Institute in Rhinebeck, New York. Curious but clueless, I went there and spent a weekend with one of the most amazing women I have ever met! Ina May Gaskin opened up doors to a world I didn't even know existed, and really empowered me as a woman. Her teachings led me to realize that, as a woman, I could make choices that I didn't even know I had, and be in control of my body and birth. It sounds silly now when I say it, but if I had not learned all of that, I would have just taken the route that so many women follow: listening to and doing everything my Ob/Gyn said, without ever knowing that I could take control of my birth and create what I wanted!

I decided that I wanted a home birth. It just seemed like such a natural thing to do, and it appealed to me very much. I knew that a home birth was only possible if I had a very healthy pregnancy and baby, so I did more research to ensure that I knew everything I needed to do to have a successful home birth.

First I found a midwife. She had to be someone I trusted and felt great with. When I interviewed her, I had a prepared list of questions about her experience as a midwife, how and where she was trained, whom she works with, what equipment she brings to the birth, etc. (Ina May Gaskin's book, *Ina May's Guide to Childbirth*, has all of those questions, as well as questions to ask a hospital-based midwife or an Ob/Gyn.) I also looked for a connection with her. It was so important to me that I get a good feeling about her.

I read a lot about nutrition and pregnancy. I followed the Brewer diet, which was recommended to me by midwives and the childbirth class we took. It is so important to have a wonderful diet, and I really had fun making great meals. I happen to love cooking so it wasn't a hard task for me, but I took proper nutrition for my baby and me very seriously.

My midwife also worked with me to make sure I did everything right. She told me to exercise every day, which was easy to follow since our dog needed to be walked every day. I made sure I walked a little faster to get my heart pumping. I also took aqua-fitness classes—they were so awesome! I can't begin to say how wonderful my big belly felt when I got in that water. Ecstasy! I also explored prenatal yoga through two fabulous DVDs: *Prenatal*

Yoga with Shiva Rea and *The Method—Baby & Mom Pre-Natal Yoga with Gurmukh Kaur Khalsa.*

Another suggestion my midwife gave me was to see a chiropractor once a week, if possible. Chiropractors work to keep the spine aligned, which keeps all those nerves functioning well and that makes the body work better. I truly believe that those weekly adjustments contributed greatly to my wonderful pregnancy and delivery.

I loved sensing every feeling my body went through. It was all such an amazing journey. Being informed, I knew that everything had its purpose. And I trusted that and simply abandoned myself in it all.

March 23rd was my actual due date, and for some reason I did not think I would have the baby that day. But it really wasn't up to me. By mid-morning, part of my mucous plug came out and I thought, *could it be...?* Finally the day I had prepared for was here!

I had chosen to have my husband, mother and grandmother at the birth. My grandmother came from Quebec, Canada, just for the event. I thought it would be really inspiring to have four generations together. My mother didn't have natural births; she had two C-sections, so it was a great gift for her to see her grandchild born this way.

It all happened pretty quickly. I started having contractions around 2 p.m. and had the baby at 10:46 p.m. At first the contractions were small and interesting. I would tell myself, "Wow, this is really happening now, my baby and my body are working together to bring life out of me!" My husband and I just hung out, looking at each other and smiling. It was such an exciting time. I called my midwife to let her know that today was the day. She was so great; she shared my joy and made me feel very calm and confident.

Of course as the day went on the contractions became stronger. I just relaxed through each one as best I knew how through deep breathing and focusing. I knew I had to rest, and be well hydrated and fed. I drank a lot of water and had some miso soup. I tried to lie down and rest, but my body would just hurt when I did that, so I kept walking through the house or laying myself over a big birthing ball.

When contractions became so powerful that I could not even think or breathe deeply, I would just tell myself that it would only last ONE minute, and that helped a lot. When the contractions became regular and heavier, we called the midwife to ask her to come over. After we did that I went to the bathroom again. (I drank a lot so I ended up there often.) I think the baby dropped because I had a sudden urge to push. I said, "Oh my God, I have to push!" and we all kind of looked at each other, almost in a panic because we had just called the midwife and she wasn't with us yet.

Fortunately, her assistant called a minute later, and when we told her what just happened, she said to get on all fours with my head down, and that this would slow down the pushing urges. I remember my husband laying down a towel that had a picture of dolphins on it for me to lie on. I got into position and just focused on those dolphins. That helped me so much. A little while later I heard a car pull in and felt so relieved that the midwife was finally here. She walked in, not knowing what just happened, and when she saw me there on the floor she said, "OK I don't even have to check you, you are ready!"

We had decided to have a water birth, so I got up and went into the tub. It was so wonderful to get into that water; I can't even begin to tell you how much I appreciated it. It made my contractions pause for a while, and my belly feel lighter. It gave us just enough time to gather our energy for the pushing phase.

Our midwife was so wonderful, calm, happy and comforting. She talked so gently, it was very soothing. As my contractions and urge to push picked up again, she gently told me to push when I felt like it, take a breath after and push some more if I needed too. Never did she tell me to, "Push! Push! Push!" or count to ten. That would have made me crazy. We just followed my body's natural instincts. Of course, as all this was happening, she was monitoring the baby and me with a Doppler. It was just perfect.

At first the pushing felt kind of strange, and I wasn't sure I was doing it right. But after a while I started feeling my body pushing more effectively and shortly after that, my baby emerged. On that last push, the whole room became white... and then I opened my eyes and there she was! What was once inside my belly was now laying on top of it. She was the cutest thing I ever saw and I remember just thanking God and Mother Mary for helping me through.

It was the happiest day of my life. I remember saying, "Wow this was fun! I wouldn't do it every day, but I can't wait for the next one!"

A Mother's Guidance: The key to my great birth was releasing my fears, which was not easy because of the unknowns. But I am a spiritual person so I did ask for the help of Mother Mary. I truly believe she helped me immensely. Confidence and trust in your body are so important. And finally, exercise and excellent nutrition are a MUST! I did Tai Chi before and during my pregnancy. It really helped with focusing and relaxation, not to mention all the good it did for my body. I also did a lot of affirmations and visualization. One affirmation I repeated during my pregnancy and labor was: "My body's perfect, my baby is perfect, God created my body and baby perfectly!" I visualized each part of my body, especially my belly, uterus, placenta, baby and cervix, and brought a lot of light to them, seeing them as perfect, beautiful and surrounded by bright white light. I also listened to a tape, *Journeying Through Pregnancy and Birth* by Jennifer Houston. On the first side she helps you to relax and visualize your baby and pregnancy. The second side included visualizations to help you prepare for giving birth, and is only for listening to after the 38th week.

The childbirth class we took was the Bradley Method. My favorite books were *Spiritual Midwifery* and *Ina May's Guide to Childbirth*, both by Ina May Gaskin, *The Baby Catcher* by Peggy Vincent, *Gentle Birth Choices* by Barbara Harper and *Birthing from Within* by Pam England and Rob Horowitz. Magazines that I loved included *Midwifery Today*, *Mothering* and *The Compleat Mother*. I also liked the videos *Prenatal Yoga by Shiva Rae*, *Baby and Mom Prenatal Yoga with Gurmukh Kaur Khalsa*, *Gentle Birth Choices* by Barbara Harper and *WATER BABY: Experiences of Water Birth*. Another great resource is www.motherfriendly.org.

Additional Thoughts: "When they got so powerful I could not even think or breath deep I would just tell myself that 'it only will last ONE minute'...." You have to remind yourself and have others remind you to stay in the moment. Thinking about how many more surges or hours are ahead can really bring in fear, but focusing on that particular one will make you feel like you can do it.

More information on the Brewer diet can be found online at www.blueribbonbaby.org

Isabelle Scinto and her husband Daniel have a two-year-old daughter named Soleil Leia. They believe in natural family living and everything that goes along with that, including attachment parenting, organic foods, natural medicine and Waldorf education.

DOCTORS DO MAKE HOUSE CALLS

BY LAURA DOMINICK

MY HUSBAND TIM and I are currently the proud parents of six wonderful children. The first three, all girls, were born in the hospital with the usual routine: epidurals, forceps, episiotomies, monitors and Pitocin. It was in response to a rather bad experience with Pitocin during the birth of our third daughter that we decided to have our next baby at home. There was a time when I thought that this was a crazy thing to do, but grace won out and we decided to go with a physician's group that delivers babies at home.

I have to admit that this new philosophy took some getting used to. The HomeFirst doctors don't routinely do ultrasounds, and they take a very natural approach to everything. The idea of no pain medication during birth wasn't too difficult for me, since the three epidurals I had never worked very well.

When the time came for our first home birth, we were all very excited, so excited that I invited my mom and mother-in-law to witness the event! The whole idea behind home births is that you will have a safer and quicker progression of labor by staying in an atmosphere that you are comfortable with, instead of going to the hospital. In theory this does work; in my case it didn't—because I had too many anxious people staring at me all day. By the time this baby was ready to be born, I had my husband, my mom, his mom, our three children, a nurse, midwife, doctor and an intern all waiting on me!

This baby was difficult to deliver because she was face up, but the midwife and doctor were both wonderful. They remained very calm throughout the delivery. When things were not progressing very well, the doctor suggested different positions to try, and I eventually ended up giving birth to our fourth daughter on my hands and knees. They worked the baby's head out slowly so that there was no need for an episiotomy, and not much tearing. It was only afterwards that I found out how difficult this delivery really was. I had no idea that everyone was worried until much later, and I am very glad for the calm demeanor of all the professionals that were there.

After the baby was born, the doctor stayed around for a while to make sure that everything was OK with both of us. The nurse stayed for a few hours after that, but then we were on our own. This was a little intimidating, but I knew that help was only a phone call away. In the past, one of the hardest things to me about having a baby was coming home again. I always found the transition from the hospital to our home to be very traumatic. With this experience, I never had to deal with that. I was always home, so the kids could come and go whenever they wanted, or I could shut the door and get some rest when I needed it. This birth experience was so different from the first three that I knew I was hooked.

Our fifth baby was born a little less than two years later in pretty much the same fashion, except that the number of people present was slightly less. This time the delivery was much easier, so the doctor just stood off to the side and encouraged me while the midwife delivered our first son. Again I experienced that very calm demeanor from everyone, as well as the nice slow progression of the baby being delivered, which meant no episiotomy and no major tearing. Since I had bled quite a bit after the last baby, the midwife had brought along some homeopathic remedies to slow down the bleeding. They did the trick, and I didn't experience the clotting and nausea that I had before.

A little less than three years later, our sixth child was born at home, still with the same physician's group. I was convinced this was another boy, since my pregnancy had been so similar to the last one. This time there was a nurse and a doctor present, and again, things were going well (although a bit faster than ever before), so the doctor stayed on the sidelines and encouraged while the nurse delivered the baby. Since I had again delivered on my hands and knees, I couldn't see the baby once it was born, so I asked what it was. The doctor said, "It's a girl," to which I promptly responded, "You've got to be kidding me." His prompt answer was "OK, it's a boy then!" But he was right the first time. Our last child came into the world a little faster than her siblings and with the cord wrapped around her neck, but I never knew it until later because everyone remained so calm.

These past three births have been wonderful experiences. I have felt so much more in control being at home and not being at the mercy of the rules of the hospital. If I wanted to walk, I would walk. If I wanted to labor on my hands and knees or while sitting on a big rubber ball, I could do that. It was absolutely wonderful to not have any stitches afterwards, which made a big improvement in my recovery. I noticed a big difference in how alert the last three babies were after birth, when they didn't have any pain medications in their systems. They nursed better and just seemed stronger. In fact, our first daughter born at home nursed so well that she nursed non-stop for the first eight hours. Every time I tried to stop her, she screamed so loud, I put her back on. I also had a lot less engorgement with these babies because they got off to such a good start. Natural childbirth definitely has its benefits for the nursing baby. Probably the thing we enjoyed most about these experiences, however, was that each time one of our babies was born, the doctors rejoiced with us and praised God for this wonderful blessing as much as we did.

Since our last baby, we have moved to a new town that is outside of the boundaries of where HomeFirst will go to deliver. If we have another baby, I'm not sure what we will do. Both my husband

and I don't know if we can stand to go back into the hospital environment unless we had to. I have known people who lived outside the HomeFirst boundaries but wanted a home birth so much that they went and delivered at a friend's house who lived within the boundaries! Only the good Lord knows what will happen next, but I can say that I'll always vote for the natural way!

A Mother's Guidance: The doctor who started HomeFirst, Dr. Mayer Eisenstein, has written a book called *Home Birth Advantage* which discusses why home births are so much better for mom and baby.

Additional Thoughts: Most women hold a belief that epidurals always work, and rely on that as their only tool for coping with labor. They never even think about the other options available to them, and are left empty-handed if the pain medication doesn't work for them.

Although it can be wonderful to have your friends and family at the birth, for many women it is too much pressure. There can be pressure to entertain them as well as please them. You might also be comparing yourself to the births that they had. If you are going to have many people at the birth, be sure to give them jobs and to set guidelines. Let them know that you will need time alone and don't be shy about sending them out of the room if they are distracting. Everyone who is at the birth should be contributing in a positive way. People who are anxious and nervous about your birth are probably better seen after the birth. If a family member doesn't believe in home birth and you are having a home birth, do not invite them to the birth. Their negative and nervous energy will distract you.

Laura Dominick and her husband Tim have been married for 15 years. They have six children: Amanda (12), Megan (10), Teresa (8), Rebecca (5), Timmy (3) and Mary Rose (7 months). They have been home-schooling their children since Amanda was old enough to start school. They recently moved to a house on five acres and are looking forward to acquiring some animals, and growing pumpkins and other vegetables. They follow a natural approach to many aspects of their life, including natural childbirth and nursing. Tim and Laura have also been involved with The Couple to Couple League, which is an international apostolate for Natural Family Planning. CCL is also a big advocate of natural childbirth and ecological breastfeeding.

CHRISTMAS LIGHTS AND CEDAR BOUGHS

BY RENE MARTINEZ

IT WAS ONE OF THOSE momentous deci-
sions, one that stops you in your tracks and turns your life down
a new path. Although I wasn't pregnant, I signed up to attend a
series of classes at our local library on birth choices, taught by
a midwife. I felt awkward introducing myself, as I was the one
student who wasn't expecting, but by the end of the class I was
"one of the crowd," so to speak. Two of the ladies I met that night
would later be in my prenatal yoga class and become good friends.

After that first class, my husband Marti and I talked about
starting a family more and more. I don't remember ever having a
big discussion about choosing a midwife or home birth; it was just
always going to be that way. Marti has worked as a Health Services
Specialist for the Coast Guard for twelve years. For six years he was
a flight medic and helped several pregnant women get from small,
remote Alaskan villages to a hospital. He had delivered a few
babies in the back of the helicopter. I figured birthing at home had
to be easier than in the back of a helicopter, flying through southeast Alaska's temperamental weather. A home birth was the obvious choice for us.

Our family, on the other hand.... After five years of marriage,
they were thrilled to hear we were finally pregnant, and they tried

to be supportive. But I don't think they really understood our choice, and they were constantly bringing up the "what-ifs." Friends and family members were always asking about how my doctor's appointments went, or when I would have an ultrasound. I found myself reading all sorts of articles and information so I would be armed and ready with home birth safety facts.

My husband's occupation added another layer of stress to the pregnancy and birth. Marti was stationed on a Coast Guard patrol boat that went to sea for two months at a time, then returned home for a month before going out again. While he was gone we used e-mail and cell phones, but they were unreliable at best. He joined me at the midwife's appointments whenever he could, but right up until he actually got off the plane, we were unsure about whether or not he would be with me for the birth.

For some, it takes months of trying to conceive; for us, it took one encounter. I traveled to California to meet my husband when his Coast Guard boat made a stop there. This was in May, and I had not had a period since March. I went through a whole box of pregnancy tests, uncertain about the results. "You see, I told you," Marti would say. To which I would reply, "I don't know, you can't really tell," as I threw out one stick after another. I was in denial. During the entire trip I was tired, and had an upset stomach much of the time. Marti was constantly saying, "It's because you are pregnant." I would just brush him off. *Silly guy, what does he know*? The flight home from California brought me out of denial; I was sick the whole flight. The polite flight attendant said, "Turbulence can do that." When I finally got my head out of the sink and stood up, I realized that this was about the smoothest flight I'd ever had!

I went straight from the airport to my best friend's house. I felt like a giddy teenager sharing something secret in my diary with her. We locked ourselves in her bathroom. Her lovely husband was watching TV in the other room, not paying us any mind. I took another pregnancy test, and there was no questioning this one. It was about as positive as they come. The next day I was off to the clinic for a blood test. The nurse was a family friend and told me it would take about three days to get the results back. I wondered how in the world I could wait that long. Thank goodness she called the next day and said, "Better find someone else to change the cat litter box, and we might need to change your allergy medicine." *Holy cow!*

Marti was still out on the boat, so I sent him an e-mail asking, "Do you think the boat will be in on December 25th?" This was our projected due date. He was able to use the ship's cell phone that night... we were so excited!

My pregnancy went very well. My work schedule was flexible so I was able to take naps and work more when I felt better. During appointments with my midwives, we talked about my health as well as issues concerning who was going to be there to support me in labor. There were no guarantees that Marti would be home, especially with the stepped up security after September 11th. We started considering a doula.

In my second trimester I started taking a prenatal yoga class. It was just what I needed. The ladies were so welcoming and formed such a great support network for me. Our due dates spanned about a month. The instructor was also planning a home birth and we shared the same midwife. Through the class I met a lady who had just become a doula. Marti and I talked it over and agreed that it would be good to get to know her, to have a plan to fall back on if he couldn't get home in time for the birth. That first night Megan came over to our house and talked with us, I knew I wanted her there for the birth.

After months of the Coast Guard changing their minds as to whether Marti could take leave and come home for the birth, I picked him up at the airport on Thursday, December 20th. What a relief! We spent some time making sure things were ready around the house, resting and even going to a movie. Friday night, December 21st, I had trouble sleeping. I had terrible cramps and was up and down all night. The only thing that helped was draping myself over the birth ball and rocking. That birth ball was the best purchase I ever made, and at $9.99 it was a steal! Saturday morning I called my dad to say hello, since I didn't know anyone else who would be up that early. Seems like I tried everything to pass the time.

On Saturday I was supposed to pick up my mom from the airport but her flight had been delayed. She was worried that with the contractions I was having she might miss the birth. No need to worry about that; I was having one of those "slow and steady wins the race" kind of labors. At about 4 p.m. we went to the airport to get my mom, and when contractions came I would bend down on the floor, with my arms on chairs. We were all hungry so we went out to eat, but throughout dinner I would get up and lean on the table to take each contraction. They weren't evenly spaced; they just came and went. We would be eating at the table, and mid-conversation I would just do what I needed and then resume my part in the conversation.

Somehow I made it through another night of not sleeping, conducting long, lonely conversations with the birth ball. Do you remember Tom Hanks in the movie *Castaway*, and his volleyball friend? I felt like I should have named my birth ball too, since we were so close for three days. I remember trying to wake Marti to help me, but it took too much effort to get him up.

On Sunday morning, December 23rd, our friends Daina and Mike were coming into town and we had breakfast plans with them. Sunday's breakfast was very similar to Saturday's dinner: talk, eat, talk, squat down, oh ouch, bend over, lean on the chair, breathe, eat, breathe, eat, talk, walk around the table, squat, ignore the strange looks, eat, ouch!, eat, talk. Oddly enough, we made plans to go to the movies with them that night. What was I thinking?!

After breakfast we went home and called the midwives to check in. They suggested things to try, and said to call if anything changed. Marti got a nice fire going in the wood stove and then went out for a round of golf. My mom would talk me through the contractions and rub my back. I remember her saying, "You are really doing good, it shouldn't be much longer now." I snapped back at her, "My friend labored like this for four days and didn't make any progress!" I think that was the low point. I hadn't slept and was getting tired. It was time for a change.

About that time, Marti came home and ran me a bath. It was about the last thing I wanted to do, but once I was in the water it felt good. Later, my mom and Marti came up with the great idea to take a walk after dinner. Again, it was the last thing I wanted to do, but once we were outside the fresh air felt good. We walked along slowly, and then when a contraction came we would speed up. I am not sure that this technique is in any textbook, but it seemed to work. If nothing else, it makes the neighbors wonder what you're up to! As we were walking we called our doula, Megan, just to let her know what was happening.

After our walk I asked Marti, just for curiosity's sake, to check me and see if I was making any progress. When he did, he thought I was about two or three centimeters dilated. Marti helped me to the bathroom, and at approximately 8:45 p.m. the waters broke. I remember thinking, "Finally some action, let's get this party going!" We called our midwives, Rose and Kathy, and they said they were on their way. Their office was an hour away from our home. Little did we know that they wouldn't get to our house until the crowning.

When our doula Megan got to our house, she was instantly helpful. She anticipated my needs before I even knew what I wanted. She got me water and started preparing the birth tub so Marti and my mom could stay by my side. I kept them both busy, and the three of us worked perfectly together to conquer each contraction. I would ask Marti to put pressure on my back to counteract the pain, and then once the contraction had passed, I needed Mom's soothing touch to relax me. Marti used a technique we learned in our childbirth class called "scissors." I must have sounded something like: "Scissors, Mom, oh my, scissors, Mom, Maaarrrrti!"

I spent hours and hours draped over the birth ball. I remember pushing and feeling the baby come down, then slip back inside, then down again and slip back in. It was a little game we were playing, I guess. I started talking to our baby, "Be gentle to your mama now, little one." Then Marti came over and asked if he could cut my panties to make room to catch the baby. I thought to myself, "It is the only stitch of clothing I have on, but why not take off the panties too." So much for modesty.

Before we knew it, Marti saw our baby's head. He paged a 911 to our midwives. They were at a stoplight in town, about 10 minutes away. I remember Marti gently whispering into my ear, "I am going to the car to get my medical kit."

All this time, the room was calm and peaceful. I remember smelling the cedar wood by the fireplace as I listened to a relaxation tape that my prenatal yoga instructor had made for me. I got caught up in the words of the music, the soft lights and the warmth of the fire. Never once was I scared or nervous that the midwives weren't there. Looking back on it, I am not sure what they would have done had they been with us. We had our own groove going, right there in the living room. I believe that they came when they were needed. When they stepped through the front door they were a little frantic, not knowing what they were coming into. But as Rose said to me after the birth, "There was this peace and calm in the room, with the soft music and dim Christmas lights."

At 11:24 p.m. on December 23rd, Sofia Grace Martinez arrived. We were so excited to meet our new baby girl! At 11:28 p.m. I was on the phone with my dad, sharing the news. Then we started calling everyone. I kept our phone bill so that one day Sofia can see that we just had to share our joy with the world, no matter what time it was!

After the birth, things were kind of a blur. I wanted to get off that darn birth ball, yet we had become so close. After three days together nonstop, it seemed strange to be without it. My mom decided that she had better go to bed so that she would be fresh to help in the morning. Megan got our bed ready for us while Kathy and Marti took care of the baby. Rose helped me into the shower and sat on the toilet to make sure I was OK as I got cleaned up. Somehow, everything got taken care of. Kathy weighed and measured Sofia—six pounds, nine ounces and 18.5 inches long—and gave her vitamin K drops. The midwives stayed awhile longer while we tried nursing. Finally though, it was time to sleep. After not sleeping Friday and Saturday night, I was ready.

The next day was Christmas Eve. Marti had to fight last minute Christmas shoppers at Wal-Mart to find Sofia some clothes that fit. The ones we had were too large. We went to Christmas Eve service at church and Sofia was only 18 hours old. I felt that I had the greatest blessing and I just wanted to share my joy with everyone. It felt good to get out of the house too.

Soon my milk came in, and that was the beginning of a whole new adventure. I tell people, "Having the baby was a snap, breast-feeding killed me." I think if I had gotten a bit more instruction beforehand, I would have done better. My childbirth classes and the meetings with my midwife were so helpful in preparing me for labor and birth, but they failed to prepare me for breastfeeding and those first few days with my baby. I didn't even have a pump on hand. But a nurse from the hospital came for a home visit a couple of times and helped Sofia and me find our niche. We must have gotten it right eventually, because two years later she still has her "yum yums."

Sofia Grace and I have gone through so much together: my emergency gallbladder surgery when Sofia was only four months old and Marti was away, a military transfer, an exchange student, new friends and new pets. I have learned so much from this little girl, and I have learned so much about myself. Giving birth is an amazing journey and I think the most important thing to remember is that you are in charge. It is your body, your decisions, your experience and you have the power to make it what you want. Be confident in yourself and the choices you make.

Doula Megan DeBoer's letter to Sofia
Dear Sofia Grace,

Your birth was the most graceful I have witnessed, as calm as I have ever dared to imagine. Your name suits you. You will probably always act in, and with, grace. It was an honor to witness such a magical event. Perhaps someday you too will witness the birth of a child, or birth a child of your own. Let your mother's story give you courage.

I met your parents several weeks before your due date. They were both so confident and unafraid; I was sure they could birth you at home. A week before your arrival I had a dream about your parents. In that dream I went to visit them at their boathouse. We talked for a while, just as we had at our first visit. All of a sudden, both your parents looked outside and got to their feet. A boat had drifted into a large wave, several large waves actually. They watched it, holding hands with the most enormous smiles on their faces and stood calmly as each wave rocked the house successively. When I awoke the next morning I was certain you would come smoothly. Your parents took everything in stride, together.

On Saturday, December 22nd, your mother informed me of her contractions, that they were on and off—unpredictable. She said that they were "interesting," but wasn't attached to what they meant. She was taking them as they came, with patience, knowing it could be a while before you arrived. It is not easy to be so patient. I didn't hear anything again until Sunday afternoon. It was 5 p.m. and your father called me as they were walking around the block. You were moving down and getting ready for the birth. Everything was progressing smoothly and steadily.

At 8:40 p.m. your father called again and asked me to come. I was so excited to be attending a birth just before Christmas! It was really cold outside; I wondered if there would be ice on the roads. The stars were bright so I knew there would be no snow.

Your father answered the door; he was opening a pine-scented candle that burned throughout your birth. I walked into a completely serene room. Christmas tree lights and candles lit the room so softly. There was your mother, on her hands and knees, her head resting on the birth ball with your grandmother's hands on her back.

The most beautiful, rhythmic music was playing, with lulling words about sailing… and that is just how it seemed. Your mom rocked gently as though she was in water, floating with and above each wave as it came. It was often hard to determine whether or not she was having a contraction. She was at peace. The room was filled with love and it all seemed so right, so incredibly right that a baby was to be born there.

Your mother was so gracious; she immediately asked me how I was doing. Then she asked me about the intense pressure in her bum. I reminded her that it was your head turning and getting ready to be born. She was always clear with her wishes. She wanted your grandmother's touch and your dad's strong hands rubbing back and forth on her lower back through each contraction. I made water and an occasional holiday cookie available as she labored, and would relieve either your grandmother or your dad whenever they were outside or were busy getting other things together.

At 10:00 I noticed that her contractions were getting closer and perhaps a bit stronger, although she never expressed any hesitation or fear that she could not go on. I noticed her start to push slightly in the middle of some contractions, but it was so slight and so natural that I wasn't concerned for the midwife's arrival. Kathy was already on her way.

At around 10:30 p.m., I began to boil water on the stove to make the birthing tub warm enough. I knew how much your mom wanted your dad, so I relieved him of that chore. The tub was still a few degrees shy of where it needed to be; it wouldn't be ready for at least another 40 minutes. I was so frustrated, and yet she had been so comfortable in her position that I wasn't too concerned. Your grandmother was outside and your dad was at your mom's feet when I made my way from the tub to the kitchen for the last time. Your dad motioned to me with his hands and the most enormous grin I have ever seen. I came closer, and he lifted back her underwear to reveal your head, crowning! I had chills all over my body! Never have I imagined a woman to be so calm and so present in that moment. We were both shocked. Your dad was unbelievable. He remained so calm, matching her mood beautifully. I believe that you were able to come calmly because of the space that they created together there. It was so beautiful to see a father so in sync with his family at that moment.

He waited a few moments before he told your mom. I am not sure what she was thinking, but she remained in the space that she had created without a murmur. Your dad paged Kathy with an emergency 911. She responded immediately, and was extremely shocked. She was only minutes away.

Your dad switched modes at this point. It was the one thing he had most wanted to avoid, that of being your mother's caregiver rather than her emotional support. He ran to his car and got his medical kit. I stayed with your mother who was still incredibly calm; perhaps she was holding back just a bit.

Your dad was undoing his medical supplies when we heard Kathy's car lurch into the driveway. Just as the door opened your mom let out her first and only cry of pain. She had waited, I believe, for Kathy's presence to let go and allow for your arrival. It was then, Sofia, that your little head was born. Kathy coached your mom through the next push, and your mom birthed your body with ease. You were absolutely perfect, with perfect color and the sweetest cry. Your mom was frozen in her hands and knees position. She asked that you be cleaned off before she took you in her arms. I must tell you, though, that you were the cleanest newborn baby I have seen. You seemed to have slipped out pre-bathed!

While Kathy wiped you off your mom was saying your name, "Sofia Rose," but moments later you were Sofia Grace. I am not sure of the story there, but I cannot imagine a more fitting name than Grace. Your dad held you and passed you to your mom. In that moment your cries sounded just like your mother. I have heard that a newborn's first noises mimic the mother's, but it was truly amazing to hear.

And there we were, your father, your grandmother, Kathy, Rose and myself, witnesses to your arrival in this world and to the three of you becoming a family. It was an incredible moment. The three of you must never forget the beauty of your birth. Let it be the calming anchor in any rough sea that you may face. The three of you faced a challenge with loving grace, together. Thank you for allowing me to be present. I will always hold you close to my heart.

A Mother's Guidance: Let go of fear, and above all, trust your instincts about your body and your baby. You are in charge of this birth. You know yourself and your needs, and you must communicate them. If you know a particular scent drives you crazy, make sure nobody has that around. Be careful in choosing who will be in the birthing room with you. Surround yourself with those who support your decisions. Have faith in your body's ability to do what it knows how to do. A thousand years ago, no one needed a fetal monitor, or to be told when to push. A woman listened to her body and it led her. Have courage to not listen to the mainstream. Read as much as you can, including *Misconceptions* by Naomi Wolf; *The Mask of Motherhood* by Susan Maushart; and *Our Babies* by Meredith Small. I also recommend any of Sheila Kitzinger's books. Study other cultures and how they birth and parent. Ask questions as you compare their ways to American culture. And have a pump on hand to relieve a bit of the pressure when your milk comes in.

When people begin relating a horror story about birth, kindly say to them, "Thank you for wanting to share your story but I plan on having a peaceful birth."

Know yourself. I knew that I would not do well in a hospital under someone else's control. I did not want to have my progress judged by a clock or a shift rotation schedule. Even if you are having a hospital birth, you can ask for specific things. You may want a CD player for soft music, a birth ball, a yoga mat, or some lamps for soft lighting. As I mentioned before, you are in charge and if people aren't listening, yell louder. You can always blame it on the hormones!

Additional Thoughts: Prenatal yoga is a great way to exercise during labor, and it also teaches you how to breathe, which is so important to practice before labor.

Prenatal yoga instructor Gurmukh Kaur Khalsa recommends starting classes as soon as you feel good enough to go. Yoga relaxes and calms pregnant women, easing their fears and teaching them to concentrate during labor—to not to be influenced by the environment. Celebrities such as Cindy Crawford and Reese Witherspoon have drawn public attention to the benefits of prenatal yoga, and its effectiveness in creating a better birth experience.

Give serious consideration to taking a breastfeeding class during your pregnancy. The information you learn will be invaluable when it comes to establishing a successful breastfeeding relationship with your child. For tips on successful breastfeeding, visit www.JourneyIntoMotherhood.com.

Rene Martinez married Ramon (Marti) in 1996 at none other than The Chapel of Love in Las Vegas. Five years later, Sofia Grace was born. They live in Palmer, Alaska. Marti commutes to the Air Force base in Anchorage where he coordinates all the medical needs for the Coast Guard stations in Alaska.

MERRY CHRISTMAS, MOM

BY CZARINA WALKER

"MERRY CHRISTMAS, MOM! I'm in labor," I said through the phone, after waking up to the realization that my waters had broken in my sleep. "Woo hoo, good girl!" she replied. "And a very merry Christmas it is," she said. It was 4:00 a.m., the beginning of our most exciting Christmas ever, as we headed to the hospital to have our first child.

If I was quiet enough, I could sense some small cramping sensations, but most of what I was feeling was excitement and joy as my husband Brad and I laughed and joked on the way to the hospital. As soon as we arrived we were greeted by the labor-and-delivery staff. They were excited because we were the first couple to come in that would have a Christmas baby. As we handed off our copies of my patient record to the hospital staff, I was finally able to relax a little.

We had chosen to use the Bradley Method to birth our baby. We were surprised at the simplicity of Bradley, and frankly the more I read about it, the more it just made good sense. My husband and I went to classes, but it was the book *Natural Childbirth the Bradley Way* by Susan McCutcheon that gave me the knowledge I needed about labor and delivery to feel more confident about wanting a natural birth for our baby.

One of the nice side effects of a natural birth is how much you can remember about your labor. I was not scared, and to this day, I am surprised at the clarity of mind that I had while in labor. In all honesty, I found it somewhat mentally relaxing to be in labor. You see, since I was 19 years old I have been a software programmer. All day, all the time, I think of solutions to other people's problems; my mind never turns off. That is, until I was in labor. To my surprise, and that of everyone who knows me, I did not think about work once while I was in labor. It was nice to daydream and release my mind from the typical thoughts that run through.

As I labored, I remembered the exact moment I decided to birth my child naturally. I was 15 years old, and babysitting for a neighbor. For three hours that night, I marveled at how well behaved her two small children were. The kids, one and three years old, played and entertained themselves, not fussing even once. This was such a dramatic change from my regular babysitting job, where I watched one child who cried constantly. Until this memorable night, I thought all babies cried constantly. When their mom returned, I told her that I couldn't believe how good her children were and reiterated that if her regular babysitter ever quit (not likely) or was unavailable, I would be more than happy to fill in for her. Their mom laughed and said, "I know, they are good. It's because I had them naturally. In fact I was teaching a natural childbirth class tonight. You can tell the difference between a child who is born naturally versus one who is not. They're just different." I had absolutely no idea what she was talking about, but that night I did know one thing—someday, I was going to have my children naturally. If this theory had even a possibility of being correct, I could not risk ignoring it!

During my pregnancy I never brought up natural childbirth unless someone asked me about it; natural childbirth is not a mainstream idea in my hometown of Baton Rouge, Louisiana. But a lot of people, for no real reason at all, ask you a lot of questions when you're pregnant, inquiring about whether you plan to have an epidural. So those were the people who discovered that I had decided to use the Bradley Method to birth our baby. Everyone thought I was crazy and proceeded to tell me their horror stories. Even the people who believed in me the most, my mom and my husband, were not so sure about this idea of mine to have a natural childbirth. Being that I have an uptight, somewhat high-strung, fairly stressed-out personality, my husband had voiced serious concerns about natural childbirth throughout my pregnancy. "This method is based on you relaxing? Is that actually possible? Don't you think that maybe you need a back-up plan?" But I had practiced relaxing, and even visualized relaxing while in labor, throughout my entire pregnancy. Additionally, I had read about the phenomenon that some women experience where they do not feel any pain during labor. I thought about my grandmother's letter and everything I had read, and kept telling myself that I could do this despite my toughest critics.

Laboring in the hospital, it was now 9:00 a.m. — somehow five hours had passed. Boy, my Bradley teacher was right! When you don't stare at the clock, the time just passes. I spent most of this time walking around the hospital, something most laboring moms are not able to do if they have an epidural and a bunch of wires attached to them. My husband and I had elected to have only hourly monitoring of the baby, and a hep-lock instead of the traditional IV so that I could move around throughout labor. When I realized how painful it was for me to lie down in bed, in contrast to walking or sitting in a reclined position, I was really glad that we had made this decision.

When I was pregnant we had considered the two major hospitals that delivered babies in our area, and chose the one that seemed more accepting of natural childbirth methods. To our surprise, many of the labor-and-delivery nurses were trained in the Bradley Method. They were happy to allow me to walk around the ward and take showers to help relax my muscles. The warm showers felt wonderful; I temporarily forgot that I was in labor. I was convinced for a time that the contractions had actually stopped, but they had not. I joked with my mom, telling her I might just stay in the shower until I had the baby.

When I wasn't walking or showering, I passed the time in a semi-reclined position in the lounge chair in my hospital room. I tried to lie down in the hospital bed, but the contractions were much stronger and very painful when I laid down in the hospital bed. Who would have thought? From everything I had seen on TV, I thought that women who were in labor were supposed to be lying down, but you couldn't have paid me to lie down. I would not have been able to have our son naturally if I had to lie down during labor.

For about a month before labor started, I had been dilated to one centimeter. So after I had been in labor for about five hours, 2.5 centimeters didn't sound like a whole lot of progress. But I wasn't really worried about when the baby would show up or how dilated I was. I almost wished the nurses wouldn't tell me. I just kept telling myself that the baby would definitely be here today, when he was ready. My job wasn't to tell him when to show up, it was to relax and let my body do what it was designed to do naturally. I kept focusing on the uterus as a muscle that was just doing exactly what it was supposed to do.

As I relaxed through the contractions, I began to have a feeling of amazement and appreciation for the human body, an experience that would gain momentum throughout my labor. Natural labor is something that every female mammal goes through, except for some humans. Why is natural labor so unusual for American women? I think it is fear.

While I was pregnant, my mom found my baby book. Inside was a handwritten letter that my grandmother had written while my mom was pregnant with me. Her letter included many pieces of advice for my expectant mother, one of which was, "the fear of labor was much worse than the reality." My grandmother gave birth to twelve children, and for most of them she arrived at the hospital too late to receive any pain medication. Her letter helped me to touch my inner strength throughout my pregnancy, as I prepared for natural childbirth.

Soon it was already 2:00 p.m. The fact that the nurse's questions could be answered by my written birth plan was really a huge asset to me. All I had to do was focus on relaxing. I found myself repeating my little daily prayer for a healthy baby during the contractions. When I wasn't reciting that in my head, I was visualizing something peaceful. My ultimate escape from my hectic world is gardening. Throughout my labor, I spent hours daydreaming about what it would be like to hold our baby in the spring, when all of my tulips are in bloom. (I had planted 300 tulip bulbs in our flower beds prior to going into labor.) Something about that image gave me a lot of peace and happiness, and so I kept letting it run through my mind.

I finally let my husband call more of our family and friends to let them know that I was in labor. I hated for him to call any of them too early, because who knew when the baby would be here, and there was no sense in all of us spending Christmas at the hospital. Some of the closer ones had already heard and had been there all morning. Eventually my husband and mother-in-law had to break it to them that natural childbirth isn't as simple as a scheduled C-section, and that it might be later that evening before the baby arrived. During the phone calls and conversations, I'd begun to notice the importance of keeping my distractions to a minimum. I asked my husband to take all conversations and phone calls outside of the room.

If I could concentrate on relaxing, the contractions did not really bother me. If I lost my concentration, I became uncomfortable. As hard as it was, especially as the day went on and more and more family and friends arrived at the hospital, we limited the number of visitors in my room. This helped me to concentrate. To be honest, I really did not want a lot of people in there with me. I appreciated that they were there, but on the other side of that door. It was nothing personal; it was the same as if I was working on a big project at work, trying my hardest to focus.

My labor support team had been strictly my mom, my mother-in-law and my husband for quite a while, aside from a brief visit here and there from a family member or friend who stopped by. But one really nice addition to the team was our friend, Julie. A massage therapist by profession and former labor-and-delivery nurse prior to that, she was just what I needed. My husband and I regularly saw Julie for massages, both before and during my pregnancy. I am not a fan of using medication when there are alternative options, and my alternative has always been massage. We think the world of Julie for all the help she has given us. Julie had agreed to help me relax through labor with massage, and while I had made it through the first part of labor myself, I was very happy to have Julie help me through the rest. My mom and my husband's mom, my husband and Julie all took turns during the remaining hours of my labor, massaging my hands and feet to help me relax through contractions. All I had to do was relax.

By 5:00 p.m. the contractions were strong, requiring complete concentration. The nurses reported that I was at seven centimeters, and Julie let me know that these contractions were at their maximum strength, and that the rest would be downhill. I was really excited to hear this, but was trying not to get my hopes up on when the baby might arrive. I kept focusing on midnight, but I knew in my heart that it wouldn't be that long.

It was just a matter of time. I knew I could do it. Nurses and others kept stepping into the room and commenting on how well I was doing. One even said that I was doing so well, I was her hero. As I listened to their conversations through my contractions, I found out that while many of the nurses were trained in natural childbirth, they still did not see many women have a successful natural birth. I was one of very few they had seen in a while.

At this point in my labor, I really didn't want to talk to anyone. Listening to them was OK, but by the time each contraction ended, it took more energy than I had left to actually speak. Yes and no answers were possible, but anything more involved was simply not going to happen. I was suddenly even more relieved that we had a birth plan, and that our doctor had signed it prior to delivery, and that the hospital had a copy. Having people in the room with me who were familiar with our birth plan helped too. Any of the people in the room with me could explain my intentions without my needing to do anything.

As I worked through the transition stage, I heard that my father-in-law had returned to the hospital with a homemade meal packaged for each of our family members, friends, and all of the nurses in the labor-and-delivery ward. I remember thinking, "What a lucky little baby to be born into a family like this." While I was known to eat constantly throughout my pregnancy, hunger never entered my mind during labor.

I looked up at some point and said quietly to the person nearest to me, "I feel this sensation... like an urge to push?" That was when the labor-and-delivery folks shifted into high gear, changing and moving things around. During that time, I don't remember having any contractions. I don't know if this was because of my sheer excitement, or a true biological reason. All I had to do now was to push. It constantly amazes me that movies and television portray the pushing stage as excruciatingly painful. This is so far from the truth. In fact, our biological systems keep many women from feeling pain while pushing; the weight of the baby in the pelvis keeps the nerves in that region from sending a signal back to your brain to feel any pain. The pushing stage was actually exhilarating—instead of merely relaxing, I was actively helping to bring my baby into the world. This was the only portion of my labor that I spent in the hospital bed.

As I pushed, my mind kept remembering that during natural childbirth, the baby actually helps you through the final stage of delivery. Full-term newborn babies have a reflex that causes them to extend their legs when they are squeezed—they actually help to push themselves out. Of course, this only happens if the baby is not under any anesthesia.

I am told that I pushed for an hour, with friends and family sitting in the waiting room, watching the clock anxiously. It felt like no more than 20 minutes to me. Our son, Gabriel Joseph Walker, was born at 7:55 p.m. on Christmas day.

A natural birth was the best decision I ever made. Our friends and family thought I was such a trooper, but in reality, I was petrified of the things that anesthesia so often brings: a lack of control during labor that could spiral into the oh-so common emergency C-section, or the use of forceps or other extraction methods. I wanted to do everything I could to ensure that our child had the best and healthiest start that I could give him.

During my pregnancy, I could rattle off many of the benefits of natural childbirth for the baby. What I did not realize was how a natural childbirth would affect me personally. The relaxation techniques that I learned with the Bradley Method have been helpful to me in many other areas of my life that bring me a great deal of stress. Also, while I was never someone who suffered from a lack of confidence, you cannot possibly imagine how your confidence soars after having a successful natural birth. Once you realize what a huge mental and physical accomplishment natural birth truly is, it becomes difficult to think that you can't do something. I find myself thinking about my challenges from a different perspective. "I went through natural childbirth... next to that, this is nothing!"

So, the big question is, did the idealistic visions of my future children hold up? Is my child any better in temperament than other children who were not born naturally? It's a good question. He has a beautiful temperament, and I thank God constantly for giving us a happy and healthy baby. However, I'm not sure that this can be attributed directly to natural childbirth. I guess you could make the case that a child born without anesthesia would have an easier birth, be more alert, and have energy to breastfeed earlier, which might contribute to fewer stomach problems, decreased risk of colic, and less fussing—thereby creating a better-tempered child. But it's a stretch, even for me. But I don't plan on risking success with the second one. After all, labor is only temporary, and the child is forever.

A Mother's Guidance: Have a well-written and well thought-out birth plan. Writing your birth plan makes you think about each decision, and leads you to discuss them with your doctor and your labor-and-delivery partners. It will also show you which hospital can best suit your needs, and lessen any fear of the unknown that you or your partner might feel about childbirth. Something as important as how your body will be treated when you may not have a voice for yourself, and how you ultimately bring your child into the world, should not be left to the opinions and biases of the nursing staff or the doctor on call; they may have very different ideas about labor and delivery and the treatment of newborn babies than you.

Visualize a successful natural birth at least once daily—this will not only give you confidence, but it will override the false and negative programming you've picked up about how difficult labor and delivery must be. Practice relaxing your mind and body completely several times a week—think about something peaceful, and concentrate on making every muscle in your body relax.

Knowledge is your best weapon against fear. Read and be informed so that you will not be afraid of the unknown.

Have a well-written and thorough birth plan signed by your physician and packed with your hospital bag. Be sure to review your birth plan with your support team so that they know and respect your wishes, and can be a voice for you during your labor.

I read (cover to cover) *Natural Childbirth the Bradley Way* by Susan McCutcheon. I also ordered *Husband-Coached Childbirth: The Bradley Method of Natural Childbirth* by Robert Bradley. I actually ordered this book for my husband to read, but I read more than he did. *Natural Childbirth the Bradley Way* was a little easier reading for me.

We took Bradley classes, and there were three areas that we found helpful:

First, the class offered solid nutritional guidelines, which is something I did not find clearly defined in any book. We filled out daily diet logs, which made me quite conscious of what I ate at every meal… before that point, I just thought that if I ate healthy foods, that was good enough for my baby. I had always eaten healthy foods; my mother is practically a nutritionist. But I still had no idea how to eat specifically for a baby and help my body nutritionally to prepare for childbirth.

Also, the role-playing portions of the class helped us think through what it would be like to be in labor, and highlighted the decisions that either I or my husband might be called upon to make.

Lastly, our Bradley class was the first we had heard about the importance of a birth plan. It really caught our attention, and we spent several weeks looking through websites and learning more about it. Writing our birth plan put both my husband and I at ease about the whole process.

Additional Thoughts: The pause in contractions between the dilation phase and the pushing stage wasn't her imagination. Some women do experience a break from contractions after full dilation as the body recovers enough to find the energy required to push out the baby.

Czarina Walker, like most women approaching 30, wears many hats. She works full time, and owns a software development company that she founded at 19 years of age. Her company currently employs herself and seven other staff members, and continues to grow and prosper each year. She is a devoted wife to her husband of three years, Brad Walker, whom she has loved and worked along side of for many more years than they have been married. They still share an office today. She is a loving mom to her son, Gabriel. Additionally, she is blessed with an incredible mom, and many wonderful friends and family who are nearby in proximity and in spirit. In her spare time Czarina can be found with her husband in their yard. The gardens they have created around their home entice neighbors and other passersby to stop and enjoy.

THE BIRTH OF THE GODS

BY ROBIN LEE

WHEN I FOUND OUT I was pregnant, I was shocked. It wasn't planned. I had been enjoying so much time with Kanya, my first child, who was six years old. When I checked in to ask the baby why she was coming (she'd better have an outstanding reason!), I knew the timing was perfect and my only job was to let go and enjoy the flow. She told me she was coming to bring together our family, and I'll tell you, this is truly what she has already done.

Eight months into the pregnancy I decided to birth at home, for a variety of reasons. Since pain medication wasn't going to be an option at all, I knew I needed support.

I started searching for something to empower me through the process and help me let go of old beliefs around how painful birthing had to be. After searching online, I came across something called HypnoBirthing. It is a technique that puts a pregnant woman into a slight hypnotic trance, which allows her to easily respond to suggestions that her birthing partner gives to her. It resonated very strongly with me, so Scott and I started the class almost immediately. At first, I didn't want to listen to Scott suggest anything about a peaceful birth! What did he know about peaceful birthing? Then I realized this was an opportunity to heal some old wounds I had been holding onto. This was a glorious opportunity to let go, and that's exactly what I did!

We practiced the affirmations and techniques almost daily. They seemed so simple, almost too simple to actually make a difference. A little music, a little relaxation... and this is supposed to create a painless experience? I couldn't help but doubt, but I did my best to remain focused on positive intentions.

After lots of practice, my waters broke while I was sleeping on the morning of October 18th, at 3:15 a.m. There's nothing quite like waking up and thinking that you've wet the bed! Excited, scared and full of anticipation, I waited about three minutes before waking Scott. He immediately jumped up and started getting things ready around the house. As the sun came up I called friends and family to let them know today was the day.

Well, the day passed without much progress. There was a contraction here and there, but nothing to get overly excited about. As evening came we called the midwife and asked her to come over. I had this incredible need to have the baby checked to make sure all was OK. She arrived and checked both of us. My blood pressure was up and the baby's heart rate was a bit low. The midwife thought I was dehydrated, and suggested more water to get us back to ideal levels. In half an hour all was perfect with us both.

We got a nice sleep that night, since contractions were minimal. Waking up at 8:30 the next morning, I was greeted by a nasty concoction of castor oil and soymilk. The length of time that had passed since my water had broken was beginning to concern the midwife, so she thought she would help things along with this remedy. Two concoctions and four hours later, we were rocking in labor. Between lying in the bathtub, rocking on the birthing ball and walking around, contractions seem to flow regularly. After an hour or so of this, the midwife told me I was dilated to six centimeters. I felt my heart grow heavy! I still had four more centimeters to go before I could see my beautiful angel.

I lay on the bed and Scott kept me in a deep state of relaxation.

I felt a need to ask my mom to come in to rub my shoulders. It felt like contractions were coming every couple of minutes, but I later found out from my mom that they were about 30 seconds apart. She was watching my back tighten with each contraction, and was intrigued that I was not responding to them at all!

Suddenly, I felt an enormous need to go to the bathroom. As I was walking there, I knew this wasn't a normal trip to the bathroom. I asked for the midwife to come in. She looked down and told me I needed to make a decision then and there about birthing in water or on the bed.

Within several minutes I was in the birthing pool with Scott. I looked up to see my mom, brother, sister-in-law, cousin, the midwife and her helper all there around the pool. Each had something they were responsible for, and there they sat, each dutifully holding their assigned tool: mirrors, clocks and cameras. A few pushes later, a deep silence filled the room and the midwife announced that the baby's head was out of me. I clearly remember having anxiety about her head being out in the water and the rest of her still up inside of me. She looked like she must have looked as she lived in the womb. It was as if she was sleeping. I wanted to force a push to get her out but my body wouldn't let me.

I remember this feeling of being completely supported by the universe, that what I thought was good to do was being overridden by something far greater than me. I felt a depth of support that was just unbelievable. With the next push, her body was out and she was moving in the water. I scooped her up to my chest and we lay against Scott. Her body was covered with a white, Crisco-like substance that made her really slippery. It took her a moment to take her first breath. (Water-birthed babies often do take a bit longer to breathe. They sometimes seem confused about whether or not they are really out of the womb, since the watery environment of birth is so similar to the womb.)

Even though it took a moment for her to breathe, I wasn't the least bit concerned. I knew she was absolutely fine because she was still getting oxygen from the pulsating cord. It wasn't until the next morning that she wanted to breastfeed; we let her go by her own schedule.

Vismaya Devi (Goddess of Awe and Wonderment) weighed nine pounds, six ounces, and was 21 inches long. Her head was 14 centimeters around—one of the things I remember most! Gee, I wonder why!

Our daughter Kanya is doing great, adjusting to her new sibling. There are times when it is a bit hard on her, and I'm so grateful she can communicate this to us. The love that she has in her eyes for her new little sister is beyond words. My mom stayed with us for a while so I could heal and we could all bond as a family without the normal pressures and stresses of daily life. What a blessing!

I can truly say that this birth was like a birth of the gods. Until the last 20 minutes or so, it was virtually painless. The power of HypnoBirthing, and the support of your loved ones and the universe, is beyond words.

A Mother's Guidance: Don't be afraid of offending anyone, or concerned with doing the "right" thing. The right thing is to listen to yourself and do whatever feels comfortable. I am speaking mostly about who to have in the room with you while giving birth. Obligations don't apply in the birthing room.

I loved the Sears books, including *The Pregnancy Book, The Birth Book, The Breastfeeding Book* and *The Attachment Parenting Book. The Tao of Motherhood* by Vimala McClure was and still is a great book on mothering.

Robin Lee is an internationally acclaimed healer, a medical intuitive and an intuitive nutritional consultant in Leucadia, California. Robin creates individualized nutritional programs and offers lifestyle counseling.

ACING THE SUN

BY RACHEL KELLUM

Before the Birth

HOW DOES A WOMAN BEGIN to write about the day she and her child were born? I must begin to try or I will lose the details that make this story ours. But do I start with the contractions that began squeezing a month before, or with the waters the squeezing sent trickling warm from me? Or did this birth begin, crying in my lover's arms 42 weeks ago on autumn equinox, when I said yes to creating a new pattern in my life; when I sobbed in a basement apartment, thinking of how long it had taken me to walk outside alone after my first child was born, without her in my arms, to look at the stars? (I had leaned my head back as far as I could, and there they were, and had been, for the past three months. And there I was, standing on a county road, looking up. Where had I been?) Four years, afraid of losing myself again to another child. Realization in a basement: I am a different person in a different situation, with a different partner; there is not a predetermined path I must follow; I can integrate my needs with my family's; I can live differently than before.

Does this story begin in a hospital as I argued with a man in white who told me I would crush my baby's head if I didn't let him cut my perineum? Did it begin with the same man walking into the comfortably pink room (as though pink is enough), after I delivered the child he thinks he delivered, soberly informing me that had I carried Sage to full term, she wouldn't have been able to pass through my small, unusually shaped pelvis? Overwhelmed, I thanked him for this information, even though he took my daughter from my womb before she was ready; even though he came in to "examine" me during my supposedly intense (the nurses pointed to the monitors in disbelief) but painless contractions with a long hook hidden along his wrist; even though he reached inside me and burst my waters without telling me. I thanked him? I took his fear arrow and carried it in my gut for four years. Where do births begin?

I suppose Grey's birth begins at each of these points in my body and more: nurses telling me not to use my voice; to push; to hold my breath until my lips and arms were cold; writing; sobbing about feeling robbed, raped, impotent; walking in the woods, imagining my pelvis the entire horizon, the valley holding the sky and everything I could and couldn't see... matrices that radiate outward at every direction like dazzled light off wet eyelashes. I cannot see them all at once and must squint to write even some of them down. The lines of light play on the pine needles, the fluttering aspen leaves, the purply juniper berries around this little house whose wooden bones we raised and smoothed with our hands.

There. I will begin with this house, with the huge bed my mate, George, built to hold our small family just a month ago. When he first started thinking of the project, I wasn't sure he'd finish it in time for the birth. He had a few weeks to go before finishing his first year of teaching seventh grade language arts in a small not-so-nearby town. Every Friday night, we were still driving over two hours to our house on the small mountain, and then back to our dim basement apartment on Sundays. I began feeling the need to stop the traveling, to be somewhere, to be where I would birth the baby, settled. George, of course, understood and told me to go to the mountains and settle in. I did.

These couple of days alone, I began wondering how I would feel about laboring and birthing alone. This was a possibility since both George and the midwife were two hours away from the cabin. Sitting on Sage's bed, remembering the stories I'd read recently of women who birthed their babies alone in bathtubs and on toilets or in bed with no assistance, I knew—I felt in my skin—that I could do it. In fact, I began to wonder if I should call anyone at all if I began labor. The contractions I'd been having were just as strong as the ones I'd had the day Sage was born (or, I should say, induced) six weeks early. With this second pregnancy, the contractions were there every day for a month, and still no baby. Grey was finishing himself, and my womb was embracing him, preparing him, everyday.

On the Thursday and Friday before Grey's birth, Sage and I hung out at the cabin together. We lay nude in the sun on the box spring we had thrown out after George had finished the new bed. "It's a beautiful day to be naked," she said. She photographed me in jeans and the crazy orange bikini top my funky friend Maile (pronounced My-lee) gave me, baby about to burst out of my skin, and I photographed her bouncing like a star on the box spring. That day I wept... she would no longer be my only child. After asking why I was crying, and I tried to explain, she said, "But mom, I'll still be here, and Baby Grey, and Pablo [our cat], too." This made me smile; she didn't understand that I was mourning the end of an era of my life. Instead I told her I was crying because I love her so much, which is also true.

George made it back to the cabin Friday and we took Sage to her dad's for the weekend, as this was the new schedule. We bathed in the washtub, made love and ate pasta with melted cheese and asparagus, in that order. My contractions began coming five minutes apart, and I could feel my cervix opening. I could still talk through contractions, though. We called Lisa, our midwife, and told her they were coming five minutes apart. She decided to come with her assistant, Trisha, just in case. As the two hours before they arrived went by, I knew this was another practice session, not the real thing, because the contractions didn't get stronger. Lisa and Trisha were happy to come anyway, and went out to look at the stars with our telescope as we tried to sleep. When they came back into the dark cabin and went to bed, they giggled and giggled like girls at a slumber party. I smiled in the dark, listening to them. In the morning we hiked into the valley. Both Lisa and Trisha paid so much attention: evening primrose, lichen, moss, shooting stars that taste like cucumber. "If you want to have more false labor," they said cheerily as they left, "that's fine with us!"

George's last day at work was Monday. I went back with him so I could work on packing up for the summer, hoping not to have the baby in the basement. I cleaned the bathtub, just in case, and sat in it next to a burning red candle, singing to Grey an English lullaby whose words I had changed.

Come through me my baby, open up your eyes.
Loved ones waiting for you, welcoming you darling to our lives.
Great big moon is shining, high up in the sky.
Time to come through me, my little one. Come to me.

My belly was huge in the water, an island.

Finally George's day at work was over. I was so tired and uncomfortable. I wanted someone to just mother me. So I called my mom. I told her about my false labor on Saturday night. Her first words? "Oh no, maybe the baby is too big!" This made me snap. "Mom! Quit trying to scare me! I'm so tired of people trying to make me afraid!" She apologized, and I know she meant well, but I felt sad. So many doctors (not to mention the media) have made our mothers and sisters afraid of their own power. When my mom was in labor with me, her doctor told her I was too big to pass through her pelvis. I was born through a caesarean incision and have been told this story my entire life. I hung up the phone with my mom, who at least sympathized with my discomfort and tried her best to be brave for me.

I felt so heavy. I sat on the couch and drank an ale, as I've heard sometimes beer can get things going and we were about to leave for the cabin soon anyway. This didn't make me feel any brighter. George was gentle and understanding, but I was still so low. All the way to the mountains and after picking up Sage from her dad's, I was quiet, thinking of my women friends. I felt this aching to be nurtured by them, sung to, held, touched, hair brushed. I wanted their hands on my belly, to dance with them. But our lives are so separate; overlap is rare since I am always far away on the plains or in the mountains. It is something I'm learning to live with. So, I sat looking out the passenger window at the glowing orange-pink clouds, thinking of the women I love, trying not to turn my face to George while tears ran, trying not to give away the new moon of my pregnancy, my melancholy. I knew this would not last. By the time we got to the cabin, it was dark. George carried Sage to her bed, and we unloaded the boxes of clothes, food, birthing supplies and clean laundry from the car. We were tired and decided to unpack the boxes in the morning.

In bed, I got some worries out of my fisted stomach to George. He held me and I loved him for listening to me when I wasn't sure if I was being overly sensitive or, as pregnant women are so often dismissed, hormonal. Talking to him made me a lot lighter. We were finally home for the summer, ready for our child to enter our world. We had been making love often in the last few weeks to get labor started, and it was hard not to laugh sometimes in the throes because I was so immobile, beached. So much for all those tips to start labor. They only work when the baby is ready to come. Perhaps those tips are only coincidental with life's little events. *Gee, I ate spicy food, drank a beer and had sex and my baby was born! Let's publish this finding!* No amount of hiking up rocks, jostling myself up our crazy road, eating Taco Bell or being given amazing oral sex could bring this baby out. But perhaps, opening my clenched stomach, sleeping at last in our huge homemade bed on the first night of summer was enough. It wouldn't work for anyone else, I'm sure. Instead of eating spicy food or making love, that night we fell asleep.

I woke up thinking I had to have what our family affectionately calls a growl (aka, a bowel movement). Or at least pee. And of course, the contractions were there, squeezing, as usual. I crawled out of bed, noticed the waning crescent moon in the cracked-by-last-winter window at the southeast side of the bed. Clear night blue-black. I shuffled across the floor, bones popping, trying not to lose my leg-hip connection, found the toilet paper in the dark and made it down the porch steps to our portable chemical toilet, whose battery operated flush function had given out three days before (we have no plumbing). I sat and tried to push out. Nothing. Back to bed. Two or three more contractions. I glanced at our unreliable digital clock, thinking maybe I would time them if I could stay awake. It was 3:46. Each contraction felt like the urge to growl. I turned to the moon in the window, a white fingernail clipping like the ones I had washed down the sink so I could reach into myself without scratching or irritating my cervix or the baby's head. Days before, I had decided to forget the glamour, the nail polish, the same way I had removed the ring in my right nipple a month ago when the contractions began. I had been having night dreams of nursing, so I figured I needed to lose the ring. This gesture was my invitation. Perhaps my cells would send a message to Grey's cells: *I'm ready.* And now the moon was ready: a crescent, a bowl of water. I turned back to face George and closed my eyes.

Labor Begins

Belly squeeze and a gentle buried pop, like a bubble-gum bubble full of water bursting in the mouth of my childhood, a gush, a trickle, a pleasure. I whispered excitedly, shaking George's shoulder, "Babe, babe, my water broke." I scooted on my side down to the foot of our tall bed, trying not to completely soak it. I stood myself up, water dripping down my legs, George sleepy fumbling, following my movement, the clear water puddles, with a green towel, on his knees. No odor. I wish I had thought to taste it, the water of my baby's mouth.

I stood facing the center pane of the five-paned front window, rocking my hips back and forth. Shaking, because it was time to decide to be alone or to call my midwife and friends. I decided to wait. I wanted to shake. Then I realized there were boxes of clothes and food under the bed that needed to be put away, into the new rough-cut pine cabinets George built. My contractions were strong and regular, about five minutes apart, and I could still walk and talk through them. I went about lighting candles: blue apple, blood red, three-flamed vanilla, old dusty green. I didn't light the Shiva altar. Perhaps George lit the candle under Whitman, and the tall green candle under Klimt's *Three Ages of Woman*. Now, after spending an hour readying the house, feeling my body, my belly, intensify, I felt a calmness come over me: I wanted women near. Not because I felt fearful, as some may assert, but immensely powerful. I wanted to share this birth ritual not only with my blood family, but with the magical women who are also my family.

First I called my midwife, Lisa, who had been a healing force to me throughout my pregnancy as I struggled to ignore words about my pelvis that had been planted in me for years. (It took a lot of reassurance from her, reading about the softening of ligaments and bones in late pregnancy, as well as visualization and forgiveness, to quiet the voice of Sage's birth doctor in my head. My mother's voice had been there too, reminding me of my own caesarean birth.) Lisa was a little surprised I had not called earlier, since it would take her two hours to get to me, but she understood and respected my decision to wait. Then I called two dear women friends, Maile, who amazingly had the day off from work, and Monica, who would be bringing her nine-year-old daughter, Andrea. Monica later told me that when she woke Andrea to see if she wanted to go to school or to the birth, she darted out of bed, grabbed her hot water bottle and said, "Mom, we'll need sturdy hiking boots." While talking to Monica, I had to stop in the middle of a few sentences, overcome with that opening, that taking over of my body. I told her she could take her time if she wanted to sleep more. Later we laughed about such a silly suggestion.

The calls were made; I began settling into myself again. The sun was rising, filling the darkness of the cabin, erasing candlelight but not the cupped moon. Yellow-orange burst below a thinning bank of clouds. I looked into the valley, feet pressed together in front of me, holding onto my knees, leaning back on my pelvis with each contraction. I asked George to put on some music we had chosen for the birth, *Zen Kiss*.

Sheila Chandra's voice liltingly chanted into my body, called me to my power, to awaken to it. She soothingly reminded me that our womanly wisdom, our spirits, cannot be lost or broken; that as the mothers of humanity, we can seek and create images of ourselves that are powerful; that we do not need to rely on lesser images others have put before us. She urged me — and all women — to find our wisdom in dreams. So I began.

In between contractions, I remembered a night dream from weeks before in which I was giving birth, reaching between my legs, feeling my baby's head bulge the skin tight and retract, bulge and retract. Although I had never reached down to feel Sage crowning, I sensed it fully in my dream. This told me where to keep my hand during labor, to stay in touch with the work of my body. I began to weep (lots of weeping going on in those last few days!) with the power surging through me, so full. I had thought I would want a lot of touch at this time from George, but I realized that touch distracted me from centering completely in myself, from fully opening and emanating around my baby. Closing my eyes through contractions helped me become the emanation. I want to call it emanation instead of pain because, for me, "pain" carries the sensation of fear, and as I have said, I wasn't afraid. Emanation better suggests the intense sensation of expansion I felt. It took all my concentration and relaxed breathing to experience this strange dimension of my body peacefully.

I began to feel an old hum come from somewhere deep in my chest, behind my breasts. Eventually I had to move from the bed, the window, to walk. The clouds were gone, the eastern sky was creamy yellow. Lisa called and said she'd be there in an hour, so I guess two hours had passed by this time. We told her my contractions were now about four minutes apart. I put on my sandals, opened the door, and stood on our small porch. For early June in the mountains, the morning was incredibly warm. I decided to

labor outside for a while. From the porch I could see the ponderosa pine tree in front of the house, a crossroads for all kinds
of birds that feed there: hummers, blackheaded grosbeaks,
stellers jays, chickadees, chipping sparrows, juncos, green-tailed
and rufus-sided towhees, house wrens and red crossbills. This
tree is the home of hanging bells, dried shriveled gourds that
click in the wind, a rope for the hammock chair. Its broken, dead
branch drew my attention. I had heard stories of women hanging on things to get labor moving, so I thought, why not? On the
way to the tree, I stopped at the pile of boards George had been
using to build kitchen cabinets, crouched with my hands on
the pile, cracked open more. I stood up, made it to the ponderosa, and hung with the gourds, straight armed, squatting as a
huge rush poured hot through my belly and out my mouth:
ooooohhhhhOOOOOHHHHHHoooooooooohhhhhhh.

I asked George, who was busy boiling water and making coffee in the house, to bring a clean towel to hang over the branch, as
well as a clean towel and sheet for some padding and protection
under my feet. After each call I stood and leaned on the branch,
resting my head on my folded arms. I don't know how many times
I did this, hanging, pressing my face into my stretched tingling
arms, standing again to lean and rest as much as possible, but this
seemed to be the best way to keep opening. I continued with the
low moaning, concentrating on keeping my jaw slack. George later
said it was one of the most primitive sounds he's ever heard. I
knew I would not move from this place. Over a half dozen chipmunks nibbled on seeds and watched from the pocketed swell of
granite behind me.

George brought me ice in my favorite pewter moon-handled
mug, and since labor was moving along smoothly, we decided at
that moment to wake Sage. She had been a huge part of preparing
for Grey's birth. We showed her videos and photos of babies developing, laboring women and actual births, so we knew she'd be fine.
She had even been by my side holding my hand and singing as
George and I practiced perineal massage and relaxed breathing

throughout the last month of pregnancy. We had prepared her as best we could for what was to come. Why not be honest with her? When George woke her up, he took her into his arms and walked to the window. He told her Baby Grey was coming, that there was some blood and that's OK, and that mom was making some strange noises. He assured her everything was fine. She watched me from the window for a few minutes until she decided she was ready to come to me.

I was in the middle of a contraction, moaning, when she came out of the house. She stood behind me on the bloody sheet. When it subsided I turned to her and there she was, with her hand over her mouth, giggling. Then it occurred to me how silly and strange my sounds must be to her. I told her, "You're right, these sounds are pretty funny, huh? But I just have to make them to deal with the energy in my belly... Here comes another..." She nodded and stayed by me on the sheet for a while. I think I quit hanging from the branch around this time because my arms and legs were falling asleep. I began squatting with my hands in front of me like a cat on its haunches, hovering over the red rubber hot water bottle George had filled earlier. Now was the time to use it, to take the heat into my perineum. I imagined blood filling my tissues, making them soft and stretchy. The heat was so right. Sage asked me who was playing the flute in the house; it was Mary Youngblood's *The Offering*.

By this time, another hour had passed and George figured the midwives would be down at the bottom of mountain by then. Their little car would never make it up our steep and rutted four-wheel-drive road. As I watched George drive away to pick them up as we had planned, my rushing sounds began to end in *ungh*. Time to push? I decided to wait to actively push until I had no choice; for now I would just let my uterus do the work. I kept my hand at my opening feeling for a bulge, not one yet. Then I reached inside with my left longest finger to feel for the head: only the soft folds of my vaginal wall—a cord? No—only my tissues and this soft lump at the very top. Not hard enough for a head. Had my cervix even opened? I wondered. I just kept calling ooohhhhh, OOOOHHH,

Hooohhhh. Sage walked out of the house saying softly, "Baby Grey, Mommy's not ready for you to come out yet." This surprised me and I managed to say gently, "Yes, honey, I'm ready… why do you say that?" She answered, "You keep saying 'nooooo.'" I explained that I was really saying "ooooohhhh" to help myself open up. She nodded. I was carried off again into that ancient sound. Again and again and again.

The Birth

I guess on his way down, George passed Maile hiking up to me with my silver dumbek drum and special gifts in her backpack: my mother's mother's brass bracelet emblazoned with The Crab; a wooden mask; a potpourri burner in the gourd shape of a woman with three faces and spirals at her womb through which candle light would shine; and a bag of almost stale tortilla chips. The scene she walked in on: me moaning under a ponderosa on a bloodstained flowered sheet with Sage behind me, brave eyes seeming to say, *Mom's OK, right?* I looked up from my sheet and there was beautiful Maile walking up the path surrounded by groundsel flowers, with a leather beaded band stretched across her forehead, wearing the embroidered vest she used to wear when we gave massage for high prices to lonely men a few summers ago. (We were broke… what can I say?) Her eyes were shining wet; she whispered in a smoky voice, "You're so beautiful… I love you." "I love… you," I told her. "I'm so glad you're here." We hugged. Maile and Sage found a wand and soap bubbles and filled the air with them, watching me from the granite mound.

My legs were falling asleep again so the midwives, who had just arrived, helped me lean back against my George who sat with his back against the tree. I could smell smoke on his clothes, in his breath, so I knew he must've had a cigarette on his trip down the mountain. He usually never smokes unless he's having a beer, so I knew he must've been a little nervous, a little excited, even though on the surface he was as quiet and serene as always. He was so strong for me.

I kept my hand at my opening and pushed with each contraction, because I couldn't NOT push. "It burns...." I groaned. Lisa reminded me the baby was passing by the mouth of the cervix, stretching it. I kept pushing but I don't know for how long or how many times. At one point my belly jumped around and it made me laugh. Grey was looking for the best position to go through my bones. Soon I felt my skin bulging, just like my dream. "OH! The baby's coming!" I exclaimed. They told me to look in the small mirror they were holding. "Look at all that hair!" There was the top of the head! So soft and dark and beautiful. I began to feel the same skin fire I felt with Sage. "Ooh, it burns...." I repeated. "Yes, you're opening," they reminded me again with smiles. Oohh, OOOHHHH Hooohhh. It was an inescapable mantra.

I lightly rubbed my fingers around the thin perineum. This was comforting. Lisa applied olive oil to my skin and I pressed my rounded palm against the small mound, supporting the tissue. I think Lisa helped massage and support the skin as well. "Come on, baby," I said longingly. Lisa softly assured me that my baby will come when it is ready, that there was no need to hurry. After another squeeze, his head slowly passed through the thinnest skin; I felt the lip slide over his head, past the widest circle of that furry globe. Relief! *The hard part is over*, I thought, *now the body will just slide out*.

But when Lisa saw in the next couple contractions that his head was still turtle-necked by me, she said, "OK, you need to get on hands and knees." My logical thinking self remembered that meant the shoulders were stuck behind my bones. George and I had read about shoulder dystocia and how to work with it, so what Lisa and Trisha did next was no surprise. I didn't think I could move into this position without help, so they pulled me up.

George supported my shoulders; I remember his downy brown forearm under my chin and across my upper chest. I knew I needed to push harder than ever now because Lisa once showed me a video of a baby born with shoulder dystocia. The mother pushed like hell while the midwife worked on hooking the shoulder with a finger to corkscrew him down and out, and the assistant applied pressure with a fist above and behind her pubic bone to dislodge the shoulder. I guess it is important to have the baby born as quickly as possible in this situation because blood fills the head and has difficulty recirculating to the rest of the body. This is what was happening to Grey.

So what did I do? I pushed like hell. I felt the baby twisting, kicking inside me. The aggressive movement startled me and my moaning turned into a deep, throat grinding roar. I have never been so animal, so uninhibited in my life; I was becoming a lion. I began to grind my teeth into George's arm as I pushed, and a voice inside told me, *Don't bite his arm.* It was a gentle calm voice so I listened and just kept roaring. Amazingly, George didn't even flinch at my bite, although he later joked that he had started looking around for a stick. It seemed like it was taking a while to get Grey moving, so I asked Lisa what they were doing, even though I already knew. "We're working on hooking... his shoulder." A catlike screeching but simultaneously deep belly roar poured out of me and I knew he was coming.

I've read about and seen so many births in which the entire body just slips right out after the head is born. Not so with Grey. I pushed out his shoulders... his arms... and his hips. What a massive child! Lisa asked George if he wanted to catch his baby, and he held out his hands with hers, carrying him fully into the light.

After the Birth

"Is the baby out completely?" I asked. "Is everything OK?" I turned to see them wrapping him in a black towel in the bright yellow air. George was brimming, looking into the towel. "We've got a... Look!" He knew I had wanted to see for myself before anyone told me, so I looked into the blanket and saw Grey's perfect little penis and swollen testicles. "We've got a boy!" I yelled out. It's funny I didn't think to look until George told me to. I'm so glad no one told me his sex and that I got to see for myself. I could tell George was thrilled to have a son; we were both hoping for one and had a feeling all along I was carrying a boy inside me. Even Eva, the Mexican custodian at George's school, knew. (Later, she was pretty proud of her powers of prediction!) Between Lisa's watch—set 10 minutes fast—and our unreliable digital clock, they decided it was, give or take, 7:58 a.m. Although none of us could remember which song was on, Crosby Stills Nash and Young were singing in the house, *So Far*. Perfect.

The cord stretched between us. As they handed him to me, creamy and light blue, all I could say was, "My baby! My baby! Look at my baby!" over and over. Lisa and Trisha sang a sweet little welcoming song to him. I wish I could remember the words. We were all so huge and brilliant together. Grey looked amazing. Coming from a water world, his hair was in black wet swirls, his skin was still swollen with fluid, and his long fingernails were nearly swallowed by the skin around them. A little fuzz from the new black towel was sticking to his damp skin, even though I had washed it for the birth. His eyes were slits above his smashed little nose, and he gurgled and grunted so sweetly.

George reached out to Sage and said, "You're a big sister!" She looked into the towel. "He's so cute!" she announced. I was glad she thought so, because he looked so strange, so old, to me. So different from me or George. But yes, he was strangely beautiful. Lisa showed me his small caput, a little swollen cap on his head where fluid had collected under the scalp. She said I was probably dilated for the past couple of weeks and that the pressure of my contractions had probably pushed his head into the open cervix, causing some fluid to build up. This explained the soft lump I felt when I reached in to check for the cord earlier. I had touched his head. The caput disappeared after about an hour or so.

It was then I noticed that Monica and her daughter, Andrea, were there. I was thrilled they made it and asked when they arrived. She said they made it up the mountain just as Grey crowned and I began roaring him out. In a photograph, the look on her face as she walked up on us was just priceless. She must have thought I was dying or something, with all the noise I was making. I'm sure this wasn't the most peaceful sound I could have made, but it is what gave me power. And Grey was calm and undisturbed for many days, never a cry.

I offered Grey my breast soon after he was in my arms, but he was more interested in just trying to breathe. They didn't suction him because they thought he should do the work of clearing the mucus himself. I felt a little awkward holding a brand new baby again, but I knew I would learn his body and the awkwardness would wear off quickly. I felt another contraction and someone helped me squat to birth the placenta. This felt good. It just came right out on its own. Perfect and iridescent with veins. (We saved it and planted seeds from his birth tree over it on the year anniversary of his conception, a few days before autumn equinox.) After a while, Lisa asked when we wanted to cut the cord. We decided to cut it when it stopped pulsating, even though throughout the pregnancy I had thought I would want to leave it attached for a couple hours. It just seemed right to cut it then, so Daddy George did it.

I couldn't stop beaming. My whole face smiled. I asked Lisa and Trisha if I tore. They both shook their heads no (it was funny how they always seemed to say or do the same thing at the same time whenever I asked a question). Lisa added, "Even with stuck shoulders and my fingers wiggling around inside!" I'm sure the elasticity of my perineum was due to the perineal massage George and I did, as well as the hot water bottle and oil we used during the birth. What a relief to pee without burning!

I handed Grey to his dad so I could get up to wash at our outdoor water tank (we have no running water). Trisha helped support me, as my bottom felt pretty bruised. I managed to get most of the blood off of my legs and hands and thanked Trisha for her help. I noticed George with Grey at the hummingbird feeder under the firs next to the house. He was already showing his son the little birds, his passion. Trisha helped me over to the futon that Maile and the midwives carried outside for me. They laid it on top of the box spring we had been using as a trampoline/sunbathing bed for the past few weeks. It was covered with a pretty southwestern patterned pinkish sheet and a few absorbent pads to collect blood.

George brought me Grey and I cuddled up with him. My hair kept getting in the way as I tried to help Grey latch on, so Lisa pulled it back into a barrette. Grey was still trying out his gurgly-groany, deep new voice, telling me all about his morning. I pulled my faded purple-gray down duvet over our heads to keep out the light. Although the brightness of the day didn't seem to bother him at all, he didn't want or wasn't able to open his eyes past slits. I cupped my hands around his face and looked in at him the way his dad has done so many times to me. As soon as I shaded his eyes like this, they popped right open and looked at me. I laughed out loud and said, "Well, hello!"

When Sage was born, Maile's twin boys' paternal grand-mother knitted a pink blanket for her. Sage brought this (which she has begun wrapping her dolls in) to her new brother, along with the knitted lavender poof-ball hat she wore as a tiny preemie in the hospital. After a while we decided the blanket may be too scratchy for him so we covered him in a cotton one instead. Sage helped me wrap Grey in these things and said seriously, "I think I have SOME boy clothes for him to wear."

I continued to offer Grey my breast as we rested on the mat-tress outside. Lisa assured me that if he didn't want to nurse yet, not to worry because he was so chunky that he had a lot of reserve energy to burn. After a while he latched on like an old pro.

I guess it didn't occur to me how big he was until Lisa pulled out the scale to weigh him. "Anyone want to take a guess at his weight?" She wagered, "You think nine pounds?" *No way,* I thought, *nine pounds?!* She laid him in the sling on the scale and announced with a huge smile, "TEN POUNDS!!" My jaw must have dropped open. Suddenly I felt incredibly vindicated. I knew that no one, not even medical science "authorities" like the doctor who shot through me with fear after Sage's birth, has the power to name or describe the capability of my body but me. My bones moved, I opened up as wide as I needed to birth my big gorgeous son. I've never felt more powerful and sacred and immense.

Many months earlier, following his autumn equinox conception, we had named him Grey Forest Walt after the union of dark and light, my father and Gramps, and Whitman, respectively. His name and the events of his birth will teach him. He journeyed through two hours of night and two hours of morning. The crescent moon, at first an upright bowl, overturned, poured after his arrival. He came facing the sun on the first day of our summer, the warmest day in weeks and for weeks after. His birth was attended by an old ponderosa, my dead grandmother's hummingbirds, chipmunks, six wise women, and his quiet, unruffled father who was not afraid to leave me alone with my power, who held me, who never doubted my body even once. I was a gate. Four turkey vultures circled over us after his entrance, smelling birth, looking for the placenta, huge and prismatic with blood. The next day, I opened the Osho Zen Tarot deck Monica had given me as a birth gift, spread the entire deck in a circle to invite the four directions, and pulled my first card. It was The Master, a picture of Osho himself, symbolizing the transcendence of duality, the presence of a teacher. The following day, I shuffled, spread a circle, and pulled my second card: The Master, again. I am not sure what any of this means, really, or if it means anything at all to anyone else. Grey's birth was simply the holiest day of my life. Maile says, "Auspicious."

....

Prelude to an Empowered Birth: The Day Sage Was Born

In my pregnancy with Sage, at 34 weeks I had gone to the hospital to see if I was in "real labor." The nurses couldn't believe I wasn't yelling out in pain based on what the monitor said about the strength of my contractions. I was examined internally several times, was told I was dilated to five centimeters, and had a heated argument about episiotomy with the doctor on duty (unfortunately we were out of town). I tried to explain to him that hot compresses and massage would open me up, and that I did not want to be cut under any circumstances, but he insisted I could crush my premature daughter's head if I didn't have the incision. I could tell he wasn't really thrilled with my persistence. Not long after, he came in to "examine" me again, and reached in and burst my waters without telling me. THEN I started "real" labor, and Sage was born into the world unable to breathe on her own. After my pregnancy with Grey, I realize I would more than likely have been able to finish growing Sage myself if the doctor had just left me alone. I'll never know for sure. But I do know now that I am just one of those women who have regular, strong contractions and even dilate considerably throughout the last month.

I had to argue with the doctor about episiotomy once again when Sage was crowning because he began reaching for a local anesthetic while loudly exclaiming, "But you are inhibited!" With obvious frustration, he finally honored my wishes to not have an episiotomy. I ended up having only a minor internal scrape that didn't require stitches, even though he unsuccessfully tried to convince my then-husband I needed them, "Or,"whispering, he confided, "her vagina won't look right." The scrape healed nicely.

Sage was rushed to another hospital with a collapsed lung. I felt strong so I checked out of the hospital and we followed her. While in intensive care, the doctors wouldn't let me hold or breast-feed Sage for over a week, telling me that too much touch would be too stressful for her already overloaded premature nervous system (they had her hooked up to everything imaginable). All I was allowed to do was place my hands on her, talk to her softly and hope she could feel my warmth. They told me that if I tried to nurse her she might aspirate my milk because often preemies have sucking problems. I just couldn't believe what they said. Once I was finally allowed to hold her on a regular basis, I was tempted to slip her my nipple when the staff wasn't watching, but her dad told me not to. I didn't. I felt so powerless. I pumped and cried a lot, saving colostrum for her that they fed through a long tube inserted through her nose and into her tummy. I couldn't imagine that this procedure of inserting the tube could be less stressful than my suckling her. I also couldn't imagine that she would have sucking problems, and she didn't. She latched right on the first time I offered her my breast. I was elated.

A couple blood transfusions and dozens of chest x-rays later, we were allowed to take our four pound, eight ounce daughter home, hooked up to oxygen and an apnea monitor. It was three months before she could oxygenate at safe levels with no extra help.

We chose not to vaccinate her, and since then, although she has been hospitalized twice with RSV when she was two and three, her health gets better and better every year. She just turned five and is busy—as she has been since birth—learning about life at her own pace in our home and everywhere she goes. I adore her. She is a beautiful, wise, dancing, bug- and bird-loving child who talks to trees.

A Mother's Guidance:
On Perineal Massage

I want to describe how we did this because I think it really helped me not to tear as I delivered our BIG boy. We started doing the massage about a month before Grey's due date. Really, calling it massage might be misleading because there was no stroking of the tissue, just stretching.

I would lie on the bed with my back propped up on pillows, and George would apply quite a bit of oil on the fingers of one hand. When we first started, he would insert one finger into my vagina as far as possible, then he would press downward toward my rectum. He would hold this as long as was comfortable for both me and him (after a while the pressure would make his wrist ache). As he applied the pressure, I concentrated on relaxing my vaginal wall and breathing slowly and steadily. Relaxing my vaginal wall felt like pushing outward to pee, only without the releasing of urine, of course. George was really helpful here because he would tell me if the tissue felt relaxed inside, or if I was beginning to tense up.

For the first few days, one finger was all I could cope with. It was so helpful to feel that slight burning and to breathe through it. This built my confidence. Gradually, as I got more used to the sensation, George added one finger at a time, inserted up to the knuckles, using as much pressure as we both could handle. No matter how many fingers we used, I made sure to relax my tissues and to breathe as naturally and deeply as possible. Believe it or not, in the week or two before Grey came, we made it to four fingers!

On Fear

People have asked me if I was afraid when George left me and Sage alone to drive the mile down the mountain. For a fraction of a second I knew I could either be afraid or trust myself. I instantly opted for the second choice because I knew I would invite problems into my body by being afraid. Before the birth I studied the physiological effects of fear and knew I needed my blood to stay in my major organs, especially my uterus, and not rush off to my limbs…. So, really, fear wasn't even an option—I had come too far to be afraid. We had made a backup plan in case of an emergency (i.e., call Flight for Life and give the land coordinates that were posted by the phone), but I knew I could do this. What was most important to me was to determine that there was no prolapsed cord, as this would require immediate transport. And since I determined this was not an issue, I was confident I could handle anything else, even shoulder dystocia, as George and I had studied this condition closely, and our midwife has also helped women deliver babies in this situation without problems. What it comes down to is this: fear has no place in any birth, not on a mountain, not in your home, not in a hospital.

I understand having fear in a hospital, though, given the way I was treated by the doctors and nurses attending Sage's birth. They actually encouraged my fear so that I would be more willing to comply with their routine procedures. They tried to make their fears mine by forcing a premature labor, immobilizing me with uncomfortable black monitor straps across my belly, wires and an

IV line; they talked down to me, told me when and how to breathe and push. None of their birthing "strategies" felt comfortable to me, and in fact angered and confused me at a time when I knew, if left alone, my body would have made it absolutely clear what to do. If they hadn't already endangered my baby by inducing labor too early, I would not have allowed their interference. Where such "preventive" measures might decrease some women's fears, they only enhanced mine by implying I could not trust my body.

Rachel Kellum grew up in central Illinois, earned her BFA in Studio Art at Millikin University, and her MA in English Education at Colorado State. She currently spends her time homeschooling her three children, gardening, making herbal medicines, writing, reading, drumming, studying world spiritual traditions, corresponding online with mothers about birth, and practicing Tai Chi. She aspires to become a midwife who encourages freebirth.

THE BIRTH RITE OF SAMUEL RUNE

BY RACHEL KELLUM

Foreword

"[WITCH] IS JUST a vulgar word for it that can mean all kinds of things. The word we use is *doran*." Juniper went on to explain that the word *doran* came from our Gaelic word *dorus*, an entrance or way in (the English have a word very like it). It was someone who had found a way into seeing or perceiving.

"Seeing or perceiving what?"

Juniper hesitated. "The energy, the pattern."

"So what does a *doran* do then?"

"Some of us do healing things, like me and my herbs. Some of us sing or write poetry, or make beautiful things. Some of us don't do anything at all. They often stay in one place, and they just know."

"Know? Know what?"

"How things are," said Juniper mysteriously.

....

"Not everyone is familiar with the vocabulary of witchcraft," [said the inquisitor]. "Perhaps you will tell us now what a *doran* is."

"It is someone who loves all the creatures of the world, the animals, birds, plants, trees and people, and who cannot bear to do any of them any harm. It is someone who believes that they are all linked together and that therefore everything can be used to heal the pain and suffering of the world. It is someone who does not hate anybody and who is not frightened of anyone or anything."

I could see from the expression on the inquisitor's face that he had not expected such a reply.

> *From Sage's favorite book,* Wise Child, *by Monica Furlong,*
> *which I read aloud twice that winter.*

I struggled for months, trying to decide how to present Sam's story in a way that would not narrow my audience or isolate me from the readers who love Grey's birth story. For a while I considered neutralizing my language and experiences to make them more palatable to a wider audience. But my night dreams advised me against this. Women's spiritual practices and voices have been ignored and marginalized for so long that I need to silence my own internal censor, the one that clamors to make me acceptable in a world dominated by patriarchal religious and medical institutions. We've all heard the dismissals of women's wisdom mysteries, traditions and ways of knowing: "what a witch, hag, cunt (a negative derivative of the name of the Hindu goddess, Kunti)"; "that's a bunch of hocus pocus, hoodoo voodoo, mumbo jumbo"; "it's just hormones"; "she's/I'm just PMSing"; "the monthly curse"; "that's just an old wives' tale"; "quit being so illogical, irrational, anti-intellectual, superstitious"; "I'm/she's just postpartum"; "oh, that New Agey stuff." Perhaps we've even used these dismissals ourselves. I know I have.

I remember a conversation I had two summers ago with a wealthy board member of a prominent spiritual community, one that supposedly provides a space to teach the traditions of all people. When I suggested having Celtic teachers on the land, he replied, "Well, that stuff is pretty New Agey. We want to be taken seriously here. We only provide a space for the expression of traditions that have a long and traceable lineage." I explained to him that this would be impossible for most women's traditions, since an acknowledgement of lineage got our sisters and mothers and grandmothers and friends killed for hundreds of years not so very long ago. His expression was paternal and impassive. I lost steam, got frustrated. I wanted to tell him that what he calls New Agey is a profound attempt by women and men to rebuild a practice around ancient wisdom, a tradition, a lineage, which is more truth-fully and rightfully a web than a line anyway; but I didn't. He listened to me finish and soon changed the subject.

I am no longer afraid of or silenced by such dismissal. So I won't edit my perspective here, my way of seeing birth. I have too much rebuilding to do. I will speak my womanly truth, the truth of what I know about childbirth, one of the most profound women's mysteries there is, and let the reader sift my words through their own cultural filters.

Samuel Rune's story is infused with the language of my spiritual practice as a woman. In the past, and even now, as many women reclaim the power of this word, a woman who spoke or practiced in this way was sometimes called a "witch," (or cultural equivalent) from the Old English root word "wit," meaning "to know." "Witch" was transformed into a derogative term by fear and hatred of womanly knowing in a world being overrun by papal, patriarchal authority. As wise women accused of witchcraft, our properties and homes were often seized, and our tools, the domestic tools of womanhood, such as healing plants, the tools of cooking, cleaning, making and mending clothes, and the free little gifts of the earth that adorned our shelves and sills and inspired us with their simple beauty and power, were demonized. It is no secret and I need not elaborate on the horrendous ways we were tortured and killed for our knowledge. Although men were also killed, the witch hunts were predominately a holocaust of women.

I have become increasingly concerned about the ways women are still silenced or forced into compromising situations by people who think they know what is best for us. Modern childbirth "management" is a prime example of such a practice. Since making the story of my first son's birth available online, I have received countless e-mails from women who mourn the ways they and their infants were treated in birth: unnecessary scars left on their abdomens and perineal tissues; lifelong urinary tract problems caused by forceps damage; lifelong vaginal pain or rectal damage caused by incisions made too deep or improperly repaired; the intense spiking pain caused by labor inducing drugs; the inability to vocalize one's needs as more and more Demerol is injected without consent; the medical practice of taking women's drugged or frightened silence as consent; lung damage caused to babies induced or taken by cesarean section too early because of miscalculation of dates or mere impatience; babies unable to nurse properly at birth and confused for months after due to painkilling drugs reaching them in-utero during delivery; babies born ill, or worse still, with disease introduced into the birth canal by too many vaginal examinations by unclean hands. The list could go on. Where the physical scars have healed, the psychological and spiritual scars continue. They run deep. Many women don't talk about these scars, or they accept them, because they have been led to believe they should simply be happy that they and their babies are alive. But I am here to say that we matter too, women, that our womanly experience of birth really matters. We deserve to be allowed to be powerful at this time. It is not even a question of "allowance," which presupposes someone else having power over our bodies.

It is hard for me to hear about these millions of visible and invisible scars without seeing the similarities to other atrocities committed against women throughout history. The time has come for women to take the initiative to learn how far-ranging our birth choices really are, that the western medical model does have its limits, and that our births and the words we use to learn about and describe birth will affect us at many levels.

I am certain that drawing parallels between the historical mutilation/torture of women and modern birth practices may come across as harsh or extremist to many ears because those who unknowingly torture birth (this is not a blanket statement; I know there are many, many gentle birth attendants out there, and that they truly love and are loved by the women they serve) believe they are helping us, and have convinced many of us that they are indispensable to our safety. And maybe, in the rarest of circumstances, much rarer than even the best birth attendants may understand, they are.

We truly can be trusted to perform birth safely, especially when we have been well nourished and have maintained a healthy pregnancy on all levels: physically, emotionally, mentally and spiritually. In the case of extreme health problems that cannot be rectified through simple changes of habit, of course intervention can be lifesaving. However, today, even healthy women's bodies are not expected to perform birth properly or safely, and the preventative measures thus employed to avoid and detect (un)expected "problems" interfere enough with the natural functioning of our inextricably connected body/heart/mind/spirit to actually *cause* the problems they are meant to prevent.

Having said this, my critique of history and obstetrics in this essay stops here. I've worked hard to forgive, to move on to better things, better ways to direct my energy. My rage at the injustices still routinely practiced against women, with or without their consent, and against myself in the birth of my first child, has spent itself, left rich nutrients in the soil of my life. Things grow there now. This birth, and this story, for example. With this story I am offering another possibility for birth, as was offered to me so generously by other conscientious women who have chosen to share their birth stories as well. My stories would not be possible without theirs.

Now I am simply a woman whose spiritual practice, in life, and subsequently, in birth, is to see the sacred in the mundane, to work with the gifts of this planet and the daily responsibilities of my life to perpetuate, as herbalist Susun Weed would say, "health, wholeness and holiness" in my journey here. I do not claim any one title for my spiritual path, I simply adopt and adapt wisdom from both men's and women's traditions (which until the past few decades were hard to find since we've been underground so long), and create my own traditions as I go along. This is what women do best. Take a little of this, a little of that, and make do. Make beautiful. Make a web.

Even if my sense of the world and how to live in it, pray in it, and give birth in it is not similar to yours, it is my hope that you will come to know yourself better by knowing me. And that, perhaps, you will take some of what is helpful from me into yourself, as I have taken in so many of you. We overlap and enlarge each other.

To all those who, despite our differences, have offered me unconditional love and support in ways physical, spiritual, emotional, intellectual and magical throughout my pregnancies, births and life, I offer my deepest gratitude.

The Motherway Ceremony

The night before, when we three women came home to messy rooms and unmade beds after a mountain weekend of just us three, I scrubbed the grime ring from the tub, thinking, *Didn't I just do this before I left? How can a tub look like this after only three days?* We had left our kids with their dads, loaded our stuff and my dog (to ward off mountain lions and a drunk neighbor), and sped toward the little mountain for my Motherway ceremony. We had planned to do this a couple weeks before my due date, as I had become uncertain about September 11th, my forty-week mark. Glorious with independence, timeless, we drummed without interruption, sang the names of the Great Woman with Many Names, Ona's voice high and my voice low, Tera quiet, but there, over her drum. Her vocalizations rang out her humor, her magic, our laughter. We whooped and chanted as Tera broke into spontaneous poetry. And we didn't stop there; we couldn't stop, this Motherway of drums and voices, this sending off of a mother into her primal power. Our bare breasts and tattoos walked unashamed through the air; we left our bodily juices on canvas chairs where we sat in the sun, reading, undone, un-heeding our kids' pleading over 80 miles away. The air, the space, swallowed their sounds long before they reached us.

I leaned back on my arms on the bed, watching, as Tera and Ona placed an overturned bowl on my belly and traced the full moon bordered by opposing crescents around my crystal belly-ring jewel. The henna and lime spray and the sun burned the sign of The Goddess into my skin: a benediction, a blessing. I passed the archetypes illustrated on specially chosen tarot cards over that sign in the sunlight, and the henna took those images into my skin: Trust, Innocence, Rebirth, Receptivity, Courage, the wisdom of the High Priestess and the Magician, and the solitude of the Hermit (for the baby's Virgo sign) and on and on. Birth-related hematite runes, Ona's sodalite runes and my quartz runes—the ones I had painted with forgotten black nail polish when I couldn't afford to buy commercial ones—followed the cards. I packed all the power I could into that full moon flanked by crescents. Henna-stained Q-tips and paper towels and lime spray in their motherly hands became the tools of their love and magical ordination. I want to use ceremonial language here because even in our giggling casualness, we were making magic. We were making meaning. We were being women. We didn't know the sun would burn my skin, leaving the upper part of the henna moon sign lighter than the burnt skin that framed it, but the lower side of the sign a nice henna orange. The gradation of orange to bronze to burnt red made a sunset, a sunrise, on my belly, on The Belly. Yes. The sun always rises and sets there.

That night they rubbed my hands and arms and fingers with oil, and Tera was not sure about participating in this "chick thing." But this was no chick thing, this rubbing of my belly and legs and feet with almond oil—this was a woman thing, a mother thing, a magic thing. They swept energy from the top of my belly to the soles of my feet, whispering, "A nice easy birth for Rachel," over and over, and I swept my own hands down over the oiled mound, lifted that invisible bundle of child out of my vagina and into my arms and clutched it against my heart: my baby, the baby that would pass so easily from me, yes, fast and easy, a beautiful birth.

No, not a chick thing, an oily hands and belly words witch thing. We were rosily alive, laughing with our love and power to help each other with simple, joyful ritual. And we didn't stop there.

We wrapped a leather shoestring cord around my belly and then around our clasped hands as a binding of love in the upcoming birth, exchanging words of love and gratitude. They would be with me and I with them, no matter where this baby chose to enter—on the mountain (as I had hoped and dreamed for nine months), in the carriage house rental, or in the house we were about to buy on the plains. We were bound together with leather and Wyrd[1] sisterly love, and I cut the cord in three equal pieces. We tied them around each other's right wrists. I thought the right hand would be best because this is my active hand, my helping hand, the hand that would do the most in this birth. I wanted their right hands with mine, carrying this baby into the world. Our hands come from our mothers, and from our mothers' mothers' mothers, ad infinitum. They would all be there, in my hands, the three becoming all.

Over twenty-five weeks had passed since I had performed a ritual to seal my bleeding twelve-week womb by placing a lid on my iron thrift-store cauldron, which held symbols of my child. I had also laid an antler across the top to protect it further with masculine energy, an energy many call the God, He with Many Names. But that afternoon, at 38 weeks of pregnancy, I moved the antler, removed the lid, turned over all my seashells like bowls, opened all my wooden boxes on shelves, uncorked my bottles of scented oils. This action made the imminence of the upcoming birth almost palpable. I felt as though I had finally released the birth power I had been holding at bay for so long, to finally let the child pass through. From that point on was safe. The closed could now open. My magic was complete.

---

[1] The Sisters of Wyrd (meaning "fate") are an ancient Celtic triple goddess who represents the circular nature of life, the phases of the moon, and are responsible for weaving the past, present and future.

But as I napped, I felt uneasy. I dreamed I should move the symbols of the child out of the cauldron to really release her (we anticipated a girl). Somehow, leaving the tokens in the pot after I had opened it felt wrong, as though I was still clinging to her, afraid to birth her. Afraid of birth. Removing the yarrow… the feather… the rose quartz… the green sea stone… filled me with anticipation, gave me courage to face birth again, to greet my child. Now I needed to find a safe place to hold these objects. The abalone shell I had bled into when my body began threatening miscarriage in March seemed to be the right container. I filled it with the runes I had chosen for the birth and with which I had already charged my henna belly, and placed the child tokens over them. I put the shell full of child on the kitchen table where the sun and moon would bless her on their paths across that five-paned window to the sky. Finally, I was ready. I had set into motion the energy of birth in my body, and had called all my elemental and spiritual allies to come to my aid. I knew that even if I did not give birth to this child in that cabin or on that land the way Grey had been born, this altar of a house would still spin its magic for me, and that I could still go there with my inner sight to draw power. The altars of overturned shells, the shelves of opened boxes and bottles made me tremble with expectancy. This was big magic, bigger than anything I had ever done. I was facing birth's shadow: death. I was not looking away. Birth would prevail. That night I stood under the waning gibbous[2] moon and it occurred to me that the next time I would stand under Her full light, I would be holding my baby.

Before I left the cabin with those women who had given me such a special blessing that weekend, I gathered up the items I would want with me in case I did end up birthing away from home: my moon cup, my crescent knife with the salmon colored handle, my mama crystal, sage and sweetgrass, and a few other stones. I also wrapped the wooden Bahamian goddess in the rabbit fur Maile dried and stretched by hand. I packed Sally's Irish Sea

---

[2] Gibbous: more than half but not all of the moon illuminated

salt, and the tarot cards I had selected for the birth. Tera watched as I wandered around, packing these things into a green plastic box loaded with birth supplies.

"Look at Rachel gathering her power," she said, and we packed the box into the car and began the drive back to the little town on the plains where we all first met. On the way we stopped at Sage's dad's apartment and picked her up. We squeezed into the backseat with my dog, Mojo, and while the two of us shared the stories of our weekend apart, Joni Mitchell's "Big Yellow Taxi" came on the radio. Our eyes lit up. I was tickled to see Tera, who is usually shy about singing and tends more toward punk music, turn up the volume and start singing along enthusiastically, dancing in her seat, with Joni. Lovers of this song ourselves, Sage and I joined in from the backseat, "Don't it always seem to go, that you don't know what you got till it's gone... They paved paradise and put up a parking lot... Ooooooo, bop bop bop bop..."

Driving home, we knew what we did that weekend was powerful. We buzzed with it, admired our bracelets, thought we'd never take them off. And that night, when I walked to Tera's to pick up Mojo's dog collar which I had left in her car, she watched me walk away down the street, avoiding neighbors' sprinklers generously watering the sidewalks. She later told me, "I knew you'd birth either that night or the next day. You were just bouncing with energy." Did she say radiant? Maybe not, but I was. With each step, the dog's collar swung back and forth in my hand, and my belly was swinging too, radiant with heaviness, ripeness, even a touch of sadness at my life as a mother walking home to a cluttered house where clothes lay in piles and beds were unmade and I was too tired to want to do anything about it. I knew I'd do it anyway. That night I went to bed in a slightly cleaner house, luminous with late August exhaustion, my damp skin reaching for the air blowing from our pointless window fan, pleading with the Mother of and in that air, pleading with All My Relations, *Please, please, may this baby come tonight. I'm so tired.* And I slept. I slept all night.

It Begins

I heard the alarm, and my husband, Geo, stumble out of bed and across the room to turn it off, pause to shake off sleep, and leave the room. I fell asleep again, waking around 6:30 a.m. As I lay there, something felt different about my body. My regular early morning contractions registered differently in my groin, in my rectum, deep in the hollows where my inner thighs reach into my perineal muscles. I know it doesn't sound very magical, but it felt almost like constipation, or stubborn gas. All of my labors have begun this way, but I always seem to have to go through a series of tests before I believe it. As I lay there, Mojo kept nosing me to let her outside, so I pulled on my cotton robe, hobbled down the stairs to the kitchen, grabbed a scoop of dog food, hurried into the yard (which we shared with our landlord), poured her food into the bowl, latched her to the chain, and turned the leaky tap to give her water. As I squatted there: more rectal cervical pangs, but I could walk through them, back into the house. Then my tests began.

I wandered about in the early light, asking myself, *Is it gas?* Turning my attention inward: *Do I need to shit or is this it? Pay attention, Rachel. Have a shit to see if the sensation changes. Now, flush. Listen deep: no change.* I began to wander aimlessly across the family room, pacing back and forth over the latch-hook rug. *Decide what to do; nothing is changing about these sensations.* I padded back into the bright light of the bathroom. *OK, run a bath, see if that relaxes me, see if this is what I hope it is. This sensation lives deep in the rectum... or is it my cervix? Somehow both.* The pangs continued to radiate through my root, my most grounded place, the place that sat there upon the earth, in that bathtub, unchanged by water.

No, I don't think this is gas. I better call Geo, I thought. So, I stepped out of the water and called him at work around 7 to say this may be It; he wondered if I was sure.

"Remember when you thought 'maybe' with Grey and it wasn't time?"

"Yes, I remember, but this is different."

He said he'd call back in an hour. An hour. I knew then that by the time he called back, and then decided to come home, there'd be no time to drive to the mountains since the cabin is over two and a half hours away. I expected this labor to be at least as short as Grey's, and I didn't want to chance trying to drive that distance with the condition our cars were in. With the car luck we'd been having lately, we'd probably break down and I'd end up giving birth on the road in our beloved Kermit der Vonder Bus. No thanks. I love our green 1974 Volkswagen, but I didn't want to labor and birth in it, especially stranded on the side of who-knows-what road. This meant the baby would be born right where I was, in that carriage house rental next to the old county courthouse, where our backyard is a parking lot and our front yard is the landlord's backyard. No birthing outdoors this time, but I would not let this disappoint me or color my birth. I would not wish for the mountain that is always in my bones anyway. I carry that mountain in my marrow, where the blood is made, and it pumps through all my parts. And besides, I felt relieved knowing that I had already prepared the cabin, my place of power, my domestic mandala, to sing songs of openness and birth whether I would actually birth there or not. I'm glad I had the foresight to do this. I'm also glad that my magical sisters had already laid their hands on me and blessed the baby and I less than two days before. I called them both to announce my labor, and they lit candles for me. I decided not to call anyone else because I didn't want them to worry during the birth. I would never be more ready than I was on this morning, and the baby was coming now, not yesterday, not two days ago on the mountain. Now, perhaps this was his choice; perhaps this was his gift to me, his lesson. He chose that rental, the last place (besides a hospital) in which I would ever choose to give birth. And I would welcome this choice; I would flow with the pattern that was already in motion. He was ready now, not next weekend when we'd be on the mountain again. Now, two and a half weeks before I'd expected, one-and-a-half weeks after the midwife (whom I saw once at 33 weeks to "verify" my pregnancy for a child healthcare application) predicted. Now, just now.

Gathering

I went to my room and changed the sheets from rust orange to pale blue and green. Bed ready. I didn't know if I'd end up birthing there, but I wanted it to be fresh and welcoming. Then I gathered amethyst, my crescent knife and pewter moon cup, the hand-carved wooden Bahamian goddess whose two faces at once howl and remain silent, the sage bundle I made on the mountain, the sweetgrass braid from the Denver powwow, chosen tarot cards from three different decks, the chocolate-colored rabbit fur Maile prepared by hand and the mama quartz crystal she gave me years before (I missed her; but in her gifts, she was there), the two clay goddess symbols made and given to me by Tera and Ona at my Motherway, and the clay maiden's vulva made by Ona's daughter. I walked back downstairs, still able to walk through the cervical pulls, and placed these objects all about the ledge of the tub. My medicine.

By now, my eight-year-old daughter, Sage, had woken up, surprised to see me walking about nude. I'm usually cautious in town since almost all my windows face the county courthouse parking lot or the landlord's house. Although I think he and his wife are very interesting, open-minded folks, I really didn't think they'd appreciate my sharing a view of my ripe body with them or the employees of the county. I made sure the blinds and curtains were closed.

"I think we're having a baby today!" I told her. Her eyes were big. "Really? I can't believe I'll see the baby today! Oh! I'm so excited!" She paused and added with a sweet expression, "I'm a little nervous!" I calmed her as well as I could with words of encouragement and lit the bundle of sage to cleanse our energy of negativity, to release our fear, to send it out, away from this day of emergence. I smudged our bodies and every corner and wall of that little house with the smoke, knowing this would ease her, and in turn, myself. I was surprised to realize that I already felt very confident and joyfully serene with the energy of the contractions and the anticipation of holding my baby soon. Then I lit the sweetgrass braid as a call to my loving, benevolent relations from all directions, the ones I could trust to witness this birth in peace, and to remind my body and baby, once again, to relax into an easy passage. The sweetness filled the whole house, and I too was calm sweet smoke inside. My grandmothers gathered in around me. I know this now.

Having set up my medicine objects around the edges of the bathtub and bathroom floor, I asked Sage to add her own stones to the sacred arrangement, which she did with reverence. Then we went to the kitchen where I placed fragrant orange sections, the whole wheat bread Ona baked at my Motherway, and green raisins on Geo's grandma's plate—the red one, the color of the Great Mother and Her food—to sustain me. I packed dried nettles from the mountain and red raspberry leaf tea into muslin bags, plopped them into pint jars, poured boiling water over them and capped them tight with canning lids to have an infusion ready to drink during or after the birth. Sage helped me carry these things into the bathroom where I entered the water, consecrated it with Irish Sea salt given to me by an old high school friend, and called in the directions and their corresponding elements to bless this birth. I felt supported in every way. The absence of lay or professional medical personnel would earn this birth the title of being unassisted. But truly, I was assisted in every dimension of the experience.

Sage sat with me in the dark bathroom and we lit her round red candle, which she loved doing, and she closed the door. I nibbled on my food occasionally to gather strength and nourishment. We sat holding hands, whispering of the mystery of birth and what was happening to my body, what the intensifying sensations told me about my progress. By then I had to close my eyes and really concentrate and breathe calmly to surrender to them. I loved her squeezing hands, her big blue innocent eyes, giving me her undivided attention and love. My first daughter, my oldest child, the child whose birth had been so hard and scary for us both. Here we were, together, healing our births, healing birth together with our eyes and clasped hands.

Eventually I decided to leave the tub, as it seemed to restrict my movement and wasn't deep enough when I squatted. Geo called and I told him this was the day. He said he'd prep his substitute teacher and walk home. I began to sing through the contractions a beautiful song by a generous Navajo woman, Sharon Burch, called "Hooghan." I had sung this song throughout my pregnancy on the hill into the valley of aspen and cinquefoil, to the ravens and air: a prayer. Now, I sang beauty into my belly and baby, into my feet and legs, into my vulva, my vulva walking in beauty, my vagina, my deep squatting, squatting in beauty, leaning my arms and head into the futon couch and Grandma's recliner, singing about beauty, the beauty in the opening, acknowledging the intense beauty of the storm moving through my cervix and belly. "Hozhoo nashaa... Hozhoo nashaa... Hozhoo nashaa." Walking in beauty in this little house, this sacred place. Beauty all around me. I knew then that all places are sacred, even the soil under the concrete of that parking lot, the soil under that old carriage house foundation. Who was carried to and from that very spot by their horses? Whose carriages rested in that house? I was my baby's carriage, and the horses were racing, pulling me through each contraction, faster and faster. Where were the reins? Was I the carriage, the driver, the horses or a rider? I reached for my breath like a mane.

Galloping

It was a bit past 8:00 a.m. when Geo walked in. The galloping only grew stronger. Geo knew I wanted to take this ride alone, to run unhindered. I felt a weak whinny in my throat; I was beginning to whinny and quake with strength and exertion in this wide open space of birth. Sage sat on the couch, watching quietly. Geo sat at the dinner table reading, I think, so as not to interfere, to respect my wishes for solitude. But I was sweating, looking back at him after each run, panting, calling to him in my head. I began to need him at my side, his soothing hands.

"Come here," I told him gently. "Come here." I wrapped my arms around his shoulders and hung through a run. *Too much, too much, I need to squat.* I knelt down, my head resting between his hips. I could feel his sex through his denim shorts. This was comforting.

I squeezed his hands tight, squatting there, but remembered he had just smashed his fingers under a huge window in his classroom that morning. I switched to hanging on his pockets, and leaned my cheek against his ropey softness. We laughed at this position, and he joked that oral favors were probably out of the question right then. I playfully, dazedly, gnawed at the bulge and said, "Yeah, I don't think so…" and took off again.

Finally, with all the energy rushing through me, I had to go back to leaning on the futon seat in order to hold on to something solid and unmoving. I asked Geo to move the fan from the kitchen to the window overhead. "Yes… the air is nice… I'm so hot." I began to bury my face into pillows on the futon to muffle my moans, asking for music, Sheila Chandra's voice, to soothe me, to camouflage my groans in this house where all the windows were open in the heat of that parking lot behind us, that busy Monday morning parking lot where that carriage house sat long before the parking lot ever spread itself over the sage brush and yucca. Geo knelt beside me with a white glass bowl of cool water and a lavender hand towel. He pressed it gently to my face. "Oh," I moaned, "That is so good… thank you." I leaned into the towel like a cat leaning into fingernails. The cool water of my lover.

It was close to 9:30, and amazingly, Grey was still asleep. He has never slept in that late before, or since, that day. I was glad to not have to worry about him up until that point. "We are getting close… we are getting so close. Sage, go run upstairs and get your brother… wake him up," I managed to utter. She ran upstairs, and I tried sitting on the hot water bottle to bring in the heat, the heat. *Oh, even the heat is too much.* I spread some clean pads, left over from my friend's unassisted Imbolc[3] birth, under me; under these was the old faded and ripped purple-grey duvet cover that Grey and I snuggled under after his birth. This cover was over the clear plastic tarp I hoped to save to cover the woodpile with this winter.

---

[3] Imbolc is a Celtic festival observed on February 2nd, celebrating the return of spring and the triple goddess, Brighid, a guardian over spring births.

The tarp was over the latch-hook rug Geo's dad made years ago as he battled his alcoholism, trading his compulsion for alcohol for the movement of his hands, placing a thread, pulling it through, placing a thread, pulling it through; latch-hooking the mandala of the rug, the mandala of the directions I've used as an indoor medicine wheel when too shy to stretch out my arms in the backyard, within the sight of conservative neighbors. I birthed over Grandpa's latch-hooked polyester mandala, over hardwood, over concrete, over sacred soil. My feet on the earth. Squatting. My hand on my perineum. A little house fly crawling on my back, drinking my sweat, unwilling to be shooed away. I looked up and there was three-year-old Grey standing on the last step of the stairway, slightly grinning, looking sleepily amazed at this sight, at my moans which were growing louder and more guttural.

"Mommy's having the baby! Mommy's having the baby!" he began chanting joyfully, boisterously, over and over until we asked him to be quiet. I didn't want the parking lot people to hear the news and call the police.

Splash! My water broke all over my hand, all over the layers of paper and plastic and cotton and more plastic and polyester and wood and concrete and soil. Geo cheered, "Yay! Your water broke! Mommy's water broke!" There was mucus on my hand, dripping, stretching.

"The fluid is clear," I announced. "No meconium. This is good." *All is well and perfect.* I tell myself, "Everything is going perfectly."

"What?" Sage asked.

"Everything is perfect." I asked Geo for the olive oil and rubbed it generously into my folds.

Little Mountains

I was a stampede inside a narrow canyon. I looked into Geo's eyes, searching for a clearing. "I can do this. I can do this," I said, trying to convince myself. "Yes, you can do it!" he said brightly. "You can do it Mommy! You can do it Mommy! You can do it Mommy! You can do it Mommy!" shouted Grey sportingly. Although I found this very sweet and funny, I felt my concentration breaking. I thanked him and gently asked him to stop. I was barely hanging on, no longer the driver, a bare-backed rider, or the horses, but the carriage again, shaking with the force moving this baby down. So elemental at this point, I was groaning and trembling like an earthquake, my voice and breath wobbling out of me, my hand still waiting for the head. It was coming, a mound of earth flesh, stretching so thin, a mountain forming under my hand, a furry, wet, burning mountain. I was panting, not pushing, letting it come, letting the fire burn. It grew timelessly, slowly, until I felt the full diameter of the head. I stretched around the forehead, the nose, the chin.

Now I was intensely alert: this was the moment I had feared throughout my pregnancy and worked endless magic to overcome, the moment of the neck and shoulders. I had made countless affirmations throughout the pregnancy: *My body will birth this baby as easily as the earth bears trees and wildflowers. My pelvis will open wide with ample room for this baby to enter the world. Grey's birth prepared the way. This baby will be the perfect size to slide through my body. My vagina will blossom open like a flower and be a safe passage for this baby. This baby will be healthy in all ways. I trust my intuition to birth this baby in the perfect way.* I had even made a drawing during my pregnancy of myself as the trunk of the Tree of Life, a Celtic knot. My feet became the roots that became the branches that became the trunk of my body again. On either side of my face, as part of the trunk, are the faces of the Maiden and Crone. Two ravens look on from the branches; runes crown my head. My hands reach down between my spread legs and pull an open-eyed infant from my body. Only its feet remain inside me. I spent much time pondering this image, taking it in to replace the images of stuck shoulders that kept invading my thoughts in the middle of the night.

The moment of the shoulders is the moment the midwives, in their loving caution, took from me at Grey's birth. I don't regret a minute of Grey's birth, or the assistance of these women. They were my healers. I needed them at that point in my life as a wounded mother. I had been lied to at Sage's birth, and they told me the truth. I had been afraid, and they lovingly guided me back to my power. And now, in this birth, my third birth, I chose to stand alone in my truth, to trust myself, to live in this moment of almost shoulders and wait. Slowly, I closed around his neck. *Yes, I feel the length of the neck. Thank you, Mother, I feel the neck.* I wasn't turtle-necking him at the chin as I did with Grey, when the midwives knew his shoulders were lodged and took over, made me change to hands-and-knees position. From that point on, I had lost contact with Grey's head, lost touch with my birthing, while they maneuvered his shoulders and my belly and I roared him out blindly.

I later learned from others knowledgeable about unassisted birth, and women who had birthed, without assistance, babies larger even than Grey, that the best way to birth shoulders is by simply shifting into different positions until the shoulder pops. I think it was the sitting position I was in during Grey's crowning that encouraged his shoulders to lodge. If the midwives had not suggested I lean back against George during the birth, I probably would've been squatting and better able to birth those big shoulders on my own.

But this time I was completely present and responsible; I took the squatting position, as seemed natural at the time. And there was his neck, and even a bit of cord. I wasn't sure if it was looped around or just hanging out. I pulled on it a little, and it moved easily, dangled lower, not seeming to be tight, if at all, around the neck. George checked it also, and said later that it was slightly looped around, but that he easily unwrapped it. We probably could have just left it, as the cord was pretty long. Through this, I kept squatting, and eventually shifted over to my left foot, putting my weight there and extending my right knee outward, just to twist my pelvis a bit, to make more room for the shoulders if necessary. *I will birth these shoulders.* And once again, I felt the burn of another mountain rising under my skin, a foothill. The first shoulder emerged and then the other. *Yes.* "Here it comes," said Geo, as he helped my right hand support the budding body. He added, "Are you going to catch your baby?"

"Yes." He began to reload the camera, which unfortunately ran out of film just at this moment of full emergence, and I reached both hands around the baby's belly, just as I do in my drawing. He glided into them, out of my body, and I instantly sat down, cradling him in my arms. It was 9:50.

Coaxing Breath

"Oh… so much smaller than Grey, don't you think? Awww…" But then, noticing his stillness and color, I immediately suctioned his nose and mouth with the bulb syringe and pulled the creamy white child belly-down across my lap. He was so pale… so pale… no purple, no pink, no squirming, so much cream. I was covered with it. I saw vernix caked on my belly ring and nipples, on my silver torque, on the leather Motherway bracelet. Tera and Ona were there with me; our right hand rubbing, rubbing, rubbing his back.

"Come on little baby… We love you so much… We want you to breathe… Come on little baby, we're so happy you're here… Let's hear you breathe… We're so happy you're here," we chanted over and over him, that little creamy floppy baby. I looked at George and our eyes were bright with concern. I almost asked him to call 911 but I lost the concept of numbers and the words for "phone" and "call." There were no words but those we spoke to the baby, our eyes and hands and love on the baby. *How long do I rub?* I began gently patting his bottom, patting enough to rouse him. *Is he sleeping?* I didn't think to check if the cord was pulsing. I kept patting his butt and craned my neck around to see the sex, the swollen sack.

"A boy!" I said with a laugh, still patting, "We have a boy!"

"We do? Wow!" George said. We were surprised he wasn't a girl, but what could have been shallow disappointment transformed into loving urgency. Another lesson.

"We love you… We love you so much… Please breathe." I don't know how long we did this; it couldn't have been much more than a minute. We were outside of time, coaxing breath. And finally, there was his gurgly voice, a squeak, a lusty cry. We cheered.

"Yes!" Geo cried out, and time returned. Sam's hands and feet and arms and legs and torso began turning a beautiful violet, then pinking in our laughter. His crying was the song of our elation. Sage helped me put the rainbow cap, the first thing I ever knitted, over his creamy head, but we soon removed it, worried the fibers, which felt soft to my fingers, would be scratchy to his newborn skin. I always forget how soft that skin is. I fumblingly used the bulb syringe to clear his nose and just inside his mouth between his cheeks and tongue, but it wasn't very effective and he was doing fine anyway, clearing his airways himself as he cried. *So rosy... thank you, Mother. Thank you.* We wrapped him in a second-hand cotton receiving blanket. *I did it. I knew I could.*

"We did it! We did it!" We exclaimed to each other.

Spirals

I was sitting on the family room floor in a pool of fluid and mucousy blood, and there I was in that rental, in that small town, the town I used to abhor because it was not the mountains. *I am here, right now, holding my baby. It is good to be here right now.* My belly began to contract deeply so I squatted over the stainless steel bowl with the baby, whom we would not name for two days, in my arms. Sage and Grey squatted in front of me, looking at their new brother. The placenta fell out rather easily into the bowl and the kids' faces registered surprise and a bit of disgust, which made me grin. I picked the bloody thing up and examined the underside. It was fine, intact, and the cord had three spiraling veins. *All is well. All is a spiral.* I counted his breaths and heartbeats, which were within normal range. Fingers and toes all there. Full palate. Two testes. Slightly bruised forehead but nothing abnormal. Good lively color, ruby lips. Eyes a bit blood shot, but that is normal too. Perfect. The baby occasionally screeched out like a tiny raven or an angry cat and we laughed each time, cooing, "Little bird... little kitty. Keep talking to us."

I asked Geo to help me up and walk me and the bowl of placenta to the bathtub where all my sacred things still sat, waiting for us. We filled the tub with hot water, left the lights off, and I sat down. I submerged his body, blanket and all, to warm him, to assist his circulation, to see if the heat helped him become even more alert and responsive. His little fingers grasped ours, his body squirmed with strength, and he eagerly took my offered nipple into his mouth to suck.

"He's nursing!" I announced gleefully, and Geo was relieved, still a bit shaken by his son's slow start. We knew then that if he had the energy and interest to nurse, he had vitality, he had will, he was well. I was bleeding a normal amount as my uterus clamped down with his sucking, but with my crescent knife, which was still on the ledge of the tub, I sliced a half-pinky sized piece of placenta off the edge and swallowed it. I washed it down with a sip of water from my moon mug and wasn't squeamish about it. The irony flavor reminded me of the blood I used to lick off my cuts as a kid. Heck, I still do this once in a while. Of course, any other animal would have eaten the entire placenta. Some women do. But I knew a bite would have enough hormones to at least help lessen my bleeding.

As I sat in the water with him, I began to ache in my hips and wanted to sever the cord from the placenta before I left the tub. Geo brought me a pair of surgical scissors from his first-aid kit, and the white embroidery floss I had boiled, knotted at both ends, and stored in a baggie weeks before. I asked if he wanted to do the cutting. "No, I did it last time. Your turn." So, I tied off the cord an inch or so from his belly, and cut just beyond the floss. The cord had already turned white by that point, so there was little blood. I put a dab of honey, a natural disinfectant, on the stump to ward off infection.

Geo took the bowl of placenta to the kitchen where he removed the entire cord, put a lid on the bowl, and put it in the fridge so we could bury it later under a tree not far from Grey's I had hoped to give birth under. The next day I would wind the cord around and around itself, and it would dry on the windowsill in the sun into a transparent, brownish spiral disc composed of three spiraling veins that I can still see when I hold it up to the light. Spirals within spirals. This will go into a medicine bag for my son.

The Naming

None of the names we had considered before his birth seemed to fit him now, especially since we had expected a girl, had sensed a feminine presence, both before and after conception. We thought of some new ones, but couldn't agree. Sage was sad we wouldn't be using "Yarrow" or "Hill," as she and I had grown fond of, or even "Creek," which Geo had wanted all along. George kept walking in and out of the bathroom, announcing different possibilities, "Raven," "Crow," and variations on the Latin names of each, "Corvid," or "Corvidae." Maybe… but, no. After much thought, light-hearted debate, a couple of nights of quiet dreams, and the intuitive suggestion of "Odin" made over the phone by my dear Christian mystic friend (who knew nothing about Odin whatsoever), we decided on Samuel Rune. "Samuel" after Geo's beloved Twain, "a man of the people," he says, and "Rune" after "mystery," or more specifically, the symbols of the Mystery revealed to the Norse god Odin after he had hung upside down for nine days and nights, wounded by his own sword, from the Tree of Life. Odin, whose messengers are two ravens named Hugin (Thought) and Mugin (Memory), gave the runes as a gift to the world, to help us see. Ravens visited me all through the winter of my pregnancy, my first full winter on that mountain, uncannily appearing directly overhead at my most desperate times—collapsed and sobbing in a yellowed yarrow patch, fantasizing my own flight and descent over a cliff—urging me to bring light out of my own near-sighted darkness. Ravens are not only the wise companions of Odin, but also the protectors of the Dharma, and the shape-shifted form of my beloved dark goddess Morrigan, whose lessons are sharp and lethal to the ego. When the Inuit people were lost in endless night, Raven brought the Sun. "Rune" holds all these things: the ravens, my hard-earned lessons and light, the mysterious gift this child is to me and to the world. Our sweet Samuel Rune.

The Extra Ordinary

My day returned to normal, although it felt amazingly ordinary already. Maybe it felt ordinary because my cells can remember thousands upon thousands of years in which a woman would simply wash up after her birth at the nearest water source, snuggle up to her baby in a safe, cozy, uninterrupted place, and nurse contentedly, sleepily amazed at the creature who only hours before was curled up inside her belly, now curled up against her belly, and she curled around it, while the family went about its day. This is what we did. What could be more ordinary? The extent to which Grey's birth on the mountain felt holy in its grandiosity, its panoramic view, his huge body leaving mine under that ponderosa, is the same extent to which Samuel Rune's birth was holy in its quiet simplicity. This day was the sacred mundane at its finest, a blade of grass breaking through concrete.

That night, the elements celebrated Sam Rune's arrival with wind that made our bedroom curtains flap feverishly like prayer flags, thunderous lightning claps that shook the foundation of our house and made Geo startle inches off the bed without waking, and sheets of rain that drenched the thirsty soil and danced across the parking lot, seeking cracks.

A Mother's Guidance: There are so many books I've read that it is hard to remember them all. Some are by midwives and are considered midwifery manuals, such as *Spiritual Midwifery* by Ina May Gaskin and *Heart and Hands* by Elizabeth Davis. I read several books by Sheila Kitzinger, *Special Delivery* by Rahima Baldwin, *Unassisted Childbirth* by Laura Shanley, *Childbirth without Fear* by Grantly Dick-Reed, *Silent Knife* by Nancy Wainer Cohen, *Wise Woman Herbal for the Childbearing Year* and *Healing Wise* by Susun Weed, *What Every Pregnant Woman*

Should Know: The Truth about Diet and Drugs in Pregnancy by Gail Sforza Brewer, *Unassisted Homebirth: An Act of Love* by Lynn Griesemer, *Mothering* magazine, and articles by Jeannine Parvati Baker posted at www.freestone.org. I read countless stories online by other women, especially unassisted birth stories and midwife-attended birth stories. I watched home videos of women birthing at home with and without midwives. I chose very consciously NOT to watch certain television shows that document birth because I believe they often perpetuate birth fear and what Jeannine Parvati Baker calls "the cult of the expert." The documentary video, *A Clear Road to Birth* by Judy Seaman was an often-turned-to inspiration. Like many unassisted birthing mothers, I think it is important for women to look to each other as the real "experts" of childbirth, people who know first hand what their bodies have done and can do. Our womanly descriptions of childbirth are much more accurate and "embodied" than medically oriented birth texts that teach us to give up our own bodily authority to medical experts who try to pigeonhole us into neat, manageable categories. Each of us is unique and should not be expected to birth in any one way. I've never taken childbirth classes, but am grateful for instruction in sitting meditation I received at the Shambhala Mountain Center, which has helped me to live and give birth mindfully.

Rachel Kellum grew up in central Illinois, earned her BFA in Studio Art at Millikin University, and her MA in English Education at Colorado State. She currently spends her time homeschooling her three children, gardening, making herbal medicines, writing, reading, drumming, studying world spiritual traditions, corresponding online with mothers about birth, and practicing Tai Chi. She aspires to become a midwife who encourages freebirth.

A LONG-AWAITED BABY

BY KIM WILDNER

BECAUSE IT TOOK MY HUSBAND and me over five years to get pregnant, I had a lot of time to read everything I could get my hands on regarding pregnancy and birth. Ultimately, it was the melding of traditional and holistic models of healthcare that finally graced us with a pregnancy, so it was an easy decision to utilize the best of both worlds for our pregnancy and birth.

It was during our fertility search that I decided to study midwifery. Since safety was our number one concern, we chose a traditional midwife to guide us through pregnancy and birth, and developed a back-up plan for the hospital should we need medical assistance. We knew this could be (and ultimately did become) our one and only opportunity to have a healthy, happy mother-baby.

My water released during a late afternoon nap on November 14th. I called my husband, Dave, at work to let him know, and told him to go ahead and finish his shift. I'd be fine by myself for the hour and a half it would take him to finish work, pick up dinner and come home.

I listened to my baby's heart tones to make sure that the release of water hadn't compressed the umbilical cord. Although I had no surges at that point, I called my midwife to let her know she might be making a road trip that night (she lived about two hours away).

By the time Dave arrived home, I was having mild surges. We ate dinner, made up the bed with double sheets divided by a waterproof layer, and set up a Leboyer bath for the baby in an insulated, covered tub. (***Editor's note:*** If you aren't familiar with the work of Frederick Leboyer, you may want to read his groundbreaking book, *Birth without Violence*.) We got out towels, washcloths and extra clothes, and walked around the yard with our dog.

I took a shower around 8:30 p.m., and I called the midwives again, as well as my sister, mom and a friend who would be attending the birth. I asked the midwives to come, since they had quite a drive ahead, but asked the others to wait awhile longer. I'm sure it was torturous for them... everyone was there in less than an hour!

As I moved through the early stages of labor, my husband continued to dance with me, hold me, walk with me and whisper in my ear how much he loved me.

The midwives arrived sometime before midnight. I got into a warm tub and Dave poured water over my belly while softly singing spiritual songs of strength and surrender to me. I was in there for over two hours, but it seemed like moments to me. (It wasn't until after the birth, when my husband complained about how stiff his arm was, that I read the birth record and realized how long I had been in the tub!) The midwives directed me out of the tub to use the bathroom—to get things moving, I'm sure. I had relaxed so much in the tub that my labor had slowed.

Once I was up, gravity did the trick; my labor intensified quite a bit. There were times I thought, "I'm so tired! This is so much harder than I thought! I don't know if I can do this!" But then I'd look around at the people who loved me, at the candles and my familiar surroundings, at the competent women who were monitoring my safety. I'd imagine what a hospital birth would be like... getting dressed, going out into the cold rain, riding in a car, being under harsh lights, having no control and strangers poking me with fingers and needles... and I knew I was just fine where I was.

Sometime around 2 a.m., I felt an irresistible urge to bear down—an involuntary grunting at the top of some of the surges.

We moved upstairs to the bed that had been my parents', the bed that our baby had been conceived in. I labored there on my side, breathing my baby down as my body directed.

I trusted my body and my baby completely. We worked together, gently nudging her into the world.

My husband was the first to touch her. Her head slowly emerged during one surge, and the midwives helped her daddy loosen the cord that was around her neck so she could slip through the loop.

We waited, resting, as she opened her eyes and sucked at the finger the midwife placed in her mouth to check her palate. With the next surge, she moved further into the world... up to her navel.

Again we waited for what seemed an eternity while she looked around at the circle of love around her. Finally the midwife said, "You know, you could give a little push if you wanted to." I did, and Chelsea was born into the hands of her mother and father (with the midwives supporting, because babies are slippery!).

She was brought to my tummy, coughing and sputtering. She pinked up (oxygenated her body) without any crying at all. She was alert, following our voices within a few minutes and nursing soon after.

By the time she was three hours old she was napping, but we were wide awake with birth euphoria... staring at the miracle between us.

A Mother's Guidance: During the years that we were trying to conceive, I read everything available at my public library. It was there that I found several books by Shelia Kitzinger, as well as *Special Delivery* by Rahima Baldwin, a book that led to my certification as a childbirth educator. Through this training and then midwifery training, I also discovered *Spiritual Midwifery* by Ina May Gaskin and *Immaculate Deception* by Suzanne Arms. Other helpful resources include *Five Standards for Safe Childbearing* by David Stewart, and *Silent Knife* by Nancy Wainer Cohen and Lois Estner.

Additional Thoughts: The Leboyer bath for the baby is a very gentle way to welcome a baby into the world. The environment that a baby is born into can leave a lasting imprint. Moving from a warm, quiet, wet and dark space into the bright lights, cold air and noise of the delivery room can be quite a shock.

Remember the wisdom of this mother: "I trusted my body and my baby completely." Sometimes we just have to get out of our own way. Once you're in labor, don't let your conscious mind try to figure out how to birth the baby. A woman's body knows how to do this, just like every animal in the wild knows. You must trust your instincts.

Kim Wildner became a childbirth educator on the path to becoming a midwife. She sought out a midwifery apprenticeship and began going to births. Soon after, she discovered she was pregnant. She has been teaching since, but she put her aspirations to be a midwife on hold for a while to write while she stays at home to mother her daughter. Kim is the author of the powerful and intuitive book, Mother's Intention: How Belief Shapes Birth. She teaches that we need to be accountable and responsible for our own births, and how that can change the course of birth.

HOME BIRTH AFTER CESAREAN

BY JENNIFER ROBINSON

THROUGHOUT MY FIRST pregnancy, I trusted my body's capability to birth naturally. I assumed my experience of birth would be very similar to my mother's; she birthed three children vaginally, and without drugs. I had no doubt that I would do the same. I read quite a bit about breastfeeding, but very little about birth.

The day before my first daughter, Sophia, was born, I went to the doctor's office for a routine weekly checkup. For no apparent reason, the doctor wanted to do a non-stress test on her. The heartbeat dipped down below what he thought was acceptable and he sent me over to the hospital, which was a four-minute walk for me. He thought that the machines were better over there. Sophia was past her estimated due date by three days.

When I walked into the hospital, 12 nursing staff greeted me. My gut reaction was to walk right out of there. I had such a strong feeling that this was not right, that I should not be there. Unfortunately, I had never heard of people being born at home, and really had no place else to go.

I was hooked up to a fetal heart monitor and given drugs; Sophia was born the next afternoon via C-section. Postpartum depression followed; fortunately, only for a day. I'll never know what would have happened if I started out at home.

I had a *Mothering* magazine that I had not read yet, and a couple weeks after Sophia was born I finally got around to it—and loved it. It connected me with women just like me. Magazines were about the only thing I could read, because I was nursing Sophia constantly. We also did not have access to the Internet until Sophia was about six months old, so *Mothering* magazine was my link to the outside world. I loved reading every word. I found an advertisement for *The Compleat Mother* magazine, so I subscribed to that and devoured it as well. I was in heaven. I definitely wanted to have another child, and I was really starting to get turned on to home birth.

When Sophia was about five months old I found a store called Magical Child in Encinitas, California, and again, WOW! I had thought I was so alone, but suddenly I was tapping into a world of like-minded mamas. I browsed through books and videos on home births, finally selecting *Primal Mothering in a Modern World* by Hygeia Halfmoon. The book explores unassisted home birth, home schooling and raw food diets. After Sophia's birth, I had become very distrustful. I briefly entertained the idea of unassisted home birth, but when I shared this with my husband Dave, he took a strong stand against it. I now agree with him, but the very concept opened my mind. And it was helpful to discuss the idea, because in comparison to unassisted birth, a home birth did not seem so radical.

Months before we became pregnant with our second child, Dave was still uncomfortable with the idea of home births. But when I witnessed a close friend become a birthing goddess at the birth center, I thought that this might be a good compromise for us. He agreed, much to my surprise. Even though I had offered the compromise, I wasn't yet convinced that was what I wanted. So I took it back, and said that I really wanted a home birth. A few months later, I found out that the birth center won't accept women who have given birth via cesarean, so that was the deciding factor: I would have a home birth. Now, how to convince my husband?

A few months later, I was pregnant! My friend Jill suggested we interview midwives and let my husband explore home birth rather than me trying to talk him into it. Despite the recommendations of several people, we only interviewed one midwife. During the interview at her house, meeting her for the first time, I cried. I was very comfortable with her from the start. On the way home, not five blocks away from her house, I started crying again, telling Dave that I wanted to birth at home and I wanted her to be our midwife. I didn't want to interview any other midwives; I wanted Vickii. It felt so right and seemed like that was what was meant to be. He agreed, and suddenly I was bubbling over. We both felt it was right.

The next day, I did make some calls to two or three other midwives, but only because Vickii said I should. I knew that Vickii was the one; she was an advocate for me from the start. I did not sense this from the others I spoke with, and some would not even consider me because of my previous C-section.

About a year before my second pregnancy, I had started walking two miles a day at a local gym. I wanted a VBAC (vaginal birth after cesarean), and I knew physical fitness would contribute a great deal to making that happen. I continued walking two miles a day up to two months before my due date. I also lifted weights for 20 minutes a day. I cut down to just walking one mile a day in my eighth month, and in the ninth month I walked around the block and swam in my sister's pool.

During my pregnancy, I also ate very well. I was vegetarian and vegan six days a week before I was pregnant, but pregnancy made me an omnivore. I didn't have the time to prepare vegetarian meals and read about that lifestyle while I was so busy with birth books. Birth became my focus, and yes, that did include great nutrition. It was VERY hard for me to eat animal products in the beginning, but I knew that I couldn't get enough iron, protein and calcium on my limited knowledge without the animal products. I took a lot of supplements as well. I took calcium in the morning with cottage cheese, prenatals during the day and at night, iron and ⅓ cup prune juice. (The iron assimilates better when not taken with or too close to the calcium.) I drank a lot of water and a couple pots of red raspberry leaf tea almost every day. I did not have the usual nausea, constipation, leg cramps and headaches that I experienced with my first pregnancy, but I did go through the phase of intense tiredness—I was lucky that Sophia would let me sleep.

Louisa's labor started August 4th at 9 p.m., right after I nursed Sophia and went to sleep. Once I realized what was happening, so many thoughts ran through my head. I cursed the computer (but really myself), because I had spent the afternoon on it instead of napping. I had been napping every afternoon for the past two weeks to prepare for this event, but of all days, this one I blew it. But then my thoughts shifted to enthusiasm... I would see my baby soon!

That whole night I labored quietly in bed, trying to sleep between contractions. Most of the contractions were light, so I did manage to sleep a little. With the stronger contractions, I focused on the crickets chirping outside rather than the pain. This helped a lot.

It was a lot easier to control my body than my mind. I could relax my whole physical body, except for the contracting area. But my head was like a radio with an on-going dialogue, chattering with enthusiasm about the fact labor had started. It finally settled down, which helped immensely.

In the morning I called Vickii to let her know what had happened, and I told her my plans for the day. She shared her plans for the day and told me to call her later, regardless of how labor was progressing. Dave, Sophia and I went to Sophia's first day of swim class. I was so tired, but I did not want to be home by myself, so I went with them. I put my swimsuit on and was going to try to swim, but I was just too tired, so I got dressed again. I went to the bleachers with Dave to watch Sophia swim, but couldn't sit comfortably for more than a minute, so I waited in the car until her class was over.

I was really craving wonton soup, so we went out to a restaurant. We went home afterwards, despite our plans to go see Dave's mom in the hospital. I needed to rest! My mom and sister came over to be with us, and I labored all that day as quietly as possible. That night, I woke Dave up around 1:00 a.m. but he fell back asleep; I woke him again at 2 a.m. and told him to start filling up the labor pool in our kitchen. I did not want to birth in the water; I was sure of that. But I had heard that the water really makes labor so much easier to bear. I also heard that it is a good idea to wait until transition before getting into the pool… I never did go in the pool that night. Silly me, to think I was getting close to transition. I still had another day and a half to go!

Tuesday at 8:30 p.m. we all headed for bed. I nursed Sophia and WOW, did I ever start contracting. It was like one long 45-minute contraction. I've heard that nipple stimulation really helps move labor along, and boy, did it ever! I went to the other room so as to not wake Sophia. Dave came with me and proved to be a wonderful doula. Once again, he got the labor pool ready and I went in; but it simply was not helping me. It was too shallow, so we skipped the labor-in-water idea.

Dave heated some water and put lavender oil drops in it. We put wash cloths in the pot and soaked them to put on my lower abdomen. We went through so many pots of water! As we did this, he read the birth affirmations from www.attachmentscatalog.com, and that helped tremendously. I was trying so hard to be quiet and not wake Sophia. I really thought I was past early labor, but I would still be in early labor for another 12 hours or so.

Dave called my sister to come over to help, and my mom and sister arrived around 11 p.m. They were both so wonderful, massaging me, reading birth affirmations and getting fresh compresses for me. Their job was to watch Sophia in case she woke up, but oh boy, did I ever need them to watch over me!

At dawn I went into our outdoor Jacuzzi. I called Vickii from the Jacuzzi, asking her to come over. I think she got to my house around 7:30 a.m. Amy and my mom took Sophia out for the day, and as soon as they left, my labor kicked in even more. Even though it was my intention to have her there the whole time, part of me must have been waiting for Sophia to leave so I could give myself over to labor. In the end, I knew it was the right thing to have her away from me.

Active labor started around 10 a.m. and Vickii called her assistant, Aimee, who arrived shortly thereafter. Transitional labor began around noon. I was in the moment and up to the challenge. Vickii had told me when I was in transition that just when I think I can't take it anymore, it changes. There were four of us there, and I wouldn't have wanted any fewer people than I had. I really needed someone with me the whole time, either holding my hand or massaging me. Everyone was wonderful, but they were on their toes the whole time. In retrospect, they probably would have appreciated an extra helping hand.

The pushing stage started around 2:30 p.m., and in my opinion, that was the best part of labor. I could finally see, ever so clearly, the light at the end. I could feel exactly when the pushing stage began, even though I doubted it a few times. Labor eased up and became more bearable, and the pushing stage began soon after that. I pushed for awhile on the toilet. There was so much blood coming out, and then the water broke while I was sitting on the toilet.

I really wanted to birth in the squatting position—I loved that image. I had been practicing squatting for a few months and had gotten pretty good at it. When the birthing stool was set up, I made my way from the bathroom to the stool. I was facing the mirror in our bedroom, squatting and naked, marveling at my beautiful body in a whole new way. It was amazing to be watching and feeling my body open up for Louisa to come through.

In the end, I did not stay in the squatting position. I did not get to see her head come out... I didn't even feel it. I just heard Vickii and Dave tell me to breathe, and then they said that the head was out. I was turned away from the mirror, kneeling and holding on to Dave and the bed. Vickii asked if I wanted to touch the head and I said no. She also asked Dave if he wanted to catch the baby, and he said no too. With the next push, Louisa was born and placed on my stomach. There are no words to describe this moment. My cup runneth over.

The placenta came without any complications. Everything was wonderful, and soon baby Louisa was nursing beautifully. I looked at her and said, "So it was you who was in there all that time." How wonderful it was to finally meet her! I thank God for this precious gift. And I thank my angel, who was with me the entire time. I am honored and privileged to be able to take care of her. She is truly a gift.

I chose Louisa's name because I liked the meaning: "famous in battle" or "famous warrior." The battle I faced was the battle of cesarean births. In 2001, the cesarean rate in hospitals was 25.1% for first-time moms. It is an atrocity, and makes me so sad for these moms and their babies. Louisa and I won this battle, and I want to be a shining example for others.

If I had given birth in a hospital, I am sure it would have been another C-section, since I've had one already and my labor was so long. My entire labor was five hours shy of three days. I trust in the process of birth and know that all the numbers and schedules of birth that hospitals adhere to apply only to textbook examples of birth. We are all different, and birth differently.

My experience with midwives and home birth was extraordinarily powerful. The level of care and respect we received far exceeds that of hospitals and the standard medical model. At my prenatal visits with my first pregnancy, I saw the doctor for five or six minutes each time. With Vickii and/or Aimee, our visits were an hour long. My husband and I were empowered, and made all the decisions. We weren't just handed a bunch of forms to sign before leaving; we were given explanations about each form, and time to review them or freedom to take them home with us to think about.

We were always treated well and became emotionally bonded with our caregivers. Vickii said to call her when I wanted her to come over, not at a specified stage of labor. I felt a lot better with her present. Aimee and Vickii were there holding my hand, massaging me and encouraging me the whole time. They both seemed to say the right things to help me. I thought that she would leave and come back later, when labor had picked up. Who would have thought that she would stay at my home until 11:30 p.m., caring for Louisa, my house and me? She was with us for 16 hours. What doctor would give you that amount of time? I have a newfound admiration for midwifery. They are making a difference in the world with every birth.

Additional Thoughts: Please check with your medical care provider before using nipple stimulation to intervene in the way your labor is progressing. Penny Simkin recommends asking, "Is there any reason I can't try..." because people with certain conditions will respond unfavorably to some practices that are generally considered safe. For instance, in people with certain blood conditions, nipple stimulation can cause tetanic contractions (contractions that last longer than two or three minutes), which can be difficult for both mother and baby.

Jennifer Robinson wrote this story just days after her second child was born. Jennifer, Dave, Sophia and Louisa live in San Diego, California.

SHORT AND SWEET

BY KIMBERLY KING

MY STORY BEGINS on the evening of March 4th, at home in bed with my husband. As I drifted into sleep, listening to the rain pouring down, I thought about how this evening would be a perfect time to go into labor. The rain is so soothing and comforting to me, and water was a source of strength and relaxation through my two previous births. I wanted so much to hear the tapping of falling drops as I worked to bring my last child into this world.

A few hours later, around 2 a.m., I awoke to the ever so familiar cramping. I wondered if this was real labor, or just wishful thinking. Throughout my first labor, I experienced many lulls in the early stage so I was reluctant to get too excited until I knew these were true labor pains. As the moments passed and the cramping continued, I knew I needed my husband so I nudged him awake.

The rain continued to pour down, as did my labor. I headed to the shower for some warmth and the comfort of the water. I frequently prayed to God for strength and relied on my husband for encouragement. By 4:30 a.m., my husband called our midwife to invite her to our house for a birth day celebration. She lived about 45 minutes away, and with the skies opening up he wanted to give her plenty of time.

Twenty minutes later I suddenly had the urge to bear down, and so I did ever so slightly. A small amount of fluid ran down my leg. I told my husband that I might have released some amniotic fluid, but I wasn't positive. As I walked into our bedroom, the next contraction came and again I pushed lightly. *Pop!* My bag of waters burst onto the sheets that we had laid down to protect the carpet. Suddenly the contractions were coming on top of each other, and I couldn't NOT push. I told my husband that the baby was coming, and to call my midwife to see how far away she was. She was still 20 minutes away! She went over our options and we chose to birth on our own.

I knelt on the floor with my arms draped over the side of our bed. The next—and last—contraction came, and I birthed our beautiful baby boy into his daddy's arms. I quickly lay down on our bed and my husband gracefully set our baby on my stomach. We wrapped him in warm towels and suctioned his nose and mouth. Within 10 minutes my midwife arrived.

What a wonderful experience for all of us! We rejoiced in our ability to work so well together—we instinctively knew what to do. No words were spoken during those last few minutes of labor, or as our son was born. We worked off each others energy and emotions, and most of all… love.

A Mother's Guidance: My husband and I educated ourselves by taking a class on the Bradley Method and reading various books. I also got regular chiropractic adjustments. My primary tool for strength during labor, which I highly recommend, is the use of water. I also recommend the comfort of loved ones whom you trust and adore. The support and security my husband's presence brought me were tremendous. I also give my midwife a lot of credit for being nurturing and calming, and for lending an amount of strength that is immeasurable.

Additional Thoughts: If you have a particular nature sound, such as rain, that you love, use a recording of it whenever you practice relaxation in the months leading up to the birth. Your body will develop an association that bypasses the mind, and once labor begins, those sounds will effortlessly guide your body into deep states of relaxation.

Kimberly King is 28 years old and lives in Temecula, California, with her husband Joshua. All three of their children were born at home with the assistance of their midwife. Morgan (five), Macy (three) and Noah (one) are the joy of their lives.

ARRIVING WITH THE SUN

BY JUTTA KRETZBERG

JORN AND I ARE SCIENTISTS — we believe in statistics. According to the statistics most first-time moms deliver after the due date. Jacob does not care about statistics yet; he decided, 12 days before his due date, that it was time to leave the womb. And I have to admit, I am very happy about that. With 20 inches and eight pounds, four ounces, he was already big enough!

After having mild contractions for a couple of weeks my bag of waters finally broke late one night. I called the midwife on call at the hospital's birth center and she told me to come to the hospital within the next four hours, even if the contractions hadn't started yet. But it wasn't long before they started—there was certainly no time to rest, let alone bake cookies like our childbirth educator had taught us to do in early labor.

When we arrived at the hospital at 2 a.m. I was already four centimeters dilated. Labor progressed very quickly. Our doula Jewel helped me a lot, anticipating my needs and making suggestions: "Do you want the birth ball?" That was the most comfortable position for me to labor in. "Keep your eyes open, stay focused! Do you want a warm rice sack?" When she applied it to my lower back, it reduced the pain.

I relied on deep breathing until transition started; then it became difficult to do it on my own. Jewel saw I was struggling and suggested, "Let's do some O's,"—it was the best thing she did for me. I could look into her face and manage to take deep breaths. When we let them out together with an "ooo" the pain was manageable again. Jorn helped me by holding my hand, pressing the rice bag on my back, giving me ice water to drink, and just being next to me.

I had asked for a big bathtub, but it filled pretty slowly. When they finally told me at 4:30 a.m. that I could use it, I asked, "Isn't it too late?" "No, go ahead, it will help." When I had my first contraction in the tub I wanted to push. The midwife checked me: "Go ahead, push!" Hence, I left the tub again after only five minutes.

Pushing was the hard part; it took two hours. I first tried a squatting position, but that didn't work too well for me. I hadn't gotten a minute of sleep that night and was exhausted. Lying on my left side with Jorn holding up my leg was much better. Jennifer, the midwife, brought a mirror so I could see the head appearing when I pushed. That was really good motivation—and I needed motivation to push against the burning. It felt as if I would tear. The midwife applied warm compresses and did some massage which relieved the pain greatly, and I did not tear.

At 6:34 on Sunday morning, our son arrived with the rising sun. The midwife showed Jorn how to place his hands and he caught our baby. At first he had something in his hands that looked and felt like a gray bag of gelatin—but only for a couple of seconds. Then Jacob started to cry and his color changed to pink. He was placed on my belly and Jorn lay down next to us on the bed— our family was complete.

Jacob was alert; he looked around, held up his head and started nursing. He stayed awake for almost two hours. During that time the cord blood was drawn for donation and I delivered the placenta. But I hardly noticed it at all; the baby was so much more important. After two hours I was able to get up, walk around and be with my baby during his medical check-up.

The three of us stayed in the birth center for three days. Jacob and I learned how to breastfeed without cracking my nipples; Jorn and I learned how to change diapers without getting wet ourselves; and Jorn and Jacob learned how to take naps tummy to tummy. The midwives and nurses were all very helpful and extremely friendly, happy to help us with all of our questions. The birth center is a great place to give birth, and I am extremely grateful to have been there. It was one of the best decisions of my life to birth there. I had exactly the birth I wanted—without any medication, without a tear or cut, and without a minute of feeling helpless.

A Mother's Guidance: My husband and I tried to be really well informed before the birth. We read several books and attended two classes. None of them was absolutely great, but it was satisfying to feel like we had done something to prepare. I knew that it is possible to give birth naturally—all women except for the last two generations have done it. My grandmother delivered two breech babies vaginally. So why shouldn't I be able to birth naturally?

In Germany, our native country, a birth typically occurs with the help of a midwife, and many women decide to try a natural birth. When we heard the statistics on interventions (epidurals, cesarians, etc.) in United States hospitals, I was quite shocked. I wanted to participate in the experience of giving birth, not be a helpless patient.

I would absolutely recommend the assistance of a doula. She helped me remember to "be prepared and trust your body." And during labor she had a very good sense of what I was experiencing and how to respond. We first learned about doulas from friends. (As far as I know there are no doulas in Germany, but there a midwife usually stays with the mom all the time until she delivers.) We wanted to have somebody experienced with us during labor, to motivate me to give birth naturally and to help Jorn support me. (Fortunately the labor was so short that he didn't need a break.) I wanted her to make sure I was not feeling helpless. We found several doulas on the Internet and interviewed three of them. Jewel was the one who made both of us feel reassured that everything would go well.

Jewel gave me an insight that I was not aware of: while pushing, I felt like I was doing something wrong because I did not count to ten or do anything I had learned from books and the childbirth class. That did not work at all for me. Pushing became very effective once I stopped thinking about what I was doing and just listened to my body.

Trust your body. I don't know if you can call it a "technique" to listen to your body… that is mainly what I did. Deep breathing was really important, and the mirror was a great help during the pushing stage. I would recommend that to every pregnant woman—it is very motivating to see your baby appear!

Jutta Kretzberg and her husband Jorn are the proud parents of Jacob. They live in San Diego, California.

LIKE MOTHER, LIKE DAUGHTER

BY MARIA DIEHL

MY STORY BEGINS nineteen years ago, with the birth of my baby brother. My mother went into labor while my dad was working the midnight shift an hour from home. She had a midwife (which, in the mid-1980s in Ohio, was quite hard to find) who lived over two hours away. Needless to say, neither my dad nor the midwife made it in time and my brother was born into my mother's hands. It was a story I grew up with and it is one that I never tired of hearing. I was fascinated by two points: first, that a baby could be born so easily at home, and second, that my mother had a baby with no assistance whatsoever.

I suffered a head injury when I was younger that left me with severe headaches and head trauma. Specialists from far and wide said that I would never be able to conceive, much less carry a child to full term. I worked with a massage therapist and a naturopathic physician, doing everything in my power to help my body heal on its own. When I married, my husband and I thought that we would look into adoption if the doctors' predictions were correct.

I conceived shortly after we were married. Inspired by the story I had grown up with, I searched for and found a midwife in my area. My pregnancy progressed smoothly, and I defied the doctors' other prediction: I carried my baby to term.

I went into labor early in the morning. Having never experienced labor before, I interpreted the sensations as stronger Braxton-Hicks contractions. But the contractions didn't go away and I called the midwife a few hours later. She said that it sounded like labor and told me to call again when the contractions became stronger. I spent the morning on my hands and knees, with my head on the floor and my backside in the air. That position helped ease the contractions during early labor. Later in the day, as labor progressed, I spent a lot of time in the shower, which made the pain almost nonexistent. During transition, I found that hip squeezes and leaning on someone were lifesavers. I also focused on a picture of a lighthouse with the waves crashing on the rocks. It helped to think that my body was the lighthouse and that the contractions were waves trying to break through, but that as long as I was strong, the lighthouse would still stand.

Our beautiful baby girl was finally born after 45 minutes of pushing. It was so incredible to experience the bag of waters breaking and then to have a baby slip out from behind. The emotions that one goes through from transition to the delivery of the afterbirth cover such a wide range of euphoria. It is impossible to put it in words. The joy of being home and going to sleep together as a family for the first time was another ecstasy all of its own.

After a 13-hour labor with my first baby, I thought the second baby would be basically the same birth with a few variations. But those variations proved to be a lot more variable than I had expected.

After a day spent canning strawberry jam, I awoke in the night with what felt like an upset stomach. I assumed that it was because I had eaten too many strawberries the day before. The pain didn't relent, and soon turned into contractions. The contractions were strong, but not strong enough that I couldn't finish dusting my bedroom and prepare it for the birth!

During my pregnancy, I had read *Spiritual Midwifery* and *Ina May's Guide to Childbirth*, and realized that a great thing to do in labor was to simply MOVE! So, with that in mind, I puttered around. I used a birthing ball to help open me, not to mention that it really helped during the contractions to focus on rocking instead of the pain. I took a nice long shower, which helped with the growing intensity of the contractions, and helped my husband set up the birthing tub (I planned on having a water birth). When I threw down the dust rag, we all knew that transition was coming.

Soon after the midwife arrived, I had one big contraction, during which she did a hip squeeze on me, and then felt the need to push. She didn't think it was time yet; she told me to use the bathroom and then labor for a while in the birthing tub. I went to the bathroom, and lo and behold! The baby's head was beginning to crown! I immediately got into the birthing tub and within minutes had an irresistible urge to push. I got into the squatting position and pushed. After a few pushes the baby was born, and as the midwife brought her to the surface, she noticed that the baby was floating in her bag of waters! I had wondered why I never felt my water break. The baby was then placed on my chest and we sunk into an intimate bond.

A Mother's Guidance: My favorite publications were *After the Baby's Birth* by Robin Lim and *Mothering* magazine, as well as Ina May Gaskin's classics, *Spiritual Midwifery* and *Ina May's Guide to Childbirth.* To any expectant mom, I say, "One of the secrets to having a great birth is to trust, first in God, and the tremendous power He has given women's bodies to birth naturally. Our bodies are designed to give birth and we should never underestimate the power we have to birth naturally. Also, don't be afraid to let go. Birth is a powerful rite of passage into motherhood, and it is only when we surrender to the power of it that we complete our initiation into the realm of motherhood."

Additional Thoughts: Maria used a variety of wonderful tools—the hip squeeze, the birthing ball and the shower all help greatly with labor and with bringing the baby down.

Birth balls are a wonderful tool to use during your pregnancy to relieve lower back stress. During labor, the rocking motion helps bring the baby down. After the birth you can lightly bounce on it with your baby in your arms to soothe the baby and help it go to sleep. They are only about $15 to $20, and well worth the investment.

Maria Diehl lives in Michigan with her husband Warren and her two home birth "miracle girls," Catherine and Gabrielle. She is also a practicing doula, helping to change the way we look at birth, one birth at a time. She aspires to be a midwife someday.

RIDING THE WAVES

BY BETH HAND

LONG BEFORE I ever got pregnant, I knew that I wanted a natural home birth. Seven years before this pregnancy, I gave birth in a hospital, and although there wasn't enough time, I had begged for an epidural. I figured that since I had already been through one natural birth, I would have no fear in doing it again.

I decided to take a Bradley Method class this time. It enlightened me so much—I learned much more than I already knew about natural birthing. My husband was nervous about our decision to birth at home, but by the end of the class he and I were both confident about our choice.

The day of our daughter's birth began about 4:00 a.m. as I was gently awakened with mild contractions. Since this was the end of my pregnancy, it was not unusual to be awakened with Braxton-Hicks contractions; so I went to the bathroom and then back to bed. At 4:30 I woke up again, this time to more intense contractions. As I laid in bed quietly I timed them, trying to decide if I should wake my husband. By 4:45, I knew I needed his company whether this labor was real or not, so I woke him. He thought we ought to fill up our birth pool, just in case. So I took a relaxing bath and even washed my hair. My mother, who was staying with us, heard the stirring and came up to check on us. By 5:30 she convinced me to call the midwife.

While waiting on the midwife, my husband and I talked and laughed, and I worried that I had called her out of bed for nothing but strong Braxton-Hicks. I was in such good spirits that this couldn't possibly be true labor. When she arrived an hour later, she informed us that I was indeed in labor, and dilated between five and six centimeters. What a surprise! I was half way done and felt great.

After hearing how dilated I was, the reality of my labor sunk in. I have a history of very quick labor, and it wasn't long after our midwife arrived that things really got moving. I noticed a change in my demeanor. I no longer laughed or even talked; between contractions I rested my mind and body by being still and quiet. I thought about something my birth instructor had taught us about contractions… they were like waves. I imagined them coming in quietly and almost softly, then peaking to an intense sharpness before moving out and away from my body. I used the time in between to appreciate no contractions, to go within myself and relax almost euphorically. As strong as the pain was, the contrast between contractions was also an amazing feeling. The team wrung cold, wet washcloths out on my sweating forehead and chest. This felt great, especially as my contraction would begin to subside.

Between 6:30 and 8:15 I had to focus more on each contraction, and I used a lot of techniques that I learned in the Bradley class to get through each one. I worked hard, but I never felt that I couldn't get through it. I had my husband, mother, birth instructor and midwife guiding me through. As I neared transition, things got more intense and I could not allow for any distractions at all. Everyone had to be deadly silent and no one could touch me or the pool. My mother said this lasted about thirty minutes. My seven-year-old son quietly knocked on the door and asked, "Did the water break?" It was about 7:30 and he must have woken up and figured out what was going on. This was amusing to everyone! As he waited outside, I felt extreme pressure on my pelvis and wanted to lay on my side to relieve it.

When I left the pool, we discovered that I was ready to push. I got on my bed and tried to push while on my side. When this was not effective, I went to my back and performed the Rebozzo method with the help of my birth instructor (pulling on a rope or similar object as you bear down and push). This seemed to help. Although very exhausting, it felt good to push against the pain; it relieved the pressure. I pushed for an hour and a half, and many times wanted to just go back to sleep, but when you are in labor that is not one of your options.

At 9:00 a.m. our beautiful nine pound, two ounce, baby girl was laid upon my stomach, cord still attached. There is no greater joy in all the world than when your womb releases your baby into your grasp. She looked at us curiously for what seemed like forever before she decided to let out her first cry. It was such a beautiful moment for our whole family! My husband asked me that night if I would do it again, and I answered quickly, "Yes, but not today!"

A Mother's Guidance: I enjoyed a book called, *A Child is Born* by Lennart Nilsson. Natural childbirth is a wonderful experience and although you will experience the pain and physical exertion without the aid of chemical relief, so too will you feel the extreme joy and euphoria brought on naturally by your body. It far outweighs any pain felt during labor and you and your baby will be glad that you aren't numb to it. Believe in your body and trust your baby.

Beth Hand and her husband live in Neptune Beach, Florida. Her husband works for KB Home as a superintendent of construction. Beth has a full-time job of home-schooling their son John Dillon and breastfeeding their new daughter, Rebekah Elizabeth Lynn.

VBAC IN SWITZERLAND

BY ELENA PIANTINO-QUINTERO

It was 2:30 in the morning on my due date; our 22-month-old son had just come to our bed when my water broke with quite a splash. I felt as if a balloon full of water had just burst inside me. After drying up a bit and spreading some protective pads on the bed, I tried to go back to sleep but contractions started shortly after. The first one was quite scary for me—I had never felt a labor contraction before. My first child was born via C-section (probably unnecessarily), and I never had the chance to experience labor. I needed reassurance that all was fine, so we called our midwife, or sage-femme, as they are called in Switzerland. Michele arrived around 4 a.m. to see how things were doing. I was just one centimeter dilated but contractions were picking up. After reassuring me that everything was fine, she left. The contractions got stronger around 5 a.m., as if I had been waiting for her permission to start working.

I was excited, so I called my mother in Mexico to talk me through some contractions; but I was tired and wanted to rest. My husband had taken our son to his room and tried to rest there until morning. In my room I propped up some pillows on the bed. I would stand up during contractions to manage the pain, and then I would rest almost upright on the pillows and sleep profoundly for the five to eight minutes between contractions. Lying down was uncomfortable, and made it harder to get up for each contraction. By 6:30 the pain was getting a bit stronger so I filled the bathtub and stayed there for the next hour or so. The warm water helped the contractions be more effective, and also relaxed me so that the pain flowed through me and I didn't block myself. I was happy to be left alone to concentrate and rest.

As contractions increased in intensity and frequency it suddenly dawned on me… this is why its called labor… you work with your body and baby, with pain and discomfort as your guide, to bring this child into the world.

Finally, around 7:30 a.m. my husband Yves timed some of my contractions, and we decided to make our way to our sage-femme's home-office, which was about 15 minutes away in Lully sur Morges. I did not mind driving 45 minutes to the place of birth if it meant I could have the birth I wanted: a natural VBAC.

Contractions were strong but bearable. I would just hum the duration of them, and the vibration in my diaphragm would break the pain and relax me. Michele checked me and by 10:30 a.m. I was three centimeters dilated. We decided to make our way to the birth center, the Maison de Naissance. We got there around 11:30 and Michele and Yves started getting things ready in the room. I walked up the stairs to our third-floor room, and it felt good to climb stairs, even if I had to stop for contractions. Michele hooked me up to the monitor to make sure the baby was fine; 20 minutes was enough to give her what she needed.

The day was warm and the sun hit my room directly. We opened the windows to get some breeze and closed the drapes. The air was warm and the drapes glowed with the sun. No one disturbed us. No nurses, no interns, no cleaning ladies or cable guys. Just Yves, Michele and me. I completely lost track of time.

We played relaxing music with soft, rhythmic drums and chants. An image kept coming to me and helped me through contractions… electric-blue night sky, a full moon; a Bryce Canyon kind of stone formation in two almost-orange columns, and a white grey wolf. I kept wondering where it came from, since I have never been in a place like that.

Yves left to have lunch and Michele was busy setting everything up. I was happy, working with my contractions, humming along and grunting a little, swinging my hips, leaning on the wall or sitting at the edge of the bed.

As soon as Yves stepped back in the room, I walked towards him, feeling a new contraction starting. I was in bliss, and wanted to be held by him and dance a bit through the contraction, but my body had other plans. His presence seemed to mark the "go ahead" for transition; the pain got surprisingly strong and I instinctively squatted. I was a bit overwhelmed and felt like going to the toilet, but as I got there I could only hang from the handles and grunt. The contractions were long, effective and very close together... I thought I was going to lose it. I think I did for a while. Michele was wonderful at this point, helping me concentrate and listen to my body. She encouraged me and massaged my lower back while she whispered supportive words between contractions. She asked if I was ready for the tub, and I was.

Funny, I had always pondered how I would handle being naked, and at that moment I just pulled my t-shirt off and almost ran into the tub. Relief was immediate! I relaxed, and managed the sensations with renewed attention. The feeling of weightlessness was amazing. Not having to carry my belly allowed me to relax and open up.

Michele checked me again around 12:25 p.m. and I was seven centimeters dilated. She said we had about an hour or two to go. I screamed with each contraction—not a pained scream but an empowering one, like in karate, and the vibrations gave me the impression of helping my muscles adjust to the new phase. In a way it was like breathing my baby through the birth canal. It was so empowering and liberating. It helped that Michele actually told me to scream if I felt like it. I was never self conscious about it after that.

Until this point, endorphins had done a magnificent job of semi knocking me out between contractions. Only the first contraction of each new phase was scary. Yves was wonderful. I would hold onto him and he would sprinkle my back with water or rub my shoulders. The weightlessness in the water helped me adopt the weird positions my body asked for, and this was crucial to helping Annie's head into position.

A while later, I felt so exhausted. I kept saying that I wanted to sleep. The pain was getting bad, and at this point I said I couldn't handle it and I wanted "out." I think the exhaustion was harder to handle than the pain. Michele encouraged me, suggesting I try something different. She gave me some chamomile sugar drops and offered the birth stool. I agreed to get out of the tub and try the stool, but first she had to check how far along I was… I felt like pushing.

Surprise! Annie was right there, ready to come out. Just 15 minutes before, I was only seven centimeters dilated; and now we were ready to push. We decided to stay in the tub. I touched her little head as she crowned, and so did my husband. That big strong man, who wobbles when he hears anything that sounds remotely anatomical or medical, was almost crying. He was so moved when he felt her little head… just looking at his face gave me new strength. I pushed and felt the little head pressing. What an encouragement that was!

I pushed again with the next contraction but it didn't feel quite right. Michele asked how I felt and what position I thought might help, and I said "standing up." She agreed, but told me to get on all fours first and see if it was better. The next contraction came and I pushed, and the little head came out a little further this time. I told myself I didn't need another contraction, so I grabbed onto the border of the tub and jumped up. I stood with my feet in the water, holding onto my husband's shoulders. I pushed once more and Annie was born. Once her head was out, her body slid right after. Michele and Yves caught her and gave her to me, still standing.

What a joy! She's little… and big… and it's over and I love her. Thank you Annie, thank you Yves and Michele. THANK YOU GOD. It was the most incredible experience. My body knew how. What an amazing thing God created. Birth is perfect.

Everything makes sense.

After this moment of intense emotion we decided to get out of the tub and into the bed. (Since I gave birth standing, the blood and membrane flowed easily into the water and it was not very clear. I've seen births that leave water almost as clear as the beginning, until the mother stands up.) On the bed Annie and I looked in each other's eyes curiously for a long time, as if we were talking about our accomplishment. She was wide awake, watching everything around her, saying hello to Daddy, too excited to latch on.

We called my parents to tell them the news. About 15 minutes later, Yves cut the cord that had just about stopped pulsating, and he held Annie as I got into pushing position. I told Michele I did not feel like pushing, but I had to push once more for the placenta; what an incredible thing! I wanted to touch it. Michele showed me the part that faced the baby, and the sac. It was so smooth and almost purple. Yves touched it too.

Annie was ready to eat. In no time she was gulping away, holding mommy's breast with her little hands.

I got a couple of tears, but considering Annie's size I'm not surprised. I much prefer to have a tear that was needed than an unnecessary episiotomy. I was stitched, then took a shower while Michele and Yves cleaned up and Annie slept peacefully. By 5:30 p.m. we were heading home.

At home, our son Patrick was waiting eagerly to meet his sister. He was curious to see something moving in the little bassinette next to his mommy's bed. He was immediately madly in love with his sister and wanted to hold her all the time. I have to say that it was great to sleep on my own bed with my husband, to be able to hold my first-born child and be at home, in peace.

My mother-in-law was an angel. She took care of the house and Patrick, and made sure I got my rest. Michele came to visit regularly, to do the mandatory post-birth check-ups on me and Annie. The pediatrician came too.

I do recommend natural birth, and I would even try a home birth next time. To think that my OB had assured me that it was impossible for me to give birth to my babies vaginally since they were so big! She was absolutely sure that I would experience shoulder dystocia. It was great to show her how perfect nature is. Needless to say, she is no longer my OB.

Ever since this birth I feel so strong, and I have a deeper understanding of the important role our hormones play in birthing and bringing up our children. How we are born does make a difference. As humans we have great adaptability to circumstance, but this shouldn't mean that interfering with birth is right and without consequence. We have a responsibility to do what is best for the baby. We should not feel free to "help" nature when it's not needed, using the argument that it will cause "no harm," because it does. Unnecessary intervention robs baby of the best scenario in those crucial first moments of birth and life, and mom too. It interferes with the body's own signals, the internal messages that instinctively help us parent our children.

Thank you Annie, for making me a woman and teaching me what it means to give birth, to be a mom. And thank you Yves, for my babies and for being such a wonderful and supportive husband. I could not have gone through this revealing process without you. And thank you Patrick, for making me a mom, showing me the way, and for loving me in my search for a better way.

A Mother's Guidance: Choose carefully your caregiver and place of birth. Take care of yourself, eat nutritiously and stay mobile. Fill your heart and head with positive images and stories of birth. Face and accept your fears, and give them names so they don't creep up on you in labor.

I recommend the video *Birth Day*, directed by Frank Ferrel. I also recommend the following books: *Immaculate Deception II: Myth, Magic & Birth* by Suzanne Arms; *Birthing from Within* by Pam England and Rob Horowitz; *The Thinking Woman's Guide to a Better Birth* by Henci Goer; *Gentle Birth Choices* by Barbara Harper; *Ina May's Guide to Childbirth* by Ina May Gaskin; and *Birth Reborn* by Michel Odent.

In preparation for my first birth I had taken some Lamaze classes. I would now recommend the Birth Works classes or the Birthing from Within classes. Whatever you choose, be sure it isn't just a hospital-procedures class.

I feel that we really have to encourage new parents to take on the full responsibilities of the way their child is going to arrive in this world. They have to be thorough in their introspection as a couple, and have the tools to recognize the caregivers that will respect their choices in pregnancy, birth and the first few days of life. And a good way is to find the right childbirth class.

Additional Thoughts: Many women make the mistake of thinking that dilation is a linear process. For example, if it takes two hours to get from four centimeters to five centimeters then it must take two hours to get from five centimeters to six centimeters. That isn't the case, and sometimes this faulty thinking is the source of much stress and worry during labor. Elena was at seven centimeters, and then 15 minutes later she was 10 centimeters dilated and pushing.

Elena's vaginal birth after cesarean (VBAC) is a victory for every woman who has been told that her body just can't give birth to a large baby. It is rare that this is really the case, according to *Ina May's Guide to Childbirth*. Even twelve-pound babies can be birthed naturally, without any tearing.

If you are planning a VBAC, seek guidance and support from the International Cesarean Awareness Network (ICAN). Contact them online at www.ican-online.org, or call (800) 686-ICAN for more information.

A tool that Elena discovered during labor was humming, and focusing on the vibration of her diaphragm during contractions. Using your voice is very effective in opening up and releasing, and often makes the contractions much easier to bear. She also used soft, rhythmic music with drumming and chants. Use the music that you want for birth before you go into labor, so you can train your body to relax to it. Put it on while you meditate, take a shower or are just relaxing outside in beautiful weather. Before long, your body will automatically relax whenever this music is played.

Elena Piantino-Quintero has been a doula since 2003. She holds a degree in communication sciences, and her work experience includes marketing, and television and radio production. Her husband, Yves Piantino, is a lawyer. They live in Nyon, Switzerland, with their children Annie and Patrick, and have another one on the way.

A PROFOUND CONNECTION

BY RHONDA SIMPSON

I WAS PREGNANT with my third child, and my only intention for the birth was that we both come out of it alive. With my first child, I nearly died soon after the birth. My second child had a bit of a rough start and gave us quite a scare at the time he was born. So, nothing fancy on the agenda for the third time around... just a nice, safe, hopefully quick birthing would suit me fine. It turned out to be the most gentle, majestic experience I have ever had.

Somewhere along my second trimester, I decided to try HypnoBirthing. This natural method piqued my curiosity and I wanted to give it a try. Sean wasn't as willing to participate and was skeptical from the get-go. After a few classes though, he was sure that this practice would benefit him as a labor coach. He enjoyed the light meditations and the extra time we were able to spend together without the kids. For me, it became a life-altering experience. My entire way of thinking was transformed. Through the classes, I realized that the birth could be something so ceremonial and peaceful and calm; what a beautiful experience it could be for the baby, and for me. I had never realized how many choices were open to us, how much say we actually had in the delivery room. I had no idea that birthing could be pain-free; that the painlessness was natural and corresponded with allowing the body to do what it needed to do, and letting the baby do its thing as well. The central idea is that you need to give over control, and not fight the natural process that your baby and your body understand. HypnoBirthing guides you to release the idea of pain and the reins of fear, and reframe your inner vocabulary, thereby transforming your experience.

HypnoBirthing taught me something powerful. It taught me to get out of the way, to just let things happen as they are intended and to honor that process. My patience was tested quite a bit towards the middle and end of my pregnancy as contractions came and went, along with waves of excitement and frustration as we waited for this little guy to come in his own time. Since both of my previous birth experiences included induced labors, I was tickled with the idea of going into labor at any random time, not knowing when or how. But it was also driving me crazy. I was walking around town, dilated to five centimeters for three weeks, and this babe wasn't budging.

Though I had originally decided that this birth was going to be very run-of-the-mill, my standards and vision for the birth began to transform once I became familiar with the concepts of Hypno-Birthing. I became very focused on developing the kind of birth that I wanted, and I was committed to exploring HypnoBirthing and all that it could be. I switched doctors at 38 weeks, opting for an OB who was familiar with the techniques I was learning and who was more in favor of natural birth. I enlisted the help of a doula so that she could keep the birthing room (and me) calm while I concentrated on having the birth I envisioned. I worked with many healers during the last segment of the pregnancy to release fears that might get in the way of a successful birthing experience. I invited my family and friends to join us in the birth room to make this moment even more special. I felt calm. I felt supported. And it showed in how my labor proceeded.

The evening before my due date was pretty uneventful, until just after dinner. I was sitting on the couch, and all of a sudden, I felt like I needed to push. I wasn't having any contractions, and there were no other traces of labor; I just suddenly had to push. When I ruled out the possibility that it could be gas pains, I contacted my doula and doctor and we were off to the hospital. As Sean rushed us there, he echoed the words we had learned in class, "Your body knows what to do, your body knows what to do." "That's what I'm afraid of," I said, as I focused on keeping the baby in the womb until I could deliver him safely at the hospital.

When we arrived, I knew that there wasn't much time until the moment of birth. The nurses must have suspected I was being overly dramatic with my pleas for urgency. They were impatient as I resisted their poking and prodding and checking for dilation. The surges piled one on top of the other. I was in the thick of labor and although they were focused on paperwork and routine, I was focused on calm. I breathed into the relaxed and focused state that I had practiced at home for many weeks, melting into the familiar dolphin sounds that enveloped the room as I played my soothing CD. I envisioned myself alone in the forest, preparing for the coming of my son. I saw myself squatting and fearless, allowing my body to transcend to the effortless state of timeless wisdom that I knew would support the natural labor that women have experienced for ages. I lay on the bed, eyes closed, mind focused, body relaxed. I met my surges with my breath, resisting the desire to label them as pain, and thanking them for the baby en route to my arms.

My sister and best friend whispered in awe from the sidelines, unable to believe that I was calmly resting while the monitor showed that surges were coming every two minutes. I resisted bearing down, though that was what my body was screaming at me to do. I finally felt the release of the water bursting between my legs and I knew that was my body's way of giving me the go-ahead. "Here he comes," I whispered, as the nurses instructed me not to push and to wait for the doctor to get there. One of them realized that the baby was crowning and they hurried to prepare for him. I pushed once and Sean reminded me to breathe down, to breathe the baby out rather than push. At that point there was no resistance. I saw my little one making his way down the birth canal and out into the world. It was a giving over. Our little boy was born an hour and a half after we arrived at the hospital, the day before his due date; in his own time, in his own way.

A good friend of mine, who was supposed to attend the birth, arrived about an hour after the baby was delivered. She thought we were joking when we told her that he had already been born. My sister and best friend, who had so wanted to watch this birth, had stepped out just before it happened. But both agreed that even though they were disappointed to miss his first breath, they were grateful to have witnessed such a beautiful labor. The effects and power of relaxation and the techniques of HypnoBirthing were evident in so many ways. I had no tearing and recovered quickly. I was empowered by the experience of connecting with my body and my baby at such a profound level, and I reveled in the fact that I was able to transform labor into my vision of a calm and peaceful moment in time. I realized that the power to create what you desire is never out of your reach.

A Mother's Guidance: My decision to switch care providers at 38 weeks was a tough one, but my first two pregnancies had been induced, and as my due date approached, I just knew that my doctor would find a reason to induce me again. It was a decision that was in the best interest of my child and dramatically changed the course of his birth, so it was well worth the added stress and strain at the end of my pregnancy.

Baby knows what baby is doing, and your body knows what it is doing. Just give over control to your body and the baby. I used a dolphin-sounds CD that was helpful, making the whole room serene. I loved *HypnoBirthing: A Celebration of Life* by Marie Mongan, which reminded me that I had a choice about how my birth proceeded.

Rhonda Simpson is an artist, holistic healer, writer and mother of three children under four years old. Her husband Sean is a high-school teacher. They live in Carlsbad, California.

$\mathcal{A}$LONE ON A QUEST

BY PAMELA POUR

TWO MONTHS after a traumatic miscarriage, I unexpectedly found myself pregnant again. Both terrified and elated, I began my quest for the perfect birth. Now, I'm well aware that nothing in life is ever really perfect... but I was committed to getting as close as possible!

At 10 weeks pregnant, I was nervous with the thought that I just might never find what I was looking for. Suddenly I remembered a friend of a friend, someone who had learned the hard way about the need for support in labor. I called her and she willingly led me to an angel, a natural born caregiver and saint: a doula named Bonnie. Excited, I called Bonnie immediately, and we clicked instantly. I knew that the additional expense would be a small price to pay to have her as part of my birth experience. I was so relieved to have found her!

I was petrified after my last Ob/Gyn experience—I now call it puppy mill obstetrics—and eager to explore my options. Bonnie recommended a group of certified nurse midwives who were part of a local hospital, and I contacted their office right away. My husband Brian and I had our first appointment with Trish, a midwife, at 12 weeks of pregnancy. She was my second angel, so supportive and genuine. Although I was nervous, I knew she would do everything in her power to help me have a natural childbirth, without drugs, unnecessary intervention or a C-section. I felt a huge wave of relief and calmness wash over my body as I heard my baby's heartbeat for the first time. As long as my health remained strong and my blood pressure normal, I could birth in the ABC (Alternative Birth Care) unit, which is geared towards natural birth and the family experience.

Around 25 weeks along, I searched for a Bradley birthing instructor. The only class I could find that fit my husband's busy schedule was 40 minutes from our house, but we decided it was so important that we registered despite the commute. Once again, I was reminded that specific people come into our lives for a reason. I was finally able to see that "perfect" was really happening for us! Our Bradley instructor, Cindy, was such an inspiring and supportive person in my life, and she continues to be. We began our twelve-week course in the fall, "graduating" just two weeks before my due date.

Since a truly natural childbirth was a foreign concept in our families and among most of our friends, I began to feel very alone on this quest. Unsupportive people often made comments, insinuating that I was somehow ignorant because I didn't want an epidural or episiotomy, and I wasn't taking synthetic vitamins. I felt like a freak until I chose to surround myself with other pregnant women.

My pregnancy was pretty normal; I had sciatic nerve problems, heartburn, basic discomforts, but nothing abnormal. I did test positive for Group B strep, but that condition didn't threaten to derail my plans to give birth in the ABC unit.

At nine days overdue, I called Bonnie with much concern. I had been spending an hour each night in the AquaDoula to help position the baby and reduce lower back pain, and for overall relaxation. I had tried taking castor oil to initiate contractions, but had yet to feel my first. Since I was birthing in a hospital, I was concerned that their policies about being overdue would lead to chemical induction, and I wanted to avoid that if at all possible. Bonnie responded to my concerns, coming to our house to try a few of the tricks she knew about. We tried tying my belly up to raise the baby and help it into position. We tried some massage and pressure points. We tried homeopathy. We tried deep squats. And again I tried castor oil. Nothing happened.

The next day I went in for an ultrasound to assess the baby's size. According to the technician, my baby would weigh in at about 10 pounds, give or take a pound! I knew this could possibly disqualify me birthing in the ABC unit; I had an appointment with my midwife scheduled for the following morning. Hours later, at 2 a.m. on Friday morning, I got up to go to the bathroom… and I felt a pop, then a trickle of water. It wasn't urine… this was it! I was nervous and happy all at once. After preparing myself and my bed for a full water breakage, I tried to go back to sleep. At 2:30 a.m. the contractions began and I called Bonnie. She told me to go back to sleep, so I tried again. Sleeping was simply not going to happen. My contractions were one minute and 30 seconds apart, and stayed that way through my entire labor!

Lying in bed wasn't working for me. I woke Brian and he asked me what Bonnie said. I told him, "She said to get some sleep," so he told me the same thing. I knew this was impossible, so I took my Bradley workbook and watch to the sofa. The cats and I sat on the sofa, timing contractions. I kept thinking, "Something must be wrong… I must be doing this wrong… aren't they supposed to be seven to ten minutes apart?"

My mother-in-law, who was visiting and anxiously awaiting the birth of her first grandchild, joined me in the living room. She confirmed that I was indeed timing the contractions correctly. Before long my legs began to tremble uncontrollably. I decided to page Trish. She told me to take a warm shower and try to get some more sleep, and reassured me that the contractions would probably adjust to a longer span before long. But before I could get in the shower, she called back to say that the ABC unit was empty, and that maybe after my shower I should head to the hospital birth center, before the rush-hour traffic set in.

The shower helped tremendously! Then I woke my husband, and we arrived at the hospital by about 7 a.m. We made our way to the ABC somewhat unceremoniously—Brian decided the wheelchair made a fun racecar (only a man…). We were greeted by the ABC nurse, who examined me and said that I was three centimeters dilated and almost completely effaced.

I desperately wanted another shower. I needed that hot water to help with the leg trembling and the contractions. But before I could shower they needed to get an IV line started to combat the Group B strep with antibiotics. The contractions were so close together that it was difficult to get the IV in my arm. Finally they decided to put me in the shower and poke me at the same time! They also started the hot tub for me.

Bonnie arrived and began feeding my husband protein bars and breakfast, and helped me sip juice from a straw. I tried to eat some of the protein bar, but couldn't. I labored in the hot tub for a while, and by 10 a.m. I was nine centimeters dilated. I was so out of breath from the fast contractions that I was beginning to think I wasn't going to make it.

And then it was time to push. I pushed a little on the bed, a little on the toilet, and a little in the birthing chair. As much as I wanted to try more upright positions, I ended up in bed—it hurt my lower back the least. My dear sweet husband and Bonnie each looped an arm under a knee and held my hands to help me push. She counted each push for me, wiped my forehead and helped by asking my midwife lots of questions for me.

Brian was such a trooper. Although we had several weeks of Bradley classes, I don't think he realized what he had gotten himself into. But he stayed by my side, doing everything in his power to ease my pain and aid in the birth of our first child. During early contractions in the shower, he sprayed my belly with warm water. Later, as I screamed in his ear, he held my hand and helped me push. He even held me up on the toilet as I sat naked, leaning into his chest, pushing with all my might.

After two hours of pushing, my beautiful baby boy was born at 12:18 p.m. Within seconds of birth, my amazingly perfect son was placed on my chest and breastfeeding. Tears welled up in my eyes as I exclaimed, "Oh, my God! I can't believe I did this! Look at him, I did this!" For the first time in probably ten years, I saw my husband cry. He kissed my brow and said, "I love you! Let's call him Mason Joseph! Is that OK?" I smiled and nodded yes—I would have burst into tears if I spoke at that moment. He looked like a Mason. My left hand cupping his tender head, running my finger under his little hand, I reveled in my warm little bundle, gazing at the curly dark hair perched atop his perfect, round head. This was my baby. His eyes scrunched tight as he quietly cooed and suckled at my breast. Every once in a while his eyes would flutter open to reveal his dark gray-blue eyes peering up into mine. He took my breath away.

With each heartbeat I realized what I had just been through, what I had just accomplished. I became overwhelmed with instant love for this sweet little being. How could I have gone so long without him in my life? If I had known how wonderfully spiritual birthing a child would be, I would have done this a lot sooner.

Trish handed Brian the scissors and held the umbilical cord for him to cut. She quickly clamped off his cord and prepared to deliver the placenta. Once it was out, we started what I call the belly tribal dance. Trish and the nurse repeatedly pressed all over my belly to help release any blood clots and aid in shrinking the uterus. This little pressing dance on my abs was a bit difficult to take, to say the least. Fortunately, the dance only took a few minutes, and I was soon cuddling my baby boy again.

After about ten minutes of nursing, Bonnie asked me, "So, do we want to see how much he weighs?" Of course I agreed. She lifted Mason from my chest and said, "This is not a ten pound baby. I'd say he's about eight pounds, thirteen ounces."

Sure enough, as the nurses weighed Mason I heard a chuckle come from Bonnie. "Not bad… I was off by an ounce. Eight pounds, twelve ounces!" She quickly wrapped Mason back in his blanket and handed him to Brian. I was so in love with our perfect little man!

A Mother's Guidance: Have confidence in yourself. As difficult as it may be to shut out the skeptics in your life, you need to keep sight of your goal—the healthiest baby you can have!

My favorite books are: *A Good Birth, A Safe Birth* by Diane Korte and Roberta Scaer; *Birthing from Within* by Pam England and Rob Horowitz; *Husband Coached Childbirth* by Robert Bradley; *The Thinking Woman's Guide to a Better Birth* by Henci Goer; *Natural Childbirth the Bradley Way* by Susan McCutcheon; and *Mothering* magazine.

Additional Thoughts: The accuracy of ultrasound tests is highly overrated. Five different studies found that predictions of extra-big babies were incorrect ⅓ to ½ of the time, as Henci Goer discusses in her book, *The Thinking Woman's Guide to a Better Birth*. Ina May Gaskin also discusses her experiences with the inaccuracy of ultrasounds in *Ina May's Guide to Childbirth*, writing that she has seen a diagnosis of twins when there was only one baby. She has also seen weight estimates by ultrasound off by five pounds!

Pamela Pour is a fine-art photographer who spends her free time taking black-and-white photos of her beautiful baby. Mason is Pamela and Brian's first child. Pamela fondly remembers moments of Mason's birth as she nurses him to sleep each night. Although Pamela will not be returning to work, she continues to create beautiful fine-art photographs of Mason, as well as her friends and their children.

CHAOS AND SERENITY

BY CANDICE BLANCO

IT WAS FRIDAY, June 20th, and I was nine months pregnant with my third daughter. My mom and two sisters, Vanessa and Liberty, had been with us for about a week, serving as my only help with my two young daughters, and I was getting increasingly anxious… they were planning to leave Monday morning. If I didn't give birth to the baby before they left, I didn't know who would watch Skyler (four years old) and Sylvia (23 months) during the birth.

Luis's best friend, Eric, owns the house we were living in, and he and his family were visiting from out of town. Since he planned to sell the house when we moved out the following month, he and his family came over to do some work. Life was getting hectic.

Around noon, I felt that the baby and my body were both ready to go through birth, so my mom bought some (gulp) castor oil at the store. I took two ounces of castor oil with some orange juice and ice cream. It wasn't as bad as I thought it was going to be. A couple hours later, Luis came home from work, then left for a quick trip to the bank. I took another two ounces of castor oil with the orange juice and ice cream. I had felt about five small contractions in the last 30 minutes, but that was typical of the last week so I paid them no mind.

But then, fifteen minutes after my second dose of castor oil, my water broke. It was a small gush, just enough to cover my panties, and enough to make me take notice. I was sitting between my mom and my oldest sister, Vanessa. "I think my water just broke," I said. They kept talking. "I SAID I think my water broke!" They both jumped up, surprised and excited as the news sank in. I jumped up too, laughing with excitement, and waddled to the bathroom. Another small gush came as I sat on the toilet. Excitement filled the air. I wasn't going to be pregnant forever after all… we were going to have a baby!

I went upstairs to change and put on a pad, and then waited for Luis to get home so we could share the news. Just a few weeks earlier, Eric had jokingly told Luis that my water had broken, so I decided to have Eric break the real news to him. When Luis came home Eric was waiting for him, but of course Luis did not believe him. When he got in the house, I told him that he wouldn't be going to work the next day because we were going to have a baby! He was as excited as I was.

I called my midwife, who lived about two hours away, and we decided to wait an hour before she headed to my house. I was experiencing some mild contractions, but nothing to really take notice of. The castor oil had given me a bellyache, so I drank juice instead of eating dinner. The cleansing effect of the castor oil kicked in, and I spent some time in the bathroom before updating my computer friends and lying down to rest.

I took some quiet time to reflect and talk with the baby. I wanted her to know how excited I was to meet her. I still wasn't experiencing many contractions, so I wandered downstairs. Eric and Kim asked if I wanted them to stop working on the house, but I told them no. I invited Kim to witness the birth, then went to ask Luis to fill the birth pool. I knew it might be a while before I needed it, but I wanted it ready. While it was filling, Luis timed some contractions, just for the fun of it. I was surprised to hear that they were three minutes apart. They were very short, around 30 seconds, and I could easily talk through them. This was around 6:30.

Vanessa, Liberty and Kim took turns rubbing my back. Oh, the pampering… I loved it. We kept this up for a little over an hour, and then my friend and midwife, Brenda, arrived around 7:45. I chatted with her and my mom for a while, but sitting down had slowed the labor, so I got up and got moving. I thought that perhaps walking up and down the stairs would get things going again.

Eric and Luis were in the living room; Kim was trying to keep busy by scrubbing my bathroom; my mom and Brenda were up stairs chatting; Kim and Eric's kids were outside with my two daughters and Liberty; Vanessa was with me, making sure I had everything I needed. Wow, what a full house! It was more like a 4th of July picnic than a birth. It felt great to have so many loved ones around.

The intensity of the contractions started picking up. I stood in the hallway and leaned on the wall, moaning quietly. With the end of each contraction, I would rejoin the crowd, but it wasn't long before I decided it was time to get in the pool. It felt WONDERFUL! Water has always been very comforting for me—how could anyone give birth without water? As soon as my body sank into the water, I was comfortable. The inflatable pool was soft and the water level was perfect. I spent the first part of my pool time sitting up with my back against the side. The water was right at chest level, and my uterus was completely covered with water. It was now about 10:00 p.m. Sylvia was asleep, and the other kids were getting very tired. Kim and Eric decided to take their children home, and Liberty put Skyler to bed.

My mom and Brenda went down stairs, leaving Vanessa and me alone. I was excited that the contractions were getting stronger, and I was working through them with some light moaning or humming. Liberty joined us and put on soft music and lit candles. I felt very comfortable, and I believe this is what allowed labor to really get going. The house was finally quiet and peaceful. Luis got on the computer to pass the time and my mom and Brenda joined us in the bedroom. They said that they could tell by the way I sounded that things were really picking up. This was just after 11 p.m. Luis then joined the womenfolk in the bedroom, as he could also tell that labor was really moving. I needed him there too. I lost track of time, but shortly after Luis came in I went through some really powerful contractions. They were hard to work through, and I began to wonder why anyone would want a home birth, let alone a natural one. Then I threw up. I heard my mom in the background, saying that I must be in transition. I was so mad at her for saying that. I wasn't in transition, I couldn't be. With my other two labors, I threw up at about five or six centimeters.

I spent the next few contractions leaning forward on all fours. I had Luis's hands in my hands, and for some reason when a contraction would come on big and strong, I would kiss his hands and tell him that I loved him. It seemed to help with the intensity. A few contractions later, I needed to go to the bathroom. The contractions I had when I was on the toilet, partly due to the cleansing castor oil, were really hard. Hard is too light of a word to use for this kind of contraction. I lost all control, grabbing for something, anything! I halfway stood up and was really out of my mind with pain. Brenda came in and stood in front of me. I buried my face into her stomach and wrapped my arms around her. Her calming voice was wonderful and it brought me back to earth. "Breathe deeply," she said, "in through the nose, out through the mouth." The contraction passed, and I made some comment about wishing I could just blink and be back in the pool. I didn't want another contraction to start until I was in the water again. As soon as I returned to the water, another huge contraction hit. I said something about not being able to do this for very much longer. I still had no idea that I was in transition.

With the next contraction I felt my body give a little push. Could it really be? And then, with the following contraction, my body really was pushing. I said, "I am feeling kind of pushy," to no one in particular. And then with the next contraction, the feeling was more than "kind of" pushy. My body was pushing, and pushing hard. I was still in a hands-and-knees position. As I pushed, I managed to say, "Get Skyler." My four-year-old really wanted to be there for the birth, and I knew we didn't have much time. Liberty awoke Skyler, who was tired but very excited. While I was pregnant, she had asked me over and over if she could touch the baby's head when it was coming out, so as the baby was crowning Brenda picked up Skyler and helped her reach into the pool to feel the baby's head.

Luis was still holding my hands and I told him that he better get down there to catch. I could feel the baby enter the birth canal and my body felt like it was going to split in two. I adjusted my legs and the pressure eased a little, but it was still very intense. I could feel the head crowning, so I slowed down the pushing so I wouldn't tear. Brenda coached Luis on what to do. It was wonderful to feel her head slip out. As soon as the head was out I felt fantastic. I was giggling and said, "I am just so excited!" I could still feel her moving from the inside. It took a lot more work to get her shoulders and body out than it had with Sylvia. In my previous birth, I didn't even need a contraction, just a tiny little push and she slipped right out. But with this baby, I had to give a huge push to get the shoulders out and another push to get her body out. After the shoulders were out I could still feel her moving from the inside. It hurt; I wasn't expecting that. But then, out she came. I lifted one of my legs, and Luis and Brenda handed her to me, still under the water. I lifted her out of the water and sat back on my heels. There she was... oh, what a beauty! She was perfect, with dark, very curly hair and more vernix than my other two babies.

She wasn't moving... I wondered, is she breathing? It didn't look like it. She was pink, that was good. Brenda sensed my thoughts and told me not to worry, that she was still getting her oxygen through the cord. While I rubbed her and talked to her, Brenda listened to her chest with a stethoscope and reassured me that everything was fine. She was just sleeping! After all of that, she wanted to sleep—I guess it really was a peaceful birth. I woke her up a little by rubbing one of her feet, then sat back to enjoy a few moments with my new baby girl.

Sage Liberty was born at 11:37 p.m., about 30 minutes after the intense contractions started and after only four minutes of pushing. She was eight pounds, four ounces, and 21 inches long. We cut the cord about 15 minutes after the birth, and I pushed the placenta out in the pool. I handed Sage off to her daddy so I could get out of the pool, and then I nursed her 20 minutes after birth. Boy oh boy, was she excited about nursing! A strong latch this little one had. It was a wonderful birth with very few interventions… not even one vaginal exam. I was just trusting my body and trusting my baby, and trusting in my Father in heaven.

A Mother's Guidance: Trust. Trust in yourself. Trust in your baby and trust in God. Do whatever you can to gain this trust and you will be fine. I enjoyed lots of Internet resources, as well as books about Bradley birth. I also loved *Spiritual Midwifery* by Ina May Gaskin; *A Good Birth, A Safe Birth* by Diane Korte and Roberta Scaer; *Special Delivery and Pregnant Feelings* by Rahima Baldwin and Terra Palmarini Richardson; *Heart & Hands: A Midwife's Guide to Pregnancy & Birth* by Elizabeth Davis; and *Active Birth: The New Approach to Giving Birth Naturally* by Janet Balaskas. Watching the video *Birth into Being: The Russian Water Birth Experience* helped prepare my daughter to witness the birth of her sister.

Additional Thoughts: Taking castor oil is one of the most commonly used techniques to encourage labor, and is generally considered safe. However, there are risks to consider and precautions to take. Too much castor oil can make you miserable with diarrhea (which leads to dehydration), and can create very strong contractions. Remember that whatever you put into your body goes into your baby as well. Many birthing care providers believe that, in large doses, it can cause the baby to release meconium into the amniotic fluid, which the baby breathes. Others say that it doesn't cause this effect.

Dosage is very important. If you are considering using castor oil, consult your care provider for specific instructions.

Candice Blanco is a stay-at-home mom living in California with her husband Luis and their three daughters. She is in the process of becoming a certified childbirth instructor.

HOME SWEET HOME BIRTH

BY MORGAN ROBINSON

OUR FIRST CHILD'S birth was just right: about 12 hours from start to finish; in a hospital-affiliated birthing suite; unmedicated and empowering. We took Bradley Method childbirth classes to prepare, and shortly after he was born, I began the certification process to teach Bradley birth classes myself.

Through Angus's birth, as well as through the extensive teacher training, I learned to trust my body and my baby even more deeply than I had before. I also discovered that the only thing that wasn't perfect for me about our first birth was having to get into a car during the most intense part of labor, to leave my nest and go to our birthing place.

With our second birth, the only thing that made sense to me was to have everyone come to me, the birthing woman. We found the perfect midwife and planned a quiet welcome for our new family member. With over 25 years of home birth experience, our midwife had the combination of trust in birth, knowledge and respect for Spirit that we were looking for.

Another Bradley instructor and I were due around the same time. So rather than take each other's classes, and to make special time for our second pregnancies, we signed up with our husbands for Birthing from Within classes. These classes helped me investigate the connection among all birthing women, past and present. Through imagery, role play and birth art, we explored birth from emotional and psychological perspectives. In addition to enhancing my own birth experience, these classes added spiritual depth to my teaching.

When I imagined the birth of our new baby, I felt certain that this child would be born on an even day of the month. I also knew my labor would start at work, but that I wouldn't mind. Sure enough, at about 10:00 a.m. on Wednesday, May 15th, my belly started tightening at regular intervals. Labor with my first child had started in my lower back, so when I felt these belly-centered sensations, I attributed them to Braxton-Hicks contractions. Though noticeable, the tightening was very subtle—and occurring every five minutes!

My first indication that it may be true labor was a feeling of uneasiness that came over me in a shopping center during my lunch hour. I felt exposed. I wanted to be in my nest. My office was nest enough; I just needed to be in a familiar environment. Light back cramping joined in the sensations around 2:00 or 3:00 p.m. When I left at 4:30, I told my coworkers not to expect me the next day.

After work I went to the park with our three-year-old son Angus and our neighbors. It was then I called the midwife to alert her that something may be going on. That was about 5:30 p.m. and the easy contractions were still about five minutes apart.

My husband Eric, Angus and I walked to the market to pick up some dinner around 7:00 and the sensations were really starting to get my attention. I called the midwife back around 8:00 and told her, "If I remember correctly, I'm pretty sure this is labor." Eric called his parents and Angus's daytime babysitter, and we prepared the bedroom with shower curtain liners on the floor (it was new carpet!). I had already made the bed with sheets covered by a plastic liner and another set of sheets, so the liner and top set could be easily stripped away and cleaned up after the birth.

My parents lived six or seven hours away and planned to attend the birth, so they were camping about an hour away. They had made arrangements with the campground manager to convey any messages, as their cell phone didn't receive calls at the site. I tried calling the manager, but didn't have any luck, so I called their cell phone anyway. About the third or fourth time I tried the number, my mother answered. It was the only call they received on that phone for the entire two weeks they stayed at the campsite.

At about 8:45 p.m., as I was checking my phone book for numbers to call after the birth, my water broke. I was pretty surprised. My water didn't break with the first birth until I was pushing him out. I changed into my robe and straddled a rolled-up towel. My midwife and her assistant arrived about 9:00, my parents by 9:30.

By 10:00, things started to get serious. The contractions demanded my full attention. I had made a CD to use in labor; I hung my arms around Eric's neck and we swayed through and between contractions (which were two to three minutes apart). Our wedding song came on. Who would have thought that Marvin Gaye's "Let's Get It On" could carry so many different moods?

I tried many different positions over the next couple of hours: squatting, kneeling, walking, side-lying, sitting. I made my way from the bed to the toilet and back again, over and over. I remember sitting on the toilet for a while, tilting my head back as I inhaled and tucking my chin as I exhaled. I imagined this action was helping me breathe the cervix up and breathe the baby down. It gave me a wonderful rhythm for several contractions. I also started lightly bearing down during contractions to see if it would feel more comfortable, because my relaxation techniques didn't seem to be cutting it any more. It didn't help much, so at about 12:30 I climbed across the bed and tried relaxing there. My midwife and her assistant had been resting in another bedroom, giving us our intimate labor space. My parents were downstairs and Angus was asleep down the hall. It was at this point that the midwife came down and quietly lay across the end of the bed, gently assuring me that I was doing well and telling me how beautiful I was. I felt so strong.

I began to shiver and asked Eric if the heat was on. "Are you sure? I don't hear it! It's too cold!" I persisted. He turned it up so it would be warm enough for me, but also so it would be warm enough for the baby. Within a few minutes (five? 45? Who knows?) I was sweating. I wriggled out of my robe and threw it off me. I realize now, this had little to do with the actual temperature of the room.

Again, I started breathing up and down, raising my head and shoulders to inhale, then burying my face in a pillow to muffle the big, low, open sounds that were helping me bring my baby down. The muffling wasn't a conscious decision, but I was aware of our sleeping child down the hall.

I began to think that this must be how women feel when they start to doubt themselves. I didn't doubt myself even for a moment, but as a doula I have seen that moment with other women. I was working so hard. I had to push my hips forward at the peak of each contraction to ease the pain. Eric was behind me, and he leaned in and kissed my lower back and very quietly said, "Thank you." Oh, that he would feel gratitude for my efforts at bringing him another child! So sweet.

I was feeling like I had very little energy left. I remember, at that moment, hearing Peter Gabriel's "Shaking the Tree" on the CD telling me—telling *me*—"This is your life, this new life has begun. It's your day, woman's day. Turning the tide, you are on the incoming wave."

My midwife asked me if I was pushing, and I told her I was a little. She said, "Make sure it's the only thing you can do." With the very next contraction, there was nothing else my body could do. My midwife called her assistant to come in and get ready. Eric guided me to relax my shoulders, which I had curved up and around with the effort of pushing. There were no dilation checks at all. My midwife could read my laboring self to know where the baby and I were with this birth. There was no counting to ten with legs in the air. There was only quiet, and my listening to my body and my baby.

Even though it was my second birth, I was still startled by the tremendous pressure in my rectum. My midwife told me to push past it, and I could feel the baby's head move over the rectum and fill the birth canal. I reached down and felt his head bulging against my perineum. I felt his softest-of-soft little head still inside me. His head felt just like that for months after he was born.

It was at that point that I realized no one had thought to call my mother. I called out, "Maaa!" between contractions. She was the only one who recognized it as her cue, and she and my dad arrived just as the baby's head was crowning. With one more push he made his slippery way into our warm, dark, intimate space, just before 2:00 a.m. on May 16th.

We were rubbing him a little with a blanket for stimulation and when my midwife asked me to talk to him, I knew she was anxious for his response. He didn't cry immediately, so in our concern we had forgotten our curiosity about his sex. Throughout the pregnancy, Eric was convinced that this baby was a girl. What a beautiful little surprise. Our son was vigorously nursing in no time.

An hour or so later, after we were cleaned up and cuddled into bed, my midwife held Porter and told him, "Welcome to the world, sweet Porter. You have made a good choice by coming to this loving family." She and her assistant then gathered their things and went home. We settled to sleep, and waited for Angus to wake us in the morning so we could introduce him to his new brother.

Hours later, when Angus came into our room, we told him we had a surprise for him. He saw Porter and gently held him and sang to him, then said, "Where's my present?" Angus's third birthday was two days away. He didn't yet realize what a gift he had received.

A Mother's Guidance: The key to a wonderful birth is to trust your body and your baby, and have faith in the birthing process. Replace fear with the knowledge of what happens in labor, and relax. In preparing for my first birth, I loved *Natural Childbirth the Bradley Way* by Susan McCutcheon, mainly for the great illustrations that provided wonderful meditation imagery for labor. It really provides a strong sense of what the muscles of the uterus are doing. It even offers scripts for those dads who are unsure about verbal coaching. I also loved the belly gallery on www.amazingpregnancy.com. We don't see a lot of naked, full, pregnant bellies in our culture, and that website offers a wide variety of photos to illustrate the full range of "normal."

Morgan Robinson is mother to Angus and Porter, and wife of Eric. She is a certified childbirth educator in the Bradley Method, as well as a birth doula. Morgan is an editorial production manager in Philadelphia. She and her family live in Collingswood, New Jersey.

A KINDER, GENTLER BIRTH

BY CAROLINE OWEN HOUDE

MY FRIENDS LIKE TO SAY I was made to have babies. After three wonderful birth experiences it's easy to see why. But things were not always so easy. It's hard to believe that just over six years ago I was doubting what my body could do, after two back-to-back, unexplained miscarriages. Now I am truly blessed with three healthy, smart, beautiful children, all with unique and incredible entries in to the world.

My first two children, Christina and Charlie, were born very quickly... with Christina, we didn't even make it to the hospital! So when my husband Peter and I were planning Catherine's birth, we wanted to stay as close to home as possible. I was concerned that I might not have any labor pains or warning signs this time. Since insurance wouldn't pay for a home birth, we opted for The Birth Place at Wellesley, a freestanding birth center, which is 18 minutes from home, door to door.

I was very sad to leave the Ob/Gyn practice I had known for over five years, and was extremely emotional when I said good-bye to them nearly halfway through my pregnancy. The Birth Place had a lot more midwives, most of whom I had only met once, so the transition was a little tough on me.

I was hoping for a water birth, but since it takes half an hour to fill the tub, I wasn't overly optimistic about having one. Frankly, my main concern was just getting to The Birth Place in time, and having my husband with me. I knew that if I went into labor on a weekday, Peter might not have enough time to get from work to me. As I neared term, he started driving to work instead of taking the train so he could get to me faster if I went into labor. The idea that I might not have any perceivable contractions, and could end up delivering in the car or alone with the kids, was a very real possibility and a huge concern. My mom, sister-in-law and my friend Debby were all ready to take me and the kids to The Birth Place on a moment's notice.

But as it happened, the timing of Catherine's birth could not have been better. It was 8:00 on a Saturday morning when my water broke. Since it was 11 days before my due date, we were caught off guard, but we all dressed quickly, packed a few things and jumped in the car. I felt fine, the kids were excited, and we honked as we drove past the fire station where Christina had been born.

When Jennifer, one of two midwives I had never met, checked me at 9 a.m. I was only three centimeters dilated. I was surprised, but based on my history of quick labors we decided against going home. We had the whole place to ourselves, and my mom and aunt joined us there. My friend Debby and her daughter Lily also came to keep the kids company. We were all hanging out and talking until about 9:40, when I started to have noticeable contractions and climbed into the Jacuzzi tub. My mom and aunt kept me company, and I squeezed Mom's hand through a few contractions, but the water helped me relax. Peter was in the other room, and I hollered to him as I felt the baby's head crowning—without even pushing! He ran in just in time, as Catherine was born quickly and easily in the water at 10:03 a.m. It was so fast and gentle and painless, and ended with a healthy, perfect little miracle. It was an amazing birth, everything I could have hoped for.

Jennifer didn't even have time to put on gloves; she just reached in to lift Catherine up and place her on my chest. She then let the water out of the tub, which was my least favorite part.

Peter helped me to a squatting position and I delivered the placenta, with the cord still attached to Catherine.

We climbed out of the tub, put on a snuggly robe and got into bed. I was thrilled to hear that I didn't need any stitches! We waited two hours before cutting Catherine's cord, and she didn't make a peep when it happened. The rest of my family joined us for the celebratory day, and we left the birth center a few hours later. We were happy to be all settled back home in time for dinner. It is my dream for all women to have births like this. I think the world would be a better, kinder, gentler place if all babies were born this way.

A Mother's Guidance: I have a few words of wisdom for mothers to be, based on my natural birthing experiences. First and foremost, trust your body and believe in yourself. As women, we are made to have babies. Tap into your inner knowledge and let your body intuitively guide you. Try to remain calm, and focus on relaxing and opening your body. I highly recommend water birth; it was the perfect medium for birthing, relaxing and gentle to mom and baby. I also recommend waiting until after delivering the placenta, or longer, before cutting the cord. Lastly, I highly encourage breastfeeding—it's so healthy for both the mother and baby, and it's the most incredible continuation of the miracle of life.

My number one influence was my mom, who had natural childbirth with me 39 years ago, and breastfed me and my brother when both practices were uncommon in the United States. She encouraged me to look into home birth and water birth, as well as using a midwife and doula. Most importantly, she told me from a young age that my own birth was so easy and that I slid right out. If only that was the message our culture offered to women....

Books I enjoyed include: *The Complete Book of Pregnancy and Childbirth* by Sheila Kitzinger; *Easing Labor Pain: The Complete Guide to a More Comfortable and Rewarding Birth* by Adrienne Lieberman; and *Fit & Pregnant: The Pregnant Woman's Guide to Exercise* by Joan Marie Butler.

Additional Thoughts: Waiting to cut the cord has become increasingly common. Many experts feel that waiting allows some of the cord blood to return to the baby, increasing its oxygen level.

Caroline Owen Houde lives in Massachusetts with her husband and three children. Caroline hopes that by sharing her stories more women will be inspired and empowered to trust in their ability to birth naturally.

AND WE WERE BOTH CRYING

BY JESSICA A. LEWIS

I'M ONE of those women who think they know everything. When my instincts scream a direction, I take notice and listen. I knew, for an absolute fact, that my baby would be early. Not premature, mind you, but early enough to ease my aching legs and bulging stomach. I had it planned perfectly. He—I also knew he was a boy—would come just after week thirty-seven. I was expecting a home birth, and the midwives would not support staying at home if the baby came any earlier. When I strained to walk, all I could picture was a huge baby, with a head just like his daddy's, upside-down and smiling on top of my bladder. I was already dilated to four centimeters. My baby had to come early. I couldn't take it any longer.

I was blessed with three midwives. All three looked at me patiently as I moaned and groaned. "My daughter was seventeen days early, so there's no doubt he'll be here in the second week of July," I told them knowingly.

Nina looked me in the eyes. "Be prepared to go to your date, August 3rd." Frustrated, I rolled my eyes. "No offense, Nina, but if I have to make it to my next appointment, I'm blaming it all on you."

The next two weeks were frustrating. I thought he should be here already. I began to doubt myself... what if he's not even a boy?

·· 233 ··

"Maybe a little rosehips oil to help ripen your cervix?" Kelley asked.

"Oh, please, *anything!*"

I was dining with my in-laws when contractions began. I was excited, eagerly anticipating the pains to grow closer and stronger. For two hours, they came half an hour apart with the punctuality of Old Faithful. My father-in-law looked at me suspiciously. "Are you sure you should be eating that?"

I looked at my bacon burger and fries. "Of course! I'm starving."

I started to visualize the birth, and how strong and in control I would be, how I would convince everyone there that a woman can and should give birth in her home. And then, without warning, the contractions died off. So I went shopping.

The next day I re-organized every cabinet in my kitchen. I was sweating and laughing and crying. My two-year-old daughter, Hannah, looked at me nervously. "What time is Daddy coming home?"

I started on the closets, and I felt a contraction. I glanced at the clock. Ten minutes went by and another one came. I began to daydream about my baby and how wonderful it would be to see him. And then, for a moment, the doubts returned. What if he... is a girl? For the next three hours I had consistent contractions, 10 minutes apart. I called the midwives, who said they'd be ready anytime I was. But then, once again, the contractions stopped. I was glad— I just had to clean the bathroom floor!

After an extremely good night's sleep, I woke at 9:30 a.m. and made coffee. And there it was... another contraction. I didn't even look at the clock; I just knew. This was it. I called my sister-in-law, our designated picture-taker, who listened to me patiently. At her first opportunity, she asked, "Have you called Chad yet?"

"Oh... right, I'll call him now."

"And call your midwife, too!"

I know it was 11:30 a.m. when my husband arrived because my daughter had just begun to watch *Sesame Street*. He looked a little pale as he filled our AquaDoula tub. The contractions were growing in strength and there was still no midwife at my side.

Chad asked, "How did Hannah deal with you?"

I glanced over at her as she sat munching on grapes and sipping chocolate milk. "She's fine."

By noon I had reached a breaking point. The midwives' apprentice, Audra, had arrived and asked if I had emptied my bladder. I went in the bathroom and tried, but to no avail. "The baby's head is probably right there," she said.

"NO SHIT!"

I looked at her sweet, attractive face and sighed. "I think it's time to get in the water," I moaned. As I climbed into the AquaDoula tub, I noticed how my now weightless body felt better, but for a second, I got nervous. It wasn't the cure-all for pain that I had hoped for.

Chad smiled proudly. "The water is six inches from the top, just like the manual said." I groaned and thought to myself, "GOOD FOR YOU!"

At this point my mother arrived and poked her head in the room, only to hear my guttural moans and see my body flailing from side to side. "Where are the other girls?" she asked through clenched teeth. I was so glad I didn't have to deal with her.

Finally, my midwife Nina swooped in, dropped her bags and checked my dilation. She looked me in the eye and said, "You're ready to push."

I thought, "Oh, thank God." Then I thought, "Oh, oh no." I got on my knees and began to push. In the distance I could hear my mother bossing everyone around. She wondered why Nina didn't count to ten, or help in some other hospital-like way. I heard Nina telling her she thought I was doing just fine.

I remember thinking about the baby and bearing down, while Nina supported his head and prevented my body from tearing. At one point Kelley, my other midwife, got on her knees in front of me and instructed me to breathe between pushes, working with me to ease the baby out of my body and minimize any tearing. The room was muted... all I could hear was my breathing and my heart beating. And then, with one last push, he was out. Sound returned. I heard Nina say, "Pick up your baby!"

He was floating between my legs, his head down. I gently picked him up and lifted him out of the water. I sat and looked at his face, his eyes wide open, so alert. I did it. I had him at home, just the way I wanted, and without even a Tylenol to help the pain. I looked over at my husband, and we were both crying. I felt in between my son's legs. "It IS a boy!"

I looked into his face while my mother and husband examined his hands, fingers, feet and toes. I looked up into Audra's face. I don't remember this, but Audra swears I said, "That was so easy." I cannot recall it, but either way, I'll never tell Duncan. He was born at 12:57 p.m. on July 31st.

Nina and Kelley helped me out of the water, and I delivered the placenta in my favorite padded rocking chair. I still had Duncan in my arms—he was a natural breastfeeder—while Nina checked me for tears. "Not one, not even a little one," she said, beaming proudly. I will always love that woman.

I cut the cord, and then Nina helped me to my shower. I remember handing Duncan to my husband right before I entered the bathroom. It was the first time he was away from my body.

I felt so happy and relaxed in my robe, lying in my own bed. I leisurely breastfed while my mom began cooking a big pot of soup and waited on me hand and foot. I tickled Duncan's face, outlining it with my forefinger. I was right… he looked just like his daddy.

A Mother's Guidance: Let go of fear, and above all, trust your instincts about your body and your baby! *Mothering* magazine helped me to prepare for home birth, as did *Baby Catcher: Chronicles of a Modern Midwife* by Peggy Vincent, which also opened my mind to the ways different women deal with pain.

Jessica Lewis is the proud mother of two, and the wife of one brave man. She currently resides in Columbus, Ohio, and between late nights with baby Duncan and early mornings with her two year-old daughter, Hannah, she writes both fiction and non-fiction. Currently, she's researching a book on the process of incorporating homeschooling and public schools, and also is attempting to take on Ohio's lawmakers and their regulations for midwives and home birth.

COMMITMENT THROUGH CHALLENGE

BY CHERITY FOAT

FROM THE TIME we decided to start a family of our own, my husband and I always wanted a natural childbirth. It aligns with our lifestyle and philosophy; we are vegetarians, and both of us have had positive experiences with natural therapies in the past. Plus, I am distrustful of most medical interventions, as I feel they interfere with the functioning of our bodies. And my husband and I both feel that pregnancy is not an illness!

When we became pregnant, we searched for the right childbirth preparation class for us. We took a Lamaze-styled course, but it felt more like "how to prepare for your epidural" instead of focusing on how to have a natural birth experience. As we were working our way through the class, I went to purchase my Maya Wrap online and discovered a link to HypnoBirthing information. The owner of the website, Carolyn, and I decided to meet so I could pick up my purchase. When I arrived, she was speaking with a couple who had just used HypnoBirthing techniques in the birth of their baby.

After hearing their story, it seemed like the perfect match for us! We signed up for the class and attended the sessions. Because of our insurance restrictions, we were required to birth our son in a hospital, but the sessions were excellent in preparing us for that.

We learned how to work with the medical personnel to ensure they complied with the type of birth we wanted. During the sessions we met Paula, a certified hypnotherapist and HypnoBirthing instructor, who agreed to assist us during our child's birth. We did all the practice work at home with the tapes and scripts. The practice proved invaluable when the time came for our child to be born.

I started feeling surges around 5 a.m. on March 9th. I slept through most of them and was very comfortable at home. We decided around 11 a.m. to go to the hospital. I felt tightness across my belly during surges, but no pain. We called Paula and agreed to meet her at the hospital. By the time we arrived, I was six centimeters dilated with intact membranes, and having no difficulty at all! I was admitted and assigned to a birthing suite.

We met our nurse, and she was incredible. We explained our goals and birth plan to her, and Paula spent a lot of time explaining HypnoBirthing. I used the birthing ball and we walked quite a bit. During surges, I would fall into an almost trance-like state. I would breathe slowly and deeply, riding it out. Still no discomfort, just tightness! When I was checked later in the afternoon, I was eight centimeters and still walking the hallways. The nursing staff was amazed that I was so far dilated and still out in the halls!

I am glad that I brought my homemade broth to keep me strong. I also drank juices and water to maintain my strength. Many hospitals, unfortunately, don't let you ingest anything except clear liquids once you are admitted.

My husband Gerardo was wonderful and very supportive. He had made a CD of favorite songs to keep me going and focused. He also included some cheesy pop songs to make me laugh. The best part of our birth experience was that we danced in the birth suite. I thought the nurses were going to go into cardiac arrest!

While I was walking the halls, the TV program *Birth Stories* was filming births. They had never seen nor heard of Hypno-Birthing. When they heard that I was eight centimeters and walking the halls, they couldn't believe it!

During this entire time, my doctor was not present. Our nurse checked me again at midnight and she estimated nine centimeters; during the examination my water broke. She called the doctor, who arrived shortly and examined me. What she said was quite a shock: she estimated seven centimeters and diagnosed a swollen cervix. She wanted to start Pitocin, stating, "this labor is not progressing." We were crushed. With those words, the positive atmosphere we had created came crashing down around us. Gerardo, Paula and I asked to be alone for a while to discuss our options. I did not want Pitocin, but I was beginning to doubt myself. Our nurse came back into the room and told us there was NO medical reason for me to have Pitocin. I was overjoyed! I knew there was no way that she would put the hospital legally on the line without being sure of what she was saying. With her vote of confidence and my newfound resolve, we pressed forward with our birth plan. We told the doctor that we would try nipple stimulation to encourage progress before starting Pitocin, and then asked for an hour of privacy. Gerardo and I turned our focus to moving things along.

When I was checked again at 1:30, progress was being made; surges were coming more strongly and frequently. By 2 a.m. I was ten centimeters and pushing. After our negative run-in with our physician, she redeemed herself by massaging my perineum to help prevent tearing, and she was very successful! We tried many different pushing positions, working to find what would be best for my baby and me.

Our son was born at 3:16 a.m. He was seven pounds, eight ounces, and 20 inches long. Healthy, with a lot of beautiful black hair. We were thrilled—we had done it! He breastfed that night, and we have been a happy nursing pair ever since.

A Mother's Guidance: Paula's support was absolutely invaluable. She was not too personally involved, and helped us keep our heads when things got challenging. To ensure a natural birth in a hospital, the best things that a family can do are hire a doula and get the nurses on your side!

Additional Thoughts: Lamaze-styled classes that are sponsored by a hospital are not same as independent Lamaze classes. Hospital-affiliated classes often include a lot of information about using drugs, and are limited in what they are allowed to teach. If you are truly committed to a natural birth, consider an independent class.

Cherity Foat is an account executive. Her husband Gerardo is a visual artist. Cherity and Gerardo live in San Diego, California.

FROM A DISTANT PLACE

BY SARA MᶜGRATH

THE MEMORY of my daughter's birth is one of my most precious memories. But it's so different than other memories. I remember hard labor and childbirth in a much more intimate way than I remember other experiences. I remember them as I experienced them, from within myself.

Before I gave birth, the thing I most wanted to know was how well I would bear the pain. My friends and family had all used pain medication, so they couldn't explain the sensations of labor. They shuddered as they wished me luck in giving birth naturally.

I spent my nine months of pregnancy transforming my growing love for my new daughter into strength to face my fear of the pain. As it turned out, only the last five hours of the 24 I spent in labor were hard, and those five flew by. In my imagination, I thought that I would be more consciously aware of the pain than I actually was.

"This is all it is?" I asked my husband while we walked around our neighborhood, pausing every two minutes so I could relax during contractions. They were a little more intense than the earlier, less frequent ones. The pain I felt slowly swelled and receded. The contractions hurt, but they didn't stop me from walking and talking. I could almost describe them as invigorating, but that's probably because I was so excited that the time had finally come. After the walk I called our midwife. We headed to the hospital, but before checking in, I went into the bathroom. Seeing that I was pregnant, a woman showed me a picture of her young baby. She never knew I was in labor.

Not long after settling into our room, the intensity of my contractions increased dramatically. After that, I don't remember much of what went on around me until after I gave birth. I was aware of little more than a continuous, generalized sense of pain. I was no longer focusing on individual contractions, although my husband said that my facial expressions suggested rising and falling pain. I reassured myself that this was the pain of physical exertion, not of injury; that it was necessary; that it would be over when it was over; and that my baby was working too.

I understand why it was difficult for other women to explain labor pain, because it was different than any other kind of pain. I imagined it as a soft pain that rocked through me and surrounded me. I couldn't see what was happening outside of myself because the sensations blurred it out, and all of my energy was focused on staying relaxed and letting my body work. I moved around, following the cues of my body, searching for comfortable positions.

My husband was by my side the whole time, but I only saw his face as if it floated near me wherever I went. He didn't speak or do anything. He was just there, so I didn't feel alone. My mom came into the room at some point. I looked up at her and said, "It hurts." She said, "I know, honey." That was what I needed from her. I was deeply comforted by the presence of a woman who had done what I was doing, especially since she was the woman who had given birth to me. I noticed Michelle, our midwife, only when I told her that my body was pushing, and I wanted to know that it was OK.

I pushed for forty minutes, but that time also flew by. In preparing myself for labor, I had been most afraid of the pain of pushing out my baby, but honestly, that was the easy part. She seemed much smaller than she was (eight pounds, three ounces) as I felt her moving down the birth canal. After what seemed like only a few pushes, Michelle handed me my daughter. My mom cut the umbilical cord and kissed my baby's head.

My daughter stopped crying as soon as I wrapped my arms around her, held her close, and spoke her name, "Maia." Her eyes were open. I imagined that she was where she expected to be—in my arms, listening to my heart and my voice as she had when she was inside. Michelle pressed on my abdomen and told me to push out the placenta. I obeyed, hearing her distant voice speaking to me from outside the halo that surrounded me and Maia.

A Mother's Guidance: Relax and let your body do the work it was designed to do. The suggestions that carried me through labor and birth, to that euphoric moment when I first held my baby, that I pass on to expectant mothers are: don't worry, because a woman needs only to stay relaxed and let her body do the work it was designed to do; learn about the process of labor and birth, because knowing what to expect can build confidence and greatly diminish any fears; and have at least one woman present who has given birth herself, because this can be immensely comforting. During pregnancy, I took a class on the Bradley approach to natural childbirth and read several books, including *Birthing from Within* by Pam England and Rob Horowitz. I recommend both approaches.

Additional Thoughts: Just because someone says she had pain during labor doesn't mean that it was excruciating. Fear and fighting your body is what causes excruciating pain, but it doesn't have to be that way.

Sara McGrath is a freelance writer of stories and articles, including a column on natural parenting at www.suite101.com. She lives in Oregon with her husband and daughter.

ABY IN A HURRY!

BY CRYSTAL AND LEE IRWIN

Crystal's Version

I DECIDED TO EXPLORE alternatives to anesthesia after the birth of our oldest son, John. Following an extremely ineffective epidural, I had to question whether I wanted to take the risk again, however remote it might be.

I was lucky enough to be one of millions who saw a segment about childbirth hypnosis on a news magazine show. I watched with interest, and a bit of skepticism. After all, I had the same preconceived notions about hypnosis as other people who have seen the Vegas-style hypno-shows, and didn't see how that could remotely touch the intense pain I'd felt during John's birth. That is, until they showed side-by-side clips of a woman during her first birth with an ineffective epidural and her second birth, using hypnosis. While she was moaning and in obvious pain in the former, in the latter she was peaceful, relaxed and talking as needed, and the calm in the room during the birth was simply inspirational. I was intrigued! Since we weren't immediately in need of such information, I filed it away in the gray matter—it might come in handy.

Fast forward a few years; the time had come. Early in my pregnancy, I knew I wanted to explore hypnosis a little further. Since seeing the show, I'd done some reading and web-surfing, and had a better idea of what it was all about. I happened to mention my interest in home birth and hypnosis to my parenting group, and one of the women recommended her hypnosis instructor, Kerry, saying she found the class to be very effective. Ultimately we decided against a home birth; my husband Lee was still disturbed by John's birth, and he didn't think hypnosis could possibly work well enough to make a home birth feasible.

We still felt, given my lack of response to epidural anesthesia, that hypnosis was worth trying, so we enrolled in Kerry's class and spent the next five weeks learning, practicing and planning. Around this time I started having preterm labor, so Kerry provided us with a "stop pre-term labor" hypnosis tape. It worked incredibly well! Each time the contractions started, I'd lie in bed with a glass of water and listen to the tape, and they'd stop.

Three weeks before my due date, I lost my mucous plug on a Saturday morning. We had planned for John to be there for the birth, but the hospital required another adult there specifically to supervise him. Our family lives pretty far away, and since we had no back-up childcare, we had planned for my mother-in-law to arrive the week before my due date and stay until the birth. But that was still two weeks away! So I stubbornly, and somewhat comically, insisted that this couldn't mean anything. I wasn't having this baby yet, and that was that! Having the baby now meant I'd be alone in a hospital room, trying to fight off unnecessary and unwanted interventions and doing my hypnosis by myself, while Lee and John were in the waiting room half a hospital away. If I had to be in a hospital, I wanted my husband there for support, to speak for me as needed so I could focus my hypnosis. And I respected John's desire to be there to welcome his new brother into the world.

Around 10 p.m., I started having very mild contractions, only noticeable because I could feel tightening very low in my uterus, just the bottom third or so. There was absolutely no discomfort. By 3 a.m. I had a small fluid leak. The painless contractions were about five minutes apart, so I called the hospital. The nurse assured me that these were too mild to be real contractions, especially since I wasn't feeling the tightening throughout my uterus. Still unwilling to believe I was in labor, I was only too happy to believe the nurse; so I listened to my pre-term labor tape, curled up and went to sleep.

While listening to my tapes, I'd typically remain "asleep" (in reality, a deep state of hypnosis); this time I awoke a few minutes into the tape to hear the voice saying that I would stay pregnant until 37 weeks, when it would be safe for the baby to be born. It was like someone flipped on a light switch. My brain had grabbed onto that 37-week idea, and having crossed that particular finish line just hours before, went with it. I kept telling myself *no, not now!* I decided the best thing was to keep listening to the tape and relax, and try and get some sleep. I was still experiencing no pain, and after John's birth, it couldn't possibly be this easy, right? I had all the time in the world. So I thought.

Fall asleep I finally did, only to awake at 6 a.m. to what felt a bit like having someone snap a rubber band somewhere inside my uterus (I'll admit, that wasn't especially pleasant!), and a gush of water. Uh oh! I grabbed a towel to stem the tide and waddled my way into the guest room to wake my sleeping husband. Once I had him sufficiently awake, I took a quick shower, dressed and went back to bed to listen to the birth guide tapes. By then the contractions had started again, not really painful, but I was feel-ing them all the way up my uterus, and I could feel with my hand that they were very hard. They were long, maybe 90 seconds, and two minutes apart.

I was so quiet, and appeared so peaceful, Lee decided it was an ideal time to do the dishes, start a little laundry, take a shower; then he asked if he had time to shave, which earned him a snappish "no" in reply! My birthing instincts are very primal. I'd be happy to do as the animals do, and crawl away somewhere to have my baby alone, in peace and quiet. Pain or no pain, loving patience isn't my strong suit during labor!

Lee got things ready, packed our bag (yes, you really should pack your bag at 36 weeks, if not sooner!) and loaded the car while I sat on the bed. I was experiencing very mild discomfort, but more importantly, restlessness, this strange sensation of being unable to find a comfortable position, a need to be moving. I wound up standing, leaning over my bed, swaying gently from side to side, or lying hands and knees on my bed, which led to a few moments of feeling "pushy"; but I was obviously incomplete. I could tell from this sense of incompleteness that I had a "lip." And yet somehow, in spite of every possible sign of being in transition, the contractions were so mild I still thought I was in early labor.

Once Lee finally had himself and John ready, and the van loaded, I made my way downstairs, into the front seat of the van, buckled my seatbelt, and we slowly backed out of the garage.

Uuuuugggggguuuuhhhhhh…. The textbook "birthing moan," an unmistakably low, guttural sound. It was accompanied by a contraction, an urge to visit the bathroom, and the sudden understanding of what that probably meant.

My wise husband, instinctively knowing what that sound must mean turned to look at me, near panic in his eyes, and asked if he needed to call 911. Having nothing but John's birth to compare this to, the prospect of an emergency delivery had us both a little nervous. I nodded, we pulled back into the garage, he sprinted inside to grab the phone, dialed on the way back to the garage, finally saying, "My wife is having a baby," and I started to yell "head, Head, HEAD!!!" When Lee told the operator that the baby was coming, her reply was to tell me not to push. But I was a mere passenger on this wild ride, and our new son was at the wheel. Tell him, not me! Somehow, my husband managed, with the phone tucked between his head and shoulder, to reach down and catch him as he made his ten-second descent, out my body, through the side of my underwear, and headed for the floor of our van. Nice catch, Dad! My husband stood, grinning like the Cheshire cat, holding our son. He whooped out, "Next time, we'll have the baby at home!" I tried to point out the irony of planning our next child while this one was still attached, a nuance that was lost on the proud Papa. And proud we were. A mere hour after my water broke, and one and a half contractions of what must be the shortest pushing stage ever, Michael David was here.

The most remarkable thing is that even when my water broke, I didn't realize I'd been in labor. Compared to John's birth, the only accurate description of which would be painful, Michael's birth at it's worst point, transition, was easier than mild PMS. I had all the signs, the restlessness, the need to move, the long contractions with only seconds between them. Unrecognizable in comparison, because it was just that easy, that peaceful. There was no "rim of fire," just a slight sensation of warmth. I had no tearing, in spite of the rather precipitous birth, and the less-than-ideal positioning (for me that is... it seemed quite ideal for Michael!). It was as easy a birth as I could ever hope for.

As my hypnosis instructor pointed out, not only did my mind give me the gentle, peaceful, painless birth I'd worked so hard for, my longstanding desire for a home birth was realized as well, if in a somewhat unorthodox manner. What the mind believes, the mind creates!

When we unexpectedly found ourselves pregnant again four months later, there was no doubt we would be returning to hypnosis. This time we wanted a planned home birth, with a midwife whose commitment to low-intervention births was as strong as ours. Given my desire for quiet during birth, having that control was extremely important to me.

We did find such a midwife, and three weeks after Michael's first birthday, we welcomed Richard Andrew (affectionately known as Drew) to our family. They were both born on Sundays, in the early morning, at home; but under completely different circumstances. This time we knew what we wanted, and had the confidence from our last experience to make it happen.

When my water broke, Drew was so low that there was no amniotic fluid leak, just that familiar rubber band snap awaking me rather abruptly. I woke Lee, and we called the midwife and her assistant (who happened to live blocks from us). The assistant made it in record time, not knowing how much notice this baby was going to give her, tying her shoes as she ran in the door. When she checked me, I was five centimeters, which led my husband and

I to think we were in for a bit of a wait (we were wrong, he came an hour and a half later). The midwife came, checked the fetal heart rate, pronounced all to be progressing well, and I snuggled into the nest of pillows the assistant had put together for me.

I have to admit, this time it was a bit more intense, but as I explained to those who ask, on a scale of 1 to 10, John's birth was an 11, Michael's was .25, and Drew was maybe .75. While Michael was accidentally born at home, with Drew we'd made the choice, which I took full responsibility for. But the "what ifs" were an unwanted distraction from the mental work of hypnosis. I had to put those worries aside, keep them in perspective so I could stay calm and relaxed. The tapes were a big help with this, urging me to focus on my body, my hypnotic anesthesia and my baby. Just as I'd always wanted, the midwife and assistant sat quietly in a corner, checking the heart rate periodically while I rested in my pillow nest, looking limp, peaceful and relaxed according to Lee. Every so often he'd come to stroke my arm in loving support, and I'd impatiently brush him away, just wanting dark, quiet, peace. Thankfully he was amused, rather than offended by my unusual reaction to his gentle touch.

I can't describe how wonderful it is to feel only minimal discomfort, but feel with absolute clarity the process of a baby making his way into the world, every twist, turn, wriggle, slowly working his way out, feeling where the cervix is in the way and where it's dilated. Once again, I issued forth with the birthing moan. The midwife came and placed my top leg on her shoulder while the assistant went to get my husband and our sons. I did what's called "breathing the baby down," meaning, between contractions, inhaling, and gently, slowly pushing, ensuring a slower, more controlled crowning and less chance of tearing. It worked wonders. Drew's birth was a bit longer than Michael's, but not by much. One little contraction, but just as easy. It was the experience of a lifetime, the quiet, gentle birth of my dreams. No counting, no "cheerleading," no "push, Push PUSH!", no hospital bed, bright lights, IVs. I was allowed to do what came naturally, and it was absolutely blissful and beautiful.

I am so lucky that we found Kerry, and were able to have the tools and knowledge we needed to have a birth that was optimal for us all; for me, the baby and for our family. They were wonderful experiences, more wonderful than I could have imagined until they'd happened. As a natural skeptic, I had my moments of doubt. But there's no doubting the results. All it takes is the time, commitment and the willingness to set your fears aside.

Lee's Version

Michaels' birth was simply the most awesome experience I have ever been a part of. So when Crystal told me she was pregnant again, we both knew we'd be attending another Hypnobabies class. We were able to get into a class, but I was only able to attend the last two sessions due to child care problems. (The last time around, I was only able to attend the first three classes, so now I can say I've attended a full Hypnobabies course.)

In the beginning of the class series, Crystal was experiencing some preterm pressure waves, so she wasn't able to completely practice all of the techniques and tools we were taught. Kerry gave Crystal a script to stop the preterm labor and it worked well. With that help, Crystal was able to hit the magical 37-week threshold. And funny enough, once she hit that threshold, her preterm pressure waves stopped almost altogether.

Then one morning, about 7 a.m., I was awoken with, "I think my water broke, and I'm starting to feel uncomfortable." The adrenaline started to pump, and I started preparing our bedroom for the arrival of the baby. Crystal called the midwife, who lives not too far from us, and she was over in about 10 minutes. The midwife, Cheryl, helped me get everything ready and get Crystal into a comfortable position. She checked Crystal and said she was five centimeters or a stretchy six centimeters; it was about 7:30 a.m. My focus was to get Crystal listening to the *Birth Affirmations* CD and get her focused, as I thought things were just starting up.

Crystal got situated and started listening to her CD. I had to go let the other midwife, Leslie, in and check on my two sons. Leslie got set up in our room, and did so very quietly. I would check in occasionally to see how things were progressing, and to ensure that Crystal was "doing her thing." She seemed very peaceful and focused. After the *Birth Affirmations* CD finished, I put in the *Birth Guide* CD. I left the room because I needed to check on my sons again, and the midwives were so great at letting Crystal stay focused and not interfering with her.

At one point I heard Cheryl talking on the phone to someone, saying she wouldn't be very long, so I figured things were progressing faster than I expected. And sure enough, right then Cheryl told me it was time. I got into the room just in time to hear Crystal let out a good moan. Not a scream, not a yell, just a calm moan like Kerry described in the class; it was exactly what I heard from Crystal last time around. With that moan, I saw Drew's head come out. And with the next moan, he slid right out, screaming up a storm. Wow!!! It was truly amazing to see, Drew in Crystal's arms, and she wasn't panting like she'd run a marathon. After a few minutes I cut the cord, and the midwives finished cleaning up Drew and delivering the placenta.

I must admit that I was skeptical the first time around, with our son Michael. But I figured that I would give my wife the best chance at having a truly natural drug-free childbirth. That meant going to the classes, practicing scripts with her, doing the communications exercises, and not imposing my own skepticism on her. My skepticism waned a little bit more with each class as she gained another tool, and she was able to use that tool effectively. By the time Michael arrived, and I saw first-hand how she put those tools to use, and the drastic difference from our first son's birth, I was sold.

The best part is, you get to experience one of the most amazing life experiences the way it was intended: in peace, calm and tranquility.

A Mother's Guidance: Early on, prepare for Plan B, especially if this is your first pregnancy and you're not sure how your body will respond to labor. Accept the possibility of unexpected complications, and know what your options would be should complications arise. Make the necessary decisions, and emotional preparations, and make sure at least one of your support people knows of Plan B and has it in writing. Then put Plan B out of your head. Completely! Create the birth of your dreams—first in your mind, then with your body. Let nothing, not even yourself, get in the way.

Crystal Irwin is a home-schooling mom. Her husband Lee is a systems analyst. Crystal and Lee live with their three sons in Pasadena, California.

ALREADY SO IN LOVE

BY DEANNA HLYWKA

I TRULY CANNOT remember a time when I wasn't thinking of when this little being would come into my life. I will start with when I subconsciously became aware of a life existing inside of me.

It was September and I was completing my postgraduate studies. There were signs coming from everywhere that should have clued me in. Megan, a classmate, was selling pregnancy tests and I bought some to have on hand. I had just received them when my husband Kregg left to go to Hunt Camp with his dad and brother for the weekend. I was planning a quiet weekend to myself. A good friend of mine, Carey, and I were taking part in the Run for the Cure, a breast cancer fundraiser. We met downtown and chatted the entire run, but the topic was a new one: I was baby crazy. I talked about how I was really pumped to have a baby and could not stop thinking about it. After the run, I went home and watched a movie, but for some reason I wanted to try out a pregnancy test... just to see how they worked and what a negative one would look like.

After completing the test, I watched for the results... it was not as clear as the package indicated a negative test should look. "Great," I thought, "I won't be using these tests on any of my patients."

Kregg came home on Monday night and I told him about the test. Since I took it, the idea that I could be pregnant had been playing around the edges of my mind. My last menstrual period had been a little less than one month ago. We decided to repeat the test. This time it was much more clear—clearly positive! I was not convinced, so we repeated the test. This time, Kregg took one as well. This cleared things up… his was definitely negative and mine was definitely positive. From that point on, I knew there was a very real person growing inside of me, someone I had only imagined before.

As a holistic-health-crazed newly-pregnant woman, I immediately thought about my baby's healthcare provider and my fears of being in a hospital. I began to consider my options. In Canada, pregnant women have three choices: a family physician, an obstetrician or a midwife. From the experiences of my friends and colleagues, as well as my research and intuition, I knew that the midwifery model was what I wanted. I wanted as little intervention as possible, and as much warmth and attention as I could get. Knowing that, I met with two midwifery practices and decided on The Riverdale Midwives.

I was assigned to Tia, a midwife with a wonderful quietude about her and an excellent reputation. We got to know her over the months and felt very informed and satisfied with our care. Kregg and I planned a home birth, with the assistance of a birthing pool. We still needed one more person to join our team—a labor assistant. Kregg and I met with two women who were both experienced labor assistants AND naturopathic doctors—how wonderful! We chose Julie and started working with her to ensure all bases were covered.

As my baby grew and grew (and so did I), I tried many things to help our family connect—Kregg, myself and our babe were becoming a unit. We played music and did guided meditations; we sang; we read (to baby and about baby); we massaged (amateurly and professionally); we shined lights; we sculpted and photographed. But most importantly, we loved our growing creation. And I loved having our baby inside me—it was amazing, it felt amazing. And there were only a few times that it was not amazing… due to intense heartburn that kept me awake at night.

Although our home is in Toronto, we actually traveled quite a bit that year—to Florida for Christmas to see my sister, Joyce; a cruise to the Caribbean in February for a break from the cold Canadian winter; and back to Florida to unwind from the school year in May. All of these trips provided ample opportunity for belly shots galore!

I had our baby on board for a full year of courses at the Canadian College of Naturopathic Medicine, and saw patients in the clinic for one month. This baby was becoming saturated with the principles of naturopathic medicine. Also during that time, we were on TV! City TV did a segment on the school, and one focus was on pregnant women—enter Deanna (and Roen) to receive an acupuncture demonstration!

With a due date of June 8th, everything was in place and ready by May 25th. The birthing pool was in our loft, the midwife and naturopath had come for home visits, the phone list was in place, those who were invited to the birth were notified, snacks, teas and supplies were ready and waiting. My hopes for my birth experience were that it would be a safe birth in the comfort of my home, surrounded by friends and family who could support and welcome our new babe. Kregg, our naturopath (Julie), my mom, sister, friend (Carey) and possibly midwife (Tia) would be there through the laboring process and would put the phone list into play as the pushing stage neared. The others (Kregg's family, the rest of my family and my friend Leslie) were welcome to come to see our baby's entry into the world if they wanted to.

Finally the days were getting closer and closer and the excitement grew. My sister Joyce was coming from Florida for the birth and was paranoid that she wasn't going to make it. But she did, and it was close. Monday morning, the day I picked her up at the airport, I woke with some Braxton-Hicks contractions. They did not last long, so we assumed they were just for practice.

Tuesday night we worked on the third and final belly cast, and Thursday night we went to the Marché for dinner. Joyce loves that place and was worried she wouldn't get to go once baby arrived! We had a great feast that ended with two slices of blueberry pie. Yummy. Kregg went to visit a friend for a while, and Joyce and I went home to watch a movie—*All the Pretty Horses*. I couldn't concentrate on the movie, since I was getting some pretty strong Braxton-Hicks again… every seven minutes, and lasting about one minute. By the time we were getting into bed they had subsided, but woke me up sometime around 6 a.m. Since the baby was not due for another week I just lay in bed for a while, thinking "more practicing." After about an hour, I woke up Kregg and he started timing them. Every four minutes, lasting 30 seconds to a minute. Consistently. So we got up and I took a bath, wondering if the warm water would make them go away before we got ready for work/clinic. They remained strong, and we gave Julie and Tia a call. They both said they would be right over, as it sounded like the real thing. While they were en route, Kregg prepped the pool and started filling it while also helping me along—the contractions were getting stronger. Joyce cleaned up, since there would be several people in the place for who knew how long!

Our midwife Tia arrived at 9 a.m. and did an internal exam— there was some show (which made things real to me) and I was dilated to three centimeters! She suggested that I rest and predicted that our baby would arrive early Saturday morning. She left to carry out some appointments, but promised to return shortly. We called school and told them that I would not be in, and then put the phone list into action. Carey was notified and told to round up some space heaters. Julie, our naturopath, arrived next, and time flew from this point on.

It is difficult to remember the order of events that followed. My mom arrived around 11 a.m. and I believe that we were upstairs in a bit of discomfort. I found it quite uncomfortable to lie down with the contractions, but Tia told me to get as much rest as possible and I tried to follow those instructions. Upstairs in the loft, my eyes kept going to a disgusting plaid shirt of Kregg's that I really didn't like and had asked him to get rid of. Finally I was tired of looking at it and it had to go. Julie thought it was all pretty funny. As the hours passed, my support team kept everyone informed on my progress, and I moved from bed to tub to toilet and back to the tub, which I preferred. It was so nice and warm and relaxing in the tub. Between contractions I was able to float in the warm water and recover. Tia monitored fetal heart rate while Julie and Kregg took turns massaging my back, and getting me drinks and popsicles.

I really had no concept of time that day, but eventually I began to feel a lot of pressure. I was loud with each contraction, moaning the way that I was told would help my body open up. But with the increased pressure I also felt some urge to push. Tia instructed me not to as the last time she checked me I had only been six centimeters dilated. As the urges continued she decided to check me again, and this time she found me to be nine centimeters dilated. Tia said that it was time. This freaked me right out, since it was only 5 p.m. and she had told me to expect my baby the next morning. But, there wasn't much time to freak, since in two more contractions and a few screams, his head was out. And I was touching a full head of long, dark, silky hair under the water. That was crazy. One more push and we were pulling a little baby up onto my chest. It was amazing the way the baby just molded to my skin—curled in a little ball on my chest.

I snuck a peek to see if we had a girl or boy—for a few moments I was the only one who knew! Then I told everyone. He was so cute… dark hair, red lips and just a little cry before he cuddled right up into my neck. We stayed there for a while in the tub, keeping him swaddled in warm blankets, as we waited for the cord to stop pulsating so Kregg could cut it. Once that happened, the back-up midwife arrived to help Kregg with the baby and I got out of the tub to deliver the placenta on the birthing stool. The midwives examined the placenta and announced that it had an extra lobe on it!

Then, we rested. The midwives examined both of us and made sure that we were breastfeeding successfully before they left for the day. Julie had prepared teas and compresses for me to speed my recovery along.

I was glad that I had people around who knew how I wanted things that day, because at the time I really could not have given any instructions. I did give everyone a copy of the birth plan and a list of things they could/couldn't do! Carey actually took a shower because she was wearing perfume! And people were great; they kept things quiet and warm and dark. I wanted our baby to be welcomed into this world in a peaceful and loving environment, surrounded by those who will love him the most. I was fortunate that I had such wonderful support that day, and was allowed to have the birth that I could only imagine… it was perfect. It was so unbelievable to be able to touch his little body after being so close all that time. I was extremely happy to meet our baby, since I was already so in love with him!

A Mother's Guidance: Listen to your body and honor what it tells you. Get as many caregivers and support people as you need. Become informed and educated, but allow others to educate you too. Surround yourself with people and friends who make you feel good about yourself and support you for who you are as much as possible during your pregnancy. Labor and birth in an environment that is safe and comfortable for you. Embrace the experience—it will change your life!

I consider this book a must read: Frederick Leboyer's *Birth without Violence.* I asked everyone who would be attending my birth to read it! I read *The Thinking Woman's Guide to a Better Birth* by Henci Goer, *Misconceptions* by Naomi Wolfe, *Immaculate Deception* by Suzanne Arms, *Nurturing the Unborn Child* by Thomas Verny and Pamela Weintraub, plus many others—keep an open mind and everything you experience will impact your birth!

Additional Thoughts: Predictions about the length of labor from a well-intentioned friend, nurse, doctor or midwife can scare or frustrate the laboring mom. Thankfully in this case the labor didn't stall with the belief that she would have the baby the next day, as the midwife predicted.

Labor is unpredictable. Dilation is not linear—women can move from three centimeters to crowning in less than 30 minutes.

Deanna Hlywka is a labor assistant and naturopathic doctor living and practicing in Toronto, Ontario, Canada. Her work focuses on perinatal health and pediatrics. She lives in the city with her husband Kregg and son Roen.

COFFEE, PLEASE!

BY MIRIAM PEARSON-MARTINEZ

ASK ANY WOMAN about the birth of her child, and you can expect to hear a story full of imagery, detail and emotion. I know this because I am a midwife. The profound effect birth has on a woman's soul is the reason I have dedicated my life to the families that seek my guidance. Yet even knowing this, it still catches me by surprise when I reflect on the birth of my own children.

It's funny how calm I was during my third pregnancy. I was a newly anointed midwife, and my training had given me a new-found confidence I had not experienced with my previous two pregnancies. It wasn't the book knowledge that led me to my new-found peace, but rather the flashcard images of happy, healthy mothers and babies that had become engrained in my mind. This was a perfect pregnancy.

Just shy of my 38th week, I fell while visiting the future site of a friend's backyard pool. I felt fine and my baby was moving, but I knew that had I been one of my own clients, I would strongly suggest an ultrasound and monitoring. So I made a call to my consulting physician, Dr. D., and off I went to the hospital, the last place I would want to birth a healthy baby.

The ultrasound showed everything was fine. (At 37 weeks, I was still patient enough to ask the technician not to reveal the gender of my baby.) I had not hurt either of us with the fall, but since the baby was not very active, Dr. D. suggested a follow-up appointment the next day to consider the need for an induction. I left the hospital, determined to have my baby that night—at home.

I called my midwives, Janice and Laura, and advised them that I was going to take matters into my own hands and try a natural induction. I took an herbal tincture and some castor oil (an old midwives' trick), and sat back to wait. It was not long before the surges began to wash over my belly. I was amazed at myself. The Hypno-Birthing techniques I had been teaching others for the last three years were so engrained in my head that I had no fear, no pain.

Each time I began to feel my belly harden, I would close my eyes and transport myself. I had not considered where I would mentally transport myself to during labor, but almost instinctively I found myself at a peaceful time and place, enjoying my labor. Six years earlier, I had joined my parents in Key West, Florida. Each day I would borrow the dingy from their boat and escape for a little alone time, piloting out to an empty cove to fish. As is tradition in my Cuban family, I fished with only the nylon line. There was no rod or reel, just me, the line and the fish. It was very primal. There were no instruments helping me, much like my labor. It was me, my body, and my baby, and no one else could understand or help provide what I needed at that moment.

I strolled through my home, enjoying the company of the midwives and my husband. We spent most of the time joking about our lives as midwives, and those out-of-the-ordinary births we had attended. Ironically, most outsiders would have considered this particular labor to be "out of the ordinary." At around three in the morning I asked that my friend Jennifer be called and invited. Jennifer had been a doula client of mine just a year and a half earlier, and we had grown to be good friends. She too had experienced a calm birth and I knew that if anybody would understand, it would be her.

Jennifer arrived quickly. We spent an hour or so looking through my photo albums and listening to Simon and Garfunkel. Pictures of my two sons, myself and my husband Zach were brought out as we tried to imagine what the newest member of our family would look like. On the third or fourth album, I ran into a picture of that fishing trip I was revisiting. I became so excited that I began to point and shout, "That's it! That is where I am having my baby." I am sure it seemed like gibberish to those around me; it wasn't until later that I would explain what I meant.

I suddenly felt very tired. It was close to 6:30 in the morning and the sun was rising. I stretched out on the couch with Zach at my side and took an hour-long nap, only half waking with the sound of my own voice bellowing a low groan. I was suddenly awakened by a different sort of feeling. I matter-of-factly stated, "I need to get in the tub," as I bounded in. What a shock... I was in the heat of labor, and the tub felt like ice water. Someone had shut off the heater by mistake. Just as quickly as I jumped in, I was out. I laugh now, thinking about the sight of me running through the house naked, shouting, "Warm, I need warm!" I got into my tiny bathtub and sung the songs of labor, moaning through each surge as they got stronger. Laura sat with me, assuring me that I doing fine. I saw Jennifer and Zach running back and forth with pots of what I assumed was hot water. I don't remember who or how, but someone told me that my big tub was ready. This could not have come at a better moment. I felt the baby moving down and knew it would not be long at all.

Zach called my mother, who lived upstairs, and told her it would not be much longer. She came down to join us just after I got back in the warm tub. My younger son awoke too. It was as if the baby was calling everyone to greet her. The funny thing is that at that moment, my mother began to offer Cuban coffee to those who had gathered with me. When she asked how many, I raised my hand. Nothing sounded better than an espresso at that moment. She took my son with her upstairs to get it for me.

I began to feel the control I had experienced earlier slip away. I was glad to see it go. There is something very primitive about birth and I enjoy experiencing it that way. I swayed my hips and moved my body, dancing with the baby. As I rolled onto my back and sang out, I could feel her head begin to descend. I asked Zach to get in the tub. I was on my hands and knees when Janice suggested I should turn over and let the baby slip past my cervix. I did just that, and with the next contraction I announced, "Here she comes!" I yelled out in relief and pain as I felt her head come out. With the next breath, I instructed Zach to help the first shoulder emerge. Even though he is a trained physician, he had not attended many natural births and had only caught one baby himself. He had some trouble so I uttered, "Laura, help him." She did, and seconds later I was holding my baby. I saw her face and just knew it was a girl. My first little girl.

As I looked up and out the window, I saw my mother and my son Elijah returning with the coffee. Wow… what felt like hours had been only a few minutes. My older son Seth was called into the room, and he and Eli cut the umbilical cord together.

The best part of experiencing the birth process at home came just an hour later, when my little girl (later named Ella Zeida) and I cuddled up in my bed and took a wonderful and well-deserved nap.

A Mother's Guidance: Don't ask anyone's opinion on how to have a good birth. Just enjoy the ride.

Additional Thoughts: Miriam says, "There were no instruments helping me, much like my labor. It was me, my body, and my baby and no one else could understand or help provide what I needed at that very moment." At some level, every birth is unassisted, no matter where you have it or who is attending. Only you can control your thoughts and your feelings. You have control of your reactions, and whether or not you trust your body and intuition. At the same time, you aren't in control because your body takes over and you need to get out of your own way. So many times, laboring women ask, "Am I doing this right?" The question is, are you following your body's cues?

Miriam Pearson-Martinez is a licensed and certified midwife, as well as the proud mother of three children. Her husband Zach is a pediatrician. Both are advocates of natural, out-of-hospital births.

FROM SOMEWHERE DEEP INSIDE

BY JENNIFER POWERS

THE BIRTH OF MY SECOND child, Jonathan Reynolds, was the birth that I had hoped to have with my first. But when it comes to making plans for a birth, it's important to remember that they are just that: plans. And Mother Nature often has her own plan. With my first pregnancy, leaking waters led to an induction with Pitocin. Although I was able to give birth without pain medications, I felt like I missed out on the chance to experience truly natural labor and birth. For the birth of our second child, I really wanted to know what it was like to feel unmedicated contractions, and to let my body do what came naturally.

During my first pregnancy, I had done a lot of reading and research. My second time around, I focused more on mental preparation: I had affirmations taped around my house; I did a little journaling and poetry writing; and I listened to relaxation tapes while falling asleep at night. I also did birth art with my doula and on my own. I felt a little silly about trying this at first… I don't consider myself to be an artistic person. But once my doula got me started, I loved it! I believed, and still do, that getting through birth is at least 50% mental, if not more. I knew that staying calm and positive would be essential.

Another way I prepared for the birth was with a blessing ceremony that my sister planned for me. It was an inspiring and fun way to celebrate my pregnancy and the upcoming birth. Some of the women who are special to me came to my home and each person shared a birth story, or a poem or a blessing. They had written them down on paper and pasted them into a journal for me to keep. They made a birth necklace for me, each woman choosing a bead to string. We even had two female body artists come to the house to decorate my big belly with henna! It was so beautiful! They also decorated anyone else who wanted it, and everyone did. The blessing ceremony helped me to experience this birth as a joyous rite of passage.

Two days past my due date, on a Friday night, my husband Doug and I decided to have one more date; we chose an Indian restaurant, hoping the spicy foods would get things going. My first contraction came in the car on the way there. It felt just the way people describe it, beginning in the back and squeezing around to the front, but I didn't want to get my hopes up. During dinner they came every 15 to 20 minutes, so I told Doug that I might be having contractions but wasn't sure. When we got home we took a brisk walk twice around the block. They still seemed irregular, and didn't really hurt; they just felt like a big rubber band tightening around my lower abdomen and back. As we passed a neighbor here and there on the sidewalk, we said a polite hello, but I remember wanting to tell every person I saw, "I'm having contractions! This could be it! Woo-hoo!" That night I nursed my son to sleep, and while he was nursing the contractions came regularly at five minutes apart, but slowed back down after we were done. I told my husband he should go to bed. If this was the real thing, he would need to be rested. I tried to sleep too... but I was so excited!

I called my doula, and she said to call her back when I needed help getting through the contractions. She also suggested I take a shower, which I did. I noticed the contractions came closer together while in the shower, which I now know is a sign that it's the real thing. Then I called my midwife to put her on alert, and lit my blessing ceremony candles. I tried watching television while sitting on my birth ball, and I had to lean on the back of a chair, rocking my hips back and forth during contractions. At 1:30 a.m. I tried to wake Doug to keep me company and distract me a little, but he was not about to wake up. He said, "But it's 1:30, why don't you come to bed?" I said, "It hurts too much." He said, "What hurts?" then rolled over and went back to sleep! (He says he doesn't remember this conversation.) So I called my mom, who lives next door, and she came over to keep me company. She also timed the contractions for me. They were now seven minutes apart and lasting 60 seconds. At this point I was down on all fours, rocking and sort of blowing through the contractions, trying to keep my mouth and face loose and relaxed. Doug eventually woke up and the three of us hung out, organizing photos (my labor project) and just enjoying the anticipation between contractions.

Contractions continued to get steadily more painful and a little longer each time. When they started to make me cry, I called my doula and asked her to come over. She lives about 45 minutes away. I also called my sister, our designated photographer. By the time we finished the calls, I was crying and moaning loudly, rocking on all fours to get through contractions. Fortunately my son slept through all of this in the next room!

I got to the point where I didn't want anyone talking or touching me during contractions. At one point I even told my Mom to shut up! I consciously thought about not saying, "ow, ow, ow," but instead saying to myself, "This is good, this is good." I also found myself turning down all the lights in the house. Everything I did was pure instinct; I never thought about what to do or what noises to make. These sounds were just coming from somewhere deep inside of me. Doug said later that I sounded like a cow in serious pain (thanks, honey).

It was a warm night and our windows were open. I remember thinking that a concerned neighbor just might call the cops! I asked my Mom to take my son to her house—I didn't want him to be scared by the noises. And then, all of a sudden, in the midst of a contraction I felt the baby moving down inside me!

"I think we should go now," I said. Just as we were about to walk out, in walked my sister. We called my doula on her cell phone and told her to meet us at the hospital.

What followed was the most exciting truck ride of my life! I was behind the front seat on all fours, concentrating on keeping the baby in. I was yelling things like, "Go, go, go!" to Doug, and "Stay, stay, stay," to the baby. He was flying, running every red light he could. Fortunately there wasn't much traffic at 5:30 in the morning, and the hospital was only about 20 minutes away, but it seemed like forever! I kept talking to the baby the whole way there, telling him to take a break, stay in, don't move, you don't want to be born in a truck…. Doug called the midwife from his cell phone to tell her we were on our way to the hospital. I was glad he remembered—I had forgotten we needed to do that! After the baby was born, the midwife said she knew it was serious when Doug introduced himself as "Jennifer's wife" on the phone!

We got to the hospital, but we couldn't tell where the ER entrance was. They were doing some renovations and the main entrance wasn't being used. We must have ended up at a back entrance, because when we got to the doors they wouldn't open, and there wasn't a soul around. There was a button to push to open the doors, but they still weren't opening. Doug began to bang on the door and yell, while I stood there moaning. Finally the doors opened, and a woman came over and told us to go to the ninth floor. She didn't ask any questions; I guess she could tell why we were there! We finally got onto the right floor and into a room. The nurses checked me and found that I was ten centimeters dilated and ready to go!

At this point I went through the only negative part of my whole birth experience. The nurses immediately started barking orders at me, in a very condescending way. They started hooking me up to monitors, and when I said that my midwife had agreed to intermittent monitoring, they said, "Not at this point." I asked if they would check me on all fours and they said no, I had to be on my back. I said I wanted to wait for my midwife, and they said there wasn't time. They had called a different doctor but he wasn't there yet either. They told me to begin pushing. I was yelling—well, more like a loud moaning—and they told me to be quiet! I got mad and said, "Don't tell me how to breathe!" and they said, "Fine, you'll just be pushing for two hours like you did for your first one." I couldn't believe how mean they were! Just then my doula and midwife walked in, and the whole atmosphere changed instantly. What a relief! I was so glad to see them.

My biggest moment of fear came right before pushing. I knew how much it was going to hurt, but the only way out is by going through it. I pushed while lying on my side with one leg up in the air, which felt right at the time. Doug and my doula were by my side, and the midwife was waiting to guide the baby out. After the first couple of pushes, my midwife asked if she could break my water, which I agreed to. I remember feeling like I needed to rest between pushes, but I was afraid of losing ground, or the baby's head slipping back up. My doula assured me that it was OK to rest, and catch my breath between pushes. At one point my midwife told me to reach down and feel the baby's head. I was surprised at how soft and squishy it felt, not hard at all. My sister later told me that as his head was coming out, Jonathan was moving it from side to side, trying to wiggle his way out. I felt a ring of fire and decided it was time to push this baby all the way out. I grabbed my doula by the shoulder, grabbed the bedrail with the other hand, and PUUUSHED! (After the birth I wondered if she would find bruises the next day). Suddenly, Jonathan was out! The midwife held him up and all I thought was, "Oh, he is perfect, so beautiful!"

She laid him on my chest, and within a couple minutes the cord stopped pulsating; Doug cut it. While he lay on my chest, the nurses rubbed him until he let out a little cry. Doug and I just looked at Jonathan, and felt his slippery warm soft body on mine. He began to nuzzle and suck right away.

Jonathan was born 30 minutes after we walked into the hospital, after 25 minutes of pushing, and 11 hours after that first contraction. He was eight pounds, seven ounces, and 21.5 inches long.

My midwife was awesome; she turned down the lights and made sure the nurses left us alone for about the first hour or so after he was born. I couldn't take my eyes off him. A few hours later, my two-year-old son came to the hospital to meet Jonathan. Upon seeing his little brother for the first time, he said with surprise and awe in his voice, "A tiny wittle one!"

A Mother's Guidance: If at all possible, hire a doula. And prepare yourself mentally for the birth. Don't just educate yourself on all possible procedures; prepare yourself to go with the pain, and let your body do its work (as opposed to fighting the pain and trying to avoid it). Even though you may have a birth plan, remember that it is really your body that is planning this birth and all you can control is your response to it.

I did not take any classes, but my doula did come to the house twice to talk about the upcoming birth. Resources that I enjoyed include: *The Thinking Woman's Guide to a Better Birth* by Henci Goer; *Birthing from Within* by Pam England and Rob Horowitz; *Mothering* magazine and the corresponding website (www.mothering.com); and *Spiritual Midwifery* by Ina May Gaskin.

Jennifer Powers lives in Cincinnati with her husband Doug and two sons, Bo and Jonathan. She spends most of her time with her boys, but also works a few hours each week as a speech pathologist, and enjoys singing with MUSE, the Cincinnati Women's Choir.

EWFOUND WONDER

BY SHANNON LOUCKS

I BEGAN MY JOURNEY into motherhood on September 25th, when I discovered I was pregnant with my first child. I was elated, grateful and full of questions. I had known for some time that I wanted, and was capable of having, a home birth. My husband Pucky and I quickly set about assembling our team.

With the assistance of our doula, my loving sister Lisa, we drafted a list of questions for a potential midwife. The first midwife assured us we could have a home birth, but said we would not plan for it until the 36th week of pregnancy. But I wanted to plan my home birth, mentally, from the start. The next midwife shared with us that she preferred home births. She made sure I knew that I was in charge, that decisions were mine to make, while she was there to provide information and support. It was then that I knew Susan would join my husband and sister as the fourth member of my birthing team.

My journey toward birth was a physical, mental and spiritual adventure. I maintained an exercise routine from the start, walking for an average of 30 minutes a day, four times a week. Being outside helped revive my spirit. I found morning sickness and fatigue were actually lessened when I was exercising. It was a great way to get my happy hormones hopping.

I read what I could on prenatal care, but this was tricky—the first book I picked up terrified me. It focused on what can go wrong during a pregnancy, as well as things to avoid eating, doing and even smelling. It really rattled me. I switched gears, looking for publications that were written by a midwife, doula or alternative care practitioner. I really wanted to know what was happening in my body and how best to facilitate a healthy pregnancy.

I also began a journal to my little one. I shared my hopes and dreams, and carved out a piece of time to just focus on my child. I spent time at the beach visualizing my ideal birth, breathing in the crisp salt air, breathing out the fears. Mother Earth was an incredible source of strength for me, and I communicated this energy to the baby growing in my womb. Toward the end of my pregnancy, I filled my house with the affirmations that I had been practicing since month six, reading them repeatedly as I went about my day.

My belly grew beyond what I thought possible, with my baby kicking, flipping and twisting inside. Each time I felt a rumble inside, it filled my heart with a joy I had never known. My pregnancy progressed normally, with no complications, and our plan for a home birth was on track. When I met people who were shocked by our choice for a home birth, I listened politely but quickly turned my attention back to my positive mindset. I believed in my choice. With each midwife visit our team grew closer and stronger. Susan believed in us as much as we believed in ourselves. Her support helped me feel courageous and proud.

In our seventh month we attended prenatal classes through a local doula collective. Our hope was to meet other couples preparing for a similar birth, but this was not the case in our group. We held firm to our birth plan, educating ourselves about the "what ifs" and "what coulds," but in our hearts we prayed for what we wanted. I knew that my positive mindset would help both my baby and me to have the birth we were capable of, a natural birth like so many women before me. I trusted myself to create a safe and gentle environment for my baby to be born into.

In early May, my sister/doula held a blessing ceremony for me. A collection of women who played important roles in my life came together to honor my transition into motherhood. Each woman shared how they knew me and something they appreciated about me. We ate some of my favorite foods while my feet soaked in warm rose petal water. We chanted while weaving a web of bracelets from wrist to wrist, honoring our connectedness as women. The bracelets were a symbol of the circle of strength I would carry into my birthing day. Then I received one piece of advice from each woman, priceless pieces of wisdom from those who had been where I was going.

A week past my due date, I was awakened at 2:09 a.m. by a strong urge to have a bowel movement. With no success I returned to bed, thinking it was just a little indigestion. Ten minutes later I returned to the bathroom… and then back to bed again, hoping for some sleep. Just as I fell back to sleep, there it was again, but this time I stayed put and drifted in and out of sleep. Somewhere in this hazy state, I realized that these urges were occurring every seven minutes. By 3:20 a.m. I was convinced that I was in labor, and I wanted to wake my husband, just so he could hold me. "Honey, I think the baby is coming. But we need to go back to sleep because it could be a long day." That's what they taught us in prenatal classes. So we cuddled up and tried to go back to sleep.

It wasn't to be. Things were moving; my contractions were now six minutes apart, and lying down was not helping me. It was about 4 a.m. at this point and I wanted to walk. I rocked to and fro in front of my living room window. I began to slip into a trance-like state, a place removed from the physical world where all I could know was my body and what it was feeling. I wondered how I could do this all day. I focused on the collective energy of all the birthing women before me and drew in a cleansing breath. By 4:45 my contractions were five minutes apart and my husband decided it was time to wake my sister, who was sleeping in the next room.

From that point on, I lost track of all time. I tried to eat buttered toast, but it came right back up and onto the carpet. I spent a few contractions on the birthing ball while candles where being lit all around me. Music played in the background, a CD of original music made by a friend just for the birth. Without so much as a word, my doula transformed my home into the birthing haven we had discussed long ago.

My contractions became stronger and closer together, and it was time for the bath. Beautiful candles lit the room as I slipped into the warm, soothing water. I could handle the contractions here. I moaned in the comfort of a warm bath, moving deeper into my trance. Some time later I had to leave the bath; I had vomited again.

Sitting on the toilet brought both release and relief for me. I would move from bed to toilet, bed to toilet. During one particularly strong contraction I shouted, "You need to call the midwife now!" My contractions were strong, my mind in an altered state. I lost my breath a few times and got caught in the pain of the contraction. Deep inside, the voice of my friend Susie spoke to me, "Don't fight the contraction; go into it." I did this, and could feel my body being pulled toward the earth. I said to my team, "I think I'm pushing." I allowed my body to continue doing whatever it felt necessary to do.

My husband timed the contractions while offering words of encouragement. My sister was my breath, breathing in rhythm with me, which helped me regain my composure several times. Another trip to the toilet and I felt something. Putting my hand between my legs I exclaimed, "The baby is here! Oh, poor Susan is going to miss it." Without missing a beat, my husband and doula prepared to catch the baby, encouraging me to move off the toilet. My sister could see what was happening and explained that what I felt wasn't actually the baby, it was my membranes bulging.

By 7:40 a.m. I returned to my room and collapsed at the end of the bed. Time was not real to me. Being in my body with my baby was all I could do. With the arrival of the midwife, I returned to the toilet. Seeing my bulged membranes, she encouraged me to return to my room, for the bursting of the membrane would bring my baby. I returned to the foot of the bed, intent on bursting those membranes. I pushed the kind of push only a birthing creature knows, and they ruptured.

Our secondary midwife arrived at this point. In the next push I felt my baby's head coming down. My sister was on my right side as I lay with my torso on the bed and knees on the floor pushing into the ground. She would breathe the calm breath I wanted to be breathing, which always brought me back when I lost my focus. My husband was behind me, reporting every little detail he could see. Susan was there, catching any discharge my body had. The secondary midwife, on my left, was my cheerleader.

While I pushed I could feel my baby's head advancing; when I stopped it retreated. I pushed and groaned in the most primal state. And then, with another push, the head did not retreat; I could surely feel that. I tried to push without a contraction, but with one gentle reminder waited patiently. One huge push brought my son's head into the world... beautiful black hair all over his head, and his little fist stuck to his left cheek. With one good spit he cleared his lungs for a big scream. I flopped on the bed and exclaimed, "That's my baby!" After a short rest I pushed the grand push that brought my son out, right into his proud daddy's hands. At 8:48 a.m. on May 28th, my son entered a hushed, dimly lit room filled with love. Breathless, I turned and wrapped this little piece of magic in my arms, holding him as close to me as I could, forgetting he was still attached to the placenta.

With the placenta birthed, truly easier than the child, I crawled into bed with my newfound wonder. He suckled my breast like a champion, and in that moment I knew why I existed.

A Mother's Guidance: Trust your body and all it knows how to do. My favorite resource was *The Complete Book of Pregnancy and Childbirth* by Sheila Kitzinger. I found this information to be supportive as well as informative.

My affirmations, adapted from a list by Gloria Lemay on www.birthlove.com, included such things as:

- My baby's birth is a calm, joyous experience.
- I direct my energy from my head, down through my body and out my vagina.
- This energy assists my muscles to work efficiently and helps my baby come out easily, effortlessly, comfortably.
- I reach inside and call upon my own strength that is wise, ancient and connected to all women.

Additional Thoughts: Many women find that well-practiced affirmations automatically play in your head during labor, making it easier to maintain a positive mindset.

Shannon Loucks is a new author focused on children's literature, and a mom to her son, as well as a little peanut arriving soon. Her story is a combination of memories and journal pieces. The story is in her son's treasure chest, as a keepsake of the day they met and fell more deeply in love then she ever dreamed.

THE POWER WAS MINE

BY PAMELA JORRICK

I WOKE UP THAT MORNING with a feeling. Maybe this would be the day. She was one day late already, just to let me know who was in charge, I think. Of course at that point I didn't even know that she was a she. I guess there was a lot I didn't know.

I had read enough about birth and babies and mothering; you would think that I would have been prepared. Much that I read seemed so distanced though, like it was just a medical event, not a right of passage. Some of it was akin to a horror story. I couldn't find much reading material that made this whole childbirth thing seem very empowering, but I did read a few things that gave me a glimmer of hope.

I was not going to be one of those women who went to the hospital at the first twinge of discomfort, only to find out that they were only one centimeter dilated, or worse, not even really in labor. *I would know when it was time.* The trouble was, when I woke up that morning... I wasn't sure. I had been feeling achy for a few days, but it was nothing major. Something was different that morning, but I wasn't going to jump the gun. In the birth stories I had read, it seemed that the earlier the woman went to the hospital, the longer the whole thing took, and the more unpleasant interventions were involved. I called my midwife to tell her what I was feeling. "Well, it may be today, or it may be tomorrow. Babies come when they're ready," she told me.

My husband had left before dawn that morning. He was a commercial fisherman and it was crab season. I had the boat captain's cell phone number, but I was hesitant to use it. What if this was nothing, and I made the boat come back early? Then again, what if this was the real thing and my husband missed it? I decided to just wait for a sign and go on with my morning. The tightening in my huge belly increased, but I still felt well enough to walk my dog and work in the garden. The contractions grew stronger and more regular, but I still was not ready to say that this was really labor.

Fortunately, the seas were rough that day and retrieving the crab pots was too difficult. My husband's boat returned around lunch time. When I told him what was going on, he was as excited as a little kid who just found out he's going to Disneyland. He immediately had me walking around the block to "get labor going" like we had read about. This man, who normally walks about as fast as a banana slug, was speeding down the road like one of those jog-walking old ladies, with me waddling alongside. After five or ten blocks, I wanted to rest. My husband was quick to tell me all about how walking helped labor progress and gravity would work against me if I was lying down. "Blah, blah, blah," is what I was thinking. He sounded like one of the adults in the old Charlie Brown cartoons. When he came out with a camera to capture the special memories, I had to laugh and remind myself that babies could hear in the womb. The cursing reply I had in mind would probably not be appropriate.

Things began to speed up, and I really couldn't deny that this was it. Still, for some reason, I was leery of being wrong and looking like an idiot. I could still walk and talk through most contractions, and overall I felt pretty good. I had an appointment with the midwife at 3:30 that day. By 3:00 I was trying to decide whether to go there or straight to the hospital. I opted for the midwife, not wanting to go into the hospital any earlier than I had to. Labor is a private thing for me. I didn't want to be with strangers where I knew I would have IVs and needles and drugs pushed on me.

At the midwife's office, I was having a bit more trouble talking through the contractions. When she checked me, we were all surprised to learn that I was already over halfway there! She suggested that if I was planning on going to the hospital, we ought to get going and she would meet us there.

We arrived at the hospital to find that all the lovely birthing suites with the cheerful home-like floral wallpaper were full. All I wanted at that point was to get in a hot tub of water. They put me in the post-operative room, where women go after cesareans. It only had a shower, so I made use of that. The nurses seemed really anxious to get me in an official birthing room. I am not sure what would have been the big deal about my giving birth in the post-op room. It had a bed and water, that's all I needed. But hospitals have their protocols, and I guess someone got kicked out and a room was cleaned up for me in no time.

When I moved there, I was beginning to tire of this labor business. My midwife checked again and said that I was fully dilated and could begin pushing. I don't know why, but it came as a shock to me that I was going to have to do more work. "Won't the baby just wiggle out on its own?" I asked, not feeling at all up to my task. Logically, I knew this wasn't how it worked, but there is little room for logic in labor. She told me that the baby and I were fine, so there was no hurry.

Part of me was afraid to start pushing, like maybe the baby wouldn't be OK when it came out. Finally, after about 20 minutes of waiting through the contractions, I got sick of it. I realized that I was the only one who could get this show on the road, so I got down to business. Pushing a baby out is, without a doubt, the hardest physical work I have ever done. But it was also a relief because I was doing something proactive. I had never been a physically active person, mind you. I never played sports and didn't run unless something like a rabid dog was chasing me. But birthing my baby, I felt so powerful and strong. I could have shouted, "I am woman, hear me roar!" Of course I opted not to in that setting.

Nevertheless, there was a power I found in childbirth that just doesn't get mentioned in the books and articles. And the power was mine, not some doctor's or nurse's. It was mine.

Within less than half an hour of pushing, she was born. A red-skinned baby with a head full of black hair. She was so peaceful, not crying or fussing like the babies on TV who get whacked on their behind as a welcome to the world. She wasn't all glassy eyed and loaded looking, like the babies I've seen who were born with an epidural. She was quiet, but alert. They laid her on my belly and she just looked up at me, checking out everything with one eye open and one shut. She was alive and healthy and beautiful! And then, all of a sudden, she peed all over me. Apparently that startled her because she started screaming like a banshee. We all started laughing and crying at the same time. I was amazed that I had actually grown this perfect little person inside of me. I named her Lily.

After teasing her father, who had been so sure he spotted a penis on the ultrasound, we got started with nursing. It was a bit shocking at first. I never realized that such a small thing could have such an incredibly strong suction force. But my body adjusted quickly and I was in love with the idea that I was still growing her. We adjusted the hospital bed, snuggled down and just enjoyed being together, our new little family. It was definitely the most incredible and empowering thing I had ever done.

A Mother's Guidance: I read the usual *What to Expect When You're Expecting* books, which did have good nutritional information, but they didn't give me the feeling I was very prepared for birth. I enjoyed *Your Pregnancy Week by Week* by Glade Curtis and Judith Schuler, and *A Child is Born* by Lennart Nilsson for the fetal development information. *A Child is Born* has such lovely photos of in-utero development. I was given an old copy of *Mothering* magazine and that was the first place I came across empowering birth stories. I found back issues at the library and was hooked. The information and articles gave me confidence in not only my body and ability to birth, but the birth process itself.

I also discovered *Birthing from Within* by Pam England and Rob Horowitz, which I would recommend to any pregnant woman. It covers the spiritual and emotional aspects of birth that are neglected by most books.

I took the hospital's childbirth preparation classes, which did cover some good breathing and relaxation techniques. The nurse who taught it discussed comfort measures, massage and the importance of moving around in labor. She treated natural birth as a real option, rather than just covering the medical interventions—which happens to be the main focus of some hospital classes. I think hearing about natural birth from a medical professional goes a long way towards promoting the validity of it as a choice.

My husband was very supportive and encouraging. He kept telling me how good I was doing, even though he later said he had no idea what was really going on. The midwives were so patient and caring. Their presence and calmness were very comforting. They gave me such a positive sense that my birth was flowing smoothly and naturally, and that made me feel more secure in it. My husband, bless his heart, is a good man who tries hard, but he is a carpenter, not a masseuse. For my next baby, my support included my husband as well as a friend who is a doula. She helped cover some of the back rubs that were so very helpful and relaxing for me.

Read *Mothering* magazine and *Birthing from Within* ahead of time to get a sense of empowered birth that doesn't come from mainstream books and magazines. Choose carefully who will be involved, and where the birth will be. In my experience, midwifery offered more personal one-on-one care, both prenatally and during the birth. They took time during each visit to answer all of my questions, and stayed with and supported me throughout labor. Many hospitals allow midwives to work within their facilities, and the comfort of knowing back-up emergency care is right there if you need it can be the best of both worlds. Selecting your caregiver and place of birth are very personal choices.

Surround yourself with people who not only love you, but believe in the birth process. You need this support system both during pregnancy and at the birth. Ignore people's fearful advice and horror stories. It may be therapeutic for them to share their negativity, but you don't need to accept it; just smile and nod, and ignore them. The birth is your chance to be queen for the day, and everyone there should know and respect that. If your support team has no faith that a natural birth is a normal or good thing, they won't be very helpful and supportive when you need it. Most of all, believe in yourself and your ability to birth a healthy, happy baby. Remember what one midwife told me, "Women have been doing this for millions of years. Your body was designed for this."

Pamela Jorrick is a writer, artist, doula and mother of two beautiful children, living in Northern California.

ARE YOU SURE...?

BY TERRI SHILLING

As a Lamaze childbirth educator, I spend a significant amount of time teaching classes, focusing on early labor and how to avoid getting to the hospital too early. I stress that early labor is easiest to cope with by relaxing and doing things at home, or by walking outside. When I was pregnant with my daughter, getting to the hospital early was one of my biggest fears. And since I'm an independent childbirth educator, I created my own challenges by thinking that the labor-and-delivery staff would scrutinize my birth to see if I practiced the principles I teach. Three weeks before my birth, my teaching partner gave birth, and at the height of transition she reportedly screamed, "This breathing sh-t doesn't work!" That story was a popular one to tell and re-tell in the maternity ward.

When my due date came and went, I felt comfortable and confident. My first child, my son, had arrived three weeks early, with my water breaking in a Kmart parking lot! So I had cleared my calendar three weeks before my due date, expecting the same early arrival. It was not meant to be. I didn't welcome my labor until 11 days after my due date. Just by chance, I went to church with a friend who was eight days past her due date, and we happened to sing a hymn called *Come Labor On*. It has nothing to do with birth, but we both ended up at the hospital the next day!

I woke up at 4 a.m. with the first twinges of contractions. Reality hit while I was cleaning the toilet, because labor meant my mother-in-law was coming to town. Wisely, I went back to bed. I remember going back to sleep and being awoken by the phone, and quietly whispering that my husband would not be going to work that day.

We calmly left the house, and left my son with friends who were going to bring him to the hospital later. At my husband's insistence, we stopped for breakfast. He thought for sure that labor would be long, and wanted to be prepared and well-nourished. I should have known something was happening when, for the first time ever, I told him he could drive faster, instead of my standard chant: "slow down, slow down." We got to the hospital and went to the assessment room. I tried to ignore the turmoil in my gut, my fears about how everybody was going to be watching to see if I could birth normally. I still remember the nurse asking, "Are you sure you are in labor—there are no contractions on the monitor." It was my worst nightmare... I was at the hospital too early! I was flabbergasted! And confused. I knew I had been having a few monster contractions. I instantly began to question my ability to read my body. I almost trusted the machine more than what I was feeling! She agreed to do a vaginal exam, and her expression said, "And then we'll send you home." To my relief, she did the exam and gasped, "Don't push!"

I was in the wonderful "rest and be thankful" stage, the contraction-free time between active labor and pushing. The contractions had stopped, but not for long! My doctor was summoned from her office. The search was on for my husband, who had been sent back to admitting to pay the $100 deposit. The hospital was very busy and the commotion was not calming. I was in an overflow area, with a curtain between me and another laboring woman. Once my husband came back, the doctor helped us welcome our daughter to the world—born only 20 minutes after the "Are you sure you are in labor?" exam.

My belief in the Lamaze philosophy was affirmed!

Although everyone is envious of the short birth stories, the intensity can be overwhelming, and not everything goes as planned. For example, we had given my son a Leboyer bath after his birth, and wanted to do the same with my daughter. But between births, we had moved and the new hospital was not familiar with it. During my pregnancy I had asked my doctor about it— she recommended I get a letter of support from my pediatrician. I did this and also had to get one from the head of labor and delivery, the nursery and from the administration of the hospital! I felt I had covered all my bases. I had the protocol from the old hospital, had my own floating thermometer, pictures, permissions, etc. But with such a short labor, the delivery team panicked... they tried to microwave sterile water and put it in a small tub on the slanted board under the warmer, but it all spilled out. I remember thinking, "Nothing about birth can be planned." I had jumped through all the necessary and unnecessary hoops, and then wisely released my plans for the Leboyer bath and just embraced my new, precious, warm daughter to my chest.

There are so many lessons to be learned from birth, we just have to open our hearts to learn them. My friend and I thought we had hit upon a get-rich-quick scheme for all those overdue moms-to-be: just sing *Come Labor On*. Unfortunately, the next month a mutual friend was into her second week past her due date, and we gathered around the piano and sang and sang. We had a great time, but labor didn't start. I guess we need to trust the other Lamaze tenet: let labor begin on its own!

A Mother's Guidance: There are three important words for expectant women to focus on: strength, courage and wisdom. Strength: being in tune with your body, knowing the importance of moving to facilitate birth and committing to an active birth. Courage: the hardest leap to take is to face any fears you have and surround yourself with those people who have confidence in your innate ability to give birth. Wisdom: too often birth is portrayed as a cognitive event—that you have to learn how to birth. Instead, focus on your body's wisdom—there are 300,000 women birthing each day. Birth is not a cognitive event—it is a physical, emotional and spiritual event that will challenge and change you to your core.

Teri Shilling, MS, IBCLC, CD(DONA), LCCE is the director of Passion for Birth (www.passionforbirth.com), a childbirth educator training program, and has authored The Idea Box for the Creative and Interactive Childbirth Educator. She is committed to "stomping out boring and ineffective childbirth education classes." She is a past president of Lamaze International and travels internationally training doulas, midwives, family doctors, nurses and community women supporting normal birth. She and her husband, and their two children (ages 12 and 16), are fortunate to be a National Park Service family and have lived in national parks across the United States.

BIRTH IN A CIRCLE OF LOVE

BY KRISTIN SPOSITO

A BIRTH STORY typically starts with the beginnings of labor, but for my second child, the journey from womb to my waiting arms began long before that... not necessarily the moment he was conceived, but at least as far back as my first trimester.

My daughter Maya experienced a natural birth in a hospital. My labor with her was joyful, empowered and relatively easy. For me, giving birth had a lot to do with submitting and letting go.

During my second pregnancy, sometime near the end of my first trimester, I switched my prenatal care from my allopathic doctor to a midwifery group. I will never forget the first time my midwives examined my pregnant belly. Each of them in turn rubbed their hands together, closed their eyes, and gently massaged my growing abdomen. Their hands somehow seemed like sacred instruments, coming forth in reverence and confidence to witness the miracle that is a baby in utero. They were there as a bridge between the born and the unborn, communicating, comforting and welcoming. They took their time and patiently placed our hands here and there so that my husband and I could feel too. We spent a lot of time talking about how I was doing, physically, emotionally and spiritually, and we laughed a lot. They shared their extensive knowledge about birth, nutrition, health and parenting, not to mention labor.

The way my midwives welcomed and included our daughter, then two years old, at all of our prenatal appointments was so wonderful. They suggested books to help prepare her for the arrival of a sibling, and talked a lot with her about how she was feeling about the birth. Maya spent a lot of time slathering my stomach with kisses and hugs, and she rubbed on it all the time. It was her own way of connecting with her brother and getting ready to be a sibling.

We decided not to do an ultrasound, an uncommon decision in the community where we live, where most people adhere to the standards of conventional medicine. People in my life gave me warning after warning about how "dangerous" this route could be. I heard stories about home births that ended in disaster. And truthfully, at times I felt scared and unconfident, doubting my ability to birth without the security of a hospital. But I also knew, from somewhere deep inside, that our bodies are designed for birth. There is something sacred, sexy and magical about being fully present and empowered through the birth of one's babies.

The decision to birth at home with midwives led me to confront my biggest fears about babies and birthing. It wasn't fear of a C-section or birth defects. It was really a fear of not being able to control an outcome. We can't choose our children, and so many levels of their development are out of our hands. We can't choose their personalities, disabilities, interests, health or appearances. We can't control how deeply we fall in love. And we can't choose when we live and die. But once I honestly came to terms with my fears, my relationship to the whole process of pregnancy and birth shifted to a more peaceful and centered place.

For the most part, I felt healthy and strong throughout my pregnancy. I still carried Maya around all the time. My husband and I had decided long ago that we would not change our course even if there was something wrong with our baby, so it seemed pointless to us to undergo many of the prenatal tests that were offered. It was very empowering to respectfully decline most of them. Our midwives were always there, nurturing, reassuring and providing information. It just felt like the natural thing, to wait for our baby without any revealing glimpses into the internal, secret world where he was growing and preparing to be born.

A week before our son arrived, I met with our midwives and asked them to do an internal examination to see if I was progressing. They said they preferred not to do an internal exam, as it increases the potential risk of introducing bacteria inside of me. I was assured that if I really wanted them to, they would check, but they saw no reason to intrude in the peaceful interior world of my baby. They showed my husband how to do an internal exam, explaining that his bacteria was "friendly" and familiar to my body, and if we decided we needed to know, it was preferable for him to be the one to do the exam.

A day or so later, the suspense was driving me nuts! I begged my husband to do an internal examination to see if I was at all dilated. He complied, and after fishing around sort of blindly for a few minutes, his eyes nearly popped out of his head. "Oh, my gosh. I can totally feel everything!" We had photographs from birthing books at hand, and after mustering up my nerve, I also put my fingers inside me to check. We agreed I was about six centimeters dilated, something I didn't even know was possible before labor began! We could feel my cervix as clear as day. And when we poked gently on our baby's head we could feel him kick and squirm in response. It was absolutely incredible!

The next week was bustling and busy, and exciting. We knew the baby would arrive any time. And finally, on a Monday afternoon, my labor began. I was out doing errands with Maya. I started feeling some pains in my abdomen, but ignored them, focused on completing the tasks at hand. Traffic was heavy; it was two days before Christmas. I was standing in lines, carrying my daughter. All of a sudden it hit me... *that* wasn't a stomach ache. Those were contractions! I was so ferociously nesting that I couldn't stop trying to get everything done. But every once in a while, when I felt a particularly strong sensation, I felt a fierce desire to get home now!

But I completed my errands anyway. I arrived home at 6 p.m. and ate dinner as my midwives prepared the birthing tub. I thought about how hungry I was, and knew that if I was in a hospital they would frown upon me eating. I felt a bit unsure of myself—would I really be eating if I were in true labor? How long would labor last? I was a bit concerned about my daughter. She was hungry and tired and only wanted me. Maybe it wasn't such a good idea to have her present at the birth? My husband was trying to time my contractions and it was annoying me greatly. The last time I gave birth I had needed him so much—he had been my anchor, pulling me out of each hard contraction and reminding me to take the breath that would keep me grounded.

By 6:30 p.m. I had been in labor for two hours. I sat on the toilet and looked down—it was full of blood. Yikes! I didn't remember this from before. I just wanted to be alone. I wanted someone to make my daughter happy. I started having that feeling of dread—there is no backing out of this now. I knew it was going to be hard, and it was all up to me. *Sigh.* By 7:45 p.m. I got in the tub. It was warm and nice, and it felt good to be naked. My living room was dark, except for the Christmas tree lights. Carolers came to the door, and the midwives gently explained that someone was having a baby and declined their offer to come in and sing to me.

Contractions began coming hard and strong. I was panting and sweating, and the fear was slipping away. This is part of the work that I was born to do. I slipped away into the quiet world of labor. The fear had evaporated, and I felt grateful to be conscious of all the feelings going on within my body. I started answering questions more slowly and retreated within.

Gratefully I felt the contractions turn into pushing contractions, something I had never experienced the first time. This time, there was no questioning what my body was telling me to do. I pushed for 45 minutes. It was really hard. It was painful and I wanted to stop. I don't remember it being this hard the first time around. I knew I was almost done, and I forced myself to breathe and be present while I hung in there.

Then he started to come out. There is nothing on this planet like the feeling of that slippery little person coming out in a gush with the very last push. At 9:15 p.m., our little boy arrived. He was still in the bag of waters, which hadn't broken during my labor. His face was still and calm. He was small and sweet, and he never cried at all. And yes, I was hopelessly in love.

My husband, singing a birthing song, floated around as background music while our daughter read her brother a book. He nursed and blinked his eyes at the Christmas tree lights. There was our little family—tired, but so blissed out that we were hardly aware of the work we had done that night. I had only been home for a little over three hours.

My placenta took a long time to come out. I tried moving around and sitting on the toilet. Finally I was getting silly, and told my husband to come kiss me while I sat on the toilet. I remembered reading something in *Spiritual Midwifery* about using sexual contact to encourage a slow labor. He said he wasn't in the mood, but came over and gave me a kiss anyways. And my placenta plopped out instantly! We had been waiting for it for over an hour, and I am sure the kiss is what did it.

As it turns out, my midwives think I had initially been pregnant with twins. I had two placentas, and a thick calcified mass in the middle of the smaller one was most likely Jonah's twin. They suspect that is why it took the placenta so long to come out.

I couldn't believe how calm our evening turned out. The midwives helped get our daughter to bed, cleaned up the tub, fed me and helped me get all situated. After they left, my husband and I snuggled with our newest little cherub and we all went to sleep. Jonah was so content, calm and peaceful. I know he appreciated being born at home. He never once left the circle of love and light that had surrounded him since conception. And the memory of his birth will never leave me.

A Mother's Guidance: Do not be afraid! Birth is mystical, magical and wonderful. Tune out the culture of fear that surrounds childbirth. While it is hard work, it is so amazing. Surround yourself with loving, confident and conscious support people.

It felt so right to have a baby at home, in the company of nurturing midwives. The water in the tub was soothing and comfortable. A key to the strength and confidence I felt was the research we had done—reading everything positive about birthing normally that we could get our hands on.

Knowing that women's bodies are almost always capable of bringing a baby into the world with very little intervention, I am so glad that my daughter was able to witness a birth before she even turned three years old. My hope is that she will be able to approach her own births without fear, and with strength and joy. And I feel a little wistful that I am all done having babies, because childbirth is one of the last great primal rites of passage. I wouldn't trade anything for the experience of being present and conscious while giving birth.

Kristin Sposito wrote this story because she has stars in her eyes from the birth of her second baby, and wanted to always remember the details. She lives in Oregon with her two children, husband and dog. She works part time as a civil engineering consultant, but is mostly a stay-at-home mother. She practices attachment parenting, elimination communication, co-sleeping and extended breastfeeding, and hopes to home-school and travel extensively with the entire family (except the dog). Kristin enjoys her consulting work but would love to spend more time writing and traveling.

FROM ACROSS ETERNITY

BY MICHELLE KRAETSCHMER

WE FELT SURE that our new little one would be born on Father's Day, so I prepared the birth basket the night before, and was not surprised when I had some very intense and long Braxton-Hicks contractions starting late Saturday night. I was aware of them throughout the night, and although they were not really uncomfortable, they kept me from a deep sleep.

I was up at 5:30 in the morning, feeling ravenous, so my husband Dominic got up and prepared a piece of toast for me. I timed a few contractions, finding they were roughly two minutes apart when moving around, and five minutes apart when I sat still. I noticed some blood-streaked mucous, so I decided to call our midwife at 6:00 a.m. She had made me promise to call her the very minute I went into labor, since she was convinced that it would progress quickly. In the meantime, my four-year-old son Keelian presented his Father's Day gift to his daddy, and we explained to him that our baby would be born today. What a Father's Day gift for Dom!

Our midwife arrived at 7:00, but by this point my contractions had slowed down to seven to ten minutes apart, so she went upstairs to get some more sleep. When she came downstairs by 10:00 and the contractions had not increased in intensity or frequency, she left to visit her mother, who was about 45 minutes away. We drifted around aimlessly at home for a while, and we finally decided to visit the farmer's market in a neighboring town about 30 minutes away. I had some intense contractions in the car, but they were still bearable. We bought an enormous amount of spinach (I was just addicted to spinach right then), and an apple-cherry pie for Father's Day before heading home. After lunch, we timed the contractions again; they were around six to eight minutes apart and mild enough to warrant some exercise.

Dom, Keelian and I walked down to the cove near our house to feed the fish, but there were too many people there and I felt like being alone, so we continued on, scrambling up a steep hill and down another to get to the beach. Everything around me seemed very bright and vibrant, especially the flowers lining the road and the water in the little creek. A few drops of rain started to fall from gray skies overhead. Dom was convinced we would be caught in a thunderstorm, but Keelian and I wanted to press on.

The water at the beach was quite choppy and we couldn't see any fish, so we stayed only a short while. I had one really achy contraction with a definite peak that I needed to breathe through, and at that point I realized that we'd better head back. We stopped to pick berries and wildflowers on the way, and once we got home, I was still able to arrange the flowers in a vase, although by now the contractions were very intense and I had to breathe through each one.

There was a message from our midwife on our answering machine, asking me to call and check in with her. I didn't call right away since I wanted to time a few contractions first. When I did call, they were still around six to eight minutes apart, but even more intense than before. She told me to call back when they were around five minutes apart, or in one hour's time. I had some juice and watermelon to rehydrate after the walk, and then decided to lie down for a rest before labor began in earnest. I tried to concentrate on a magazine, but found that with each, ever-more-intense contraction, I felt an intense urge to get up from the bed. Finally I gave up, called her and told her that although an hour had not passed and the contractions certainly weren't five minutes apart yet, I needed to call. She asked me if I was able to do anything during the contractions, and since I replied that I couldn't even concentrate, she said that she was on her way immediately.

I suddenly felt very crampy and needed to be on the toilet. Once there, it didn't take me long to realize that I now needed to be in the bathtub for pain relief, and I was sure that it would not be long before I held my baby in my arms. But once in the water, I realized that I had already progressed too far for the water to make any difference at all! We have an old Victorian claw-foot tub, and I was able to sit sideways and cross-legged in the tub. I tried to remember to keep my mouth open and loose, and my hands unclenched—I had read somewhere that this opens up the cervix considerably—and it seemed to help me breathe and relax more.

After a short while, our midwife arrived and quietly went about getting her supplies ready. Keelian was very excited now, running around shouting and roughhousing with her—she was amazingly patient with him! At some point I remember him repeatedly banging and shutting the door to the upstairs, and then banging on his drum and chanting, "Baby come out! Baby come out!" right outside the open bathroom door. None of this bothered me— I was in my own world, and felt like I was levitating slightly above my body at the end of each contraction. Every contraction was felt and visualized like a slowly cresting wave, with a short plateau near the top, then another short crest to the peak, and then a rapid descent and fade-off.

I suddenly felt very "grunty" and told our midwife that I needed the toilet again, and she said, "It's the baby." I was sure it was not! At the next contraction this feeling turned into a strong urge to bear down, and it felt great! Once it gripped me there was no letting go… my body just took over, leaving me grunting and groaning out loud. All I could think was that the baby could not come down while I was sitting up! I tried reclining and was swept away by this huge force, this primal wave that made me focus all my energy into pushing, pushing.

At some point I reached in and felt the baby's head… soft, yet firm underneath. My little one was almost here! My whole being was directed at pushing through the pain, bearing down and out. I heard our midwife say, "That's the bag of water," and Dom said, "Wow!" in such an awestruck voice—something I will always remember. Keelian had joined them at the foot of the tub and was shining the flashlight into the water. "Look! Look! It's coming out of Mommy's crack!" he said in a tone of utter disbelief. There was an incredible swelling and filling sensation; a few more pushes and the sac stayed bulging out. The pressure was so great, but it felt good! I reached down to feel it, and there was a soft puff as it released its contents into the water… all clear.

As if in a dream, I looked down to see her right hand come flying out, reaching ahead for the life she waited so long for. Her head came through and with it, no more pain… just pure joy and a feeling of letting go, of "giving forth." Dom and our midwife held her head and arm down under the water, to avoid her skin being exposed to air, which would lead to her taking a breath under water. The next contraction brought the exquisite slithering out of her body—feeling her bony shoulders, hips, bottom and legs pass through me—a sense of fulfillment, of being made complete, settled over me. This was what I had come here to do.…

She lay in my arms, the little girl I had loved for so long; the one we had called here from across eternity. Finally, a warm wet baby with healthy lungs, sniffing and licking at my nipple like a little kitten. And all of her perfect, so incredibly new and perfect. She has filled up our hearts, healing the wounds of six miscarriages and the challenges of infertility treatment. Our deep longing for a little girl to complete our family was finally met by baby Indya Katherine.

A Mother's Guidance: Read *The Power of Pleasurable Childbirth* by Laurie Morgan and *Unassisted Childbirth* by Laura Kaplan Shanley, and then work your way back from there to your own comfort level. Realize that the American medical community will treat you as a medical patient who needs to be "helped," and that in many cases, the fear of litigation issues will lead the hospital staff to intervene in the perfectly normal process of birth. It is up to you to educate yourself about invasive procedures before allowing them. Birth is inherently a safe, natural and non-medical occurrence. The human race would not have flourished as it has if birth was not safe! As Laurie Morgan says, "Birth is as safe as life gets."

Michelle Kraetschmer is a South African living in the United States with her husband and two beautiful home-schooled children. They plan on making the United States their permanent home, and dream of owning a large farmhouse with an organic garden and orchards in rural New York.

OH, RIGHT... A BABY!

BY MARIEKE BENDELER

I WAS DUE on May 15th, but two days before that I awoke at 4 a.m. with pain in my lower belly. It felt like the pains I have when my period comes. I tried to lie calmly in my bed and pretend that nothing was happening, but in my head I was cheering: "Will the delivery start now? Am I feeling contractions?" This was my first pregnancy, and so my first experience of labor.

My husband Sander was still deep asleep. I tried to read a little, but the cramps were coming faster and faster. I tried to clock the intervals, but I had a hard time concentrating. At 5:30 a.m. I woke up Sander to tell him that the contractions had started. Sleepy, he asked me if he could snooze a little longer.... *What?! Snooze? No way, wake up!!*

I got up to use the restroom, and there I lost my mucous plug. Immediately afterwards I lost my amniotic fluid, but I was not completely sure, so I showed it to Sander. After studying it intensely, he agreed—my water had broken.

I got into the shower, hoping it would speed up contractions... and it did. As I finished my shower, I asked Sander when we should call the midwife/obstetrician. He didn't know either, so I grabbed the *Big Delivery Book* and read that we can call when the contractions are coming every five minutes, or whenever you feel that you need to call. I thought it was time to call, but Sander wondered if the contractions were indeed already happening every five minutes. Sander thought we should count from peak to peak, but I thought they should be counted from the finish of the first contraction to the start of the next one. We couldn't seem to agree, so Sander called the midwife. She told us that I was right, and I was having contractions every two minutes. The midwife was on her way.

In the meantime, I was having a hard time thinking straight. The pain seemed to be coming in a big wave, and required my full attention. I didn't have the patience or time anymore to read or watch TV. Then, all of a sudden, our midwife was with us. She asked me to lie down so she could check my dilation: three centimeters—still seven to go! She told me that the rest of my dilation could take 12 to 24 hours. She left the room and I was by myself. I talked to myself: *You can do this! So many women have done this before you, so you can do this too.* I lost track of time, but before long I was exhausted, and my internal dialogue changed. *If I need to do this for 12 or more hours, I don't want to do it this way. I want anesthesia! And to be honest, I don't want to deliver at all anymore!*

After another 30 minutes I asked for our midwife again. She examined me, and I was so relieved to hear that I was now at eight centimeters. *Well now, that's better. Still two to go, but that shouldn't be too hard!*

Then everything started happening really fast. I didn't have any sense of time anymore; I was only able to concentrate on my body and myself. It seemed only a moment passed before I felt pressure and the midwife told me that I could start to push.... *Push?* I had completely lost all knowledge about deliveries... I had no clue anymore what I need to do. Our midwife reassured and guided me.

I tried to push really carefully; I was afraid I would break something. After a while the midwife assured me that it's fine to feel some anger, to use all the power I had to push. With the next contraction, I pushed hard and felt a huge ball pressing against my perineum. After the contraction passed, the ball moved back, but with the next one it was there again. The midwife told us that she could see hair, black hair! And in a split second, I realize that I am having a baby! It seems that I had forgotten, but the hair gave me new strength to keep going. Each time, the ball came and went. I started to get a little discouraged about it... but then the ball stayed put. And with the next contraction, I pushed as if my life depended on it—and then: the release. I felt the little head coming outside of me, immediately followed by the small body, and very soon after that a total relaxation washed over me.

Our little one was resting on my belly; tears of happiness and tension release washed out of me. *I can be proud of myself; I did it!* Nothing mattered anymore. The delivery was over and the little baby was with me. It was exactly 10 a.m. when our healthy girl was born. When the midwife asked me what her name was, I didn't know anymore! Sander spoke up with pride, "This is Lotte Maria." She had ten fingers and ten toes, a clear little voice, and she curiously looked into the world. Sander cut the umbilical cord, and from that moment Lotte had to "fend for herself."

I felt another contraction come and I got a little scared: *not another one, not more work?* But the midwife assured me that this was the placenta, and it came very quickly and easily. The home baby nurse helped me put Lotte to my breast.... what power has such a little baby!

The first day without the home baby nurse was a little scary, but very soon I knew that Lotte and I could take care of each other so very well!

About Deliveries in the Netherlands

In the Netherlands you can deliver your baby in many different ways. Most women opt for a natural delivery at home with the assistance of a midwife, who has trained at a university for four years. While a woman is pregnant, the midwife handles most of the prenatal care, building a relationship with the pregnant woman. If a woman decides to have her baby in a hospital, the midwife will be there to assist too.

The Ob/Gyn only takes care of pregnant women who have difficulties during their pregnancy, or when it is expected to be a complicated pregnancy or delivery. When multiple births are expected, the Ob/Gyn will be there as well to assist during the pregnancy and delivery of the babies. Ob/Gyn's also handle all cesarean sections.

Sometimes, although a woman prefers to have her baby at home, complications occur during the delivery. In this case the woman is transported to a hospital (which, in the Netherlands, is almost always within 15 miles distance) where an Ob/Gyn will assist with the delivery.

You can have your baby at home in many different ways. You can be lying flat in a bed, or on a little delivery stool. This is a small toilet-bowl-shaped stool that the woman sits on to allow gravity to help with the delivery. You can also choose to deliver in a large bathtub. In this case, women rent a bathtub that is specially designed for deliveries, because the regular bathtubs in the Netherlands are too small.

It is common to have your baby in a natural way. Only in certain occasions will something be given to a woman in labor to ease her pain. For example, anesthesia may be used when the delivery is taking too long and the woman is completely exhausted, or when a woman really cannot take more pain and asks for painkillers. Most often, women are given nitrogen, but epidurals are used in some cases. If a woman prefers to use pain medication, she must birth in a hospital.

A home baby nurse assists the mother and newborn for the first eight days. She is trained to teach parents how to care for a newborn. For example, she teaches them how to wash the little one and how often. She teaches them how they can keep their newborn warm, how a baby sleeps safely, and she offers tips and advice on breastfeeding. She will also take care of any other children in the family, keep the house clean and cook. Depending on the wishes of the parents, she will come for three-and-a-half to eight hours a day. The parents pay a small deductible for each hour of this service, and the remaining cost is paid by health insurance.

A Mother's Guidance: My husband and I took a class in Haptonomy, which works with the relationship a child and its parents establish even before birth. More information can be found at www.haptonomy.net. Get prepared: birth is going to be very, very heavy with nothing to compare. It will turn out better than was expected.

Marieke Bendeler is 31 years old. She and her husband live in The Hague, the seat of government in The Netherlands. In 2002 their first child, Lotte, was born.

OWNING EVERY MOMENT

BY JODY NIEKAMP

I WANTED TO DELIVER my children at home, but my husband felt differently. Eventually we agreed that we would labor at home and deliver at the hospital.

Preparation for the birth of my second child was based on the birth of our first child. I spent a lot of time working through my residual emotions about my first delivery. It took me a long time to resolve my disappointment, frustration and sadness about the loss of control, the doctor yelling at me to push harder, and the fact it didn't go as I had hoped. I meditated a lot. For an hour a day for my entire third trimester, I would rest my head on an ottoman and rock back and forth while listening to a relaxation tape. I also read everything I could get my hands on, searching for material that supported my commitment to a natural, comfortable birth. I practiced Lamaze and HypnoBirthing techniques, but the most important element of our preparation was hiring a very knowledgeable, highly experienced doula.

Labor started around 9 p.m. on a Saturday evening, two days before my due date. My in-laws were visiting, and I was getting ready to put Alexander, our three-year-old son, to bed. He asked to stay up for a few minutes to play with his grandmother, and since I had been feeling a little out of it, I wasn't in the mood to disagree with him. The three of us sat down at the kitchen table to play with stamps, and after a few minutes I got up to get Alexander some ice cream. As soon as I stood up, I felt an overwhelming need to lie down. I knew it was going to be a long night.

By 10 p.m. I was certain I was in labor. I'd had three contractions about 15 minutes apart, and I lost the mucus plug. We called LaNette, our doula, and told her I was in labor but that everything was going well and we would call her later.

At 11 p.m., my husband Scott decided to get some sleep so he would be ready for a very eventful night. I tried to lie down too, but when I did the contractions became very strong. If I stood and kept my mind active they were barely noticeable—the difference was amazing.

Thinking ahead, I had frozen some ripe bananas. This was an idea I'd gotten from an old episode of *The Cosby Show*, where a laboring woman brought in banana bread for the entire OB staff. I made the batter for the bread, washed the pan, talked with Stacie, my sister-in-law who was living with us at the time, and watched the end of *Saturday Night Live*. But as the evening progressed, so did my contractions; I had to stop moving to focus on breathing to get through each contraction. I put the bread batter into the fridge and started crawling up and down the stairs. As odd as it sounds it was soothing, and soon it was after midnight.

After getting bored with the steps I decided to try a hot shower. The hot water felt so wonderful. Before the hot water ran out I decided to try rocking on my hands and knees in a bath. It was helpful, but suddenly the bathroom lighting seemed far too bright. I woke up Scott to get the night light out of Alexander's room, and to keep me company. Scott was exactly what I needed. My contractions were getting intense. In the bathtub we would talk and laugh during the down times, but during a contraction I would rock while Scott would rub my back. I also found the Lamaze breathing very helpful, and I *hee hee hee hoo*'d my way through the intense pressure of my contractions. Scott would breathe with me through them, and it made all the difference for me.

It was almost 1:00 a.m. when I decided I had enough with the bathtub and tried lying on the birthing ball. The contractions shifted, coming every few minutes but not lasting as long. They became inconsistent too; it felt like every third contraction was hard and the ones in between were much easier. I really didn't know how my labor was progressing.

As time went on I became more easily frustrated. Scott tried to talk me through the contractions and he tried to put in my favorite relaxation tape, but I snapped at him. Now, not only were lights bothering me but sounds were too. Not knowing how to help, he decided to call LaNette and ask her to come over. It was about 1:25 a.m. Only minutes later, things got very intense and uncomfortable.

I climbed into bed and the contractions came really hard. We tried to time them but it didn't really matter, so I asked Scott to turn all the clocks around. I was having a lot of trouble breathing through the contractions, so I started moaning and the noise released a lot of tension. Soon the moaning wasn't working as well as before, so I started repeating, "Help help help." It wasn't that I really wanted help; it was the only word I could think of, and there was something comforting about the rhythm and repetition of the word.

I wasn't in bed very long before I felt the urge to push. I tried to suppress the urge, knowing that if I started pushing before I was fully dilated, it would cause my cervix to swell and would make labor last longer. I held in the urge to push for a couple of contractions and then decided to see what happened if I pushed though one. If felt really nice! It was so much easier to push than to hold back. This made me really nervous. I told Scott that it was time to go to the hospital, even though LaNette wasn't with us yet. It had only been about five minutes since we called her.

It took a few more contractions before I felt ready to try to walk to the car… I never made it. I was about to walk to the car when a contraction came… I looked down at my hands and they were covered with blood. I turned around and ran downstairs into the bathroom, knowing we were not going to make it to the hospital. Scott was wonderful; he never left my side, but I'm sure he was scared out of his mind.

LaNette arrived around 1:45 a.m., about twenty minutes after we called her. I was sitting on the toilet; it was the only place I felt almost comfortable. Sitting on something hard was so much more comfortable than lying in bed; the contractions did not feel as intense. Such small changes made a world of difference.

It was a relief when LaNette came; she has been to many births and proved to be most valuable. When she walked in the door I remember asking her for a hug, and she smelled really nice, a very motherly feel. Her voice was so calm and happy, and she assured me that it wasn't out of the ordinary to see blood during the second stage of labor. As she spoke, every worry in my body disappeared and was replaced with excitement. We were going to have our baby right here, right now.

We discussed whether we should stay home or go to the hospital. At this point I knew home was the only answer—there was no way anyone was going to get me to move anywhere. She asked Scott if he was OK with my decision to stay home and he said, "She is doing great, let's stay here." He was so supportive. We also discussed whether or not to call 911, and Scott and I agreed that it would be better to wait until after the baby was born. We were doing very well on our own.

Within seconds, I was cussing and screaming, "Ring of fire!" He must have been crowning. As soon as his head was out, the rest of him came with ease. LaNette was there to catch him and knew exactly what to do. My water never broke prior to his birth. Zachary let out a beautiful cry. He was born at 1:53 a.m., about ten minutes after LaNette arrived. He was never suctioned, and I am thankful for this because it wasn't necessary.

I tried to nurse him but was having trouble. LaNette assessed my injuries, and since we were concerned that they may not heal properly without medical attention, Scott called 911. The ambulance arrived, and one man came to talk with Scott, LaNette and my mother-in-law, who was patiently waiting on the other side of the bathroom door. He was the only paramedic who came in the room. Everyone was very respectful of our wishes for privacy. Scott looked so happy holding our six pound, 13 ounce, 20-inch long, very healthy baby boy.

I tried to deliver the placenta at home, but a half hour after he was born I was feeling light headed, and wanted the cord cut. Soon the paramedics brought me a blanket and helped me up the steps. I climbed into the ambulance bed and off to the hospital we went.

After my obstetrician finished the stitches, she said, "Well, I'm sorry this was such a traumatic experience for you." Wow, did she have it wrong! I have no regrets.

Before I had Zachary, I thought that the only thing that was important during delivery was to have a healthy baby. Now I recognize that while this is the primary goal, it is not the only goal. Birth is such an emotional experience; it can give or take away so much more than I ever realized. If it is handled with care, it will change you in such a wonderful and powerful way. It gave me more strength than I ever imagined. Since then, whenever I become overwhelmed, all I have to do is say, "I had a baby in my home!" I am instantly empowered. While in labor with Zachary, Scott and I consciously made every decision. I was able to accept everything as it happened. We own every moment of that experience.

A Mother's Guidance: Giving birth is an amazing spiritual event. There is so much to do to prepare for a child, like getting the baby's room ready and going to prenatal visits, but don't overlook the emotional and spiritual work. Spend time getting to know yourself and your body. If you are not sure where to start, find a doula. I worked with some meditation techniques and attended a brief class on Lamaze-type breathing techniques provided by our doula.

There are too many good books to mention what helped me during labor. The most influential resources were: *Easing Labor*

Pain: The Complete Guide to a More Comfortable and Rewarding Birth by Adrienne Lieberman; *A Good Birth, A Safe Birth* by Diane Korte and Roberta Scaer; and the website www.spinningbabies.com.

Jody Niekamp lives in Waukesha, Wisconsin. She has a wonderful husband, Scott, and two terrific boys. She is a stay-at-home mom with a home-based business. She is currently working on an organic clothing website (www.mothernaturescloset.com) and a website informing people why they should add organic foods, clothing and parenting to their life (www.naturalbychoice.com).

IN MY DEEPEST MEDITATION

BY YAEL SOLOMON

To my dearest Yakir Daniel,

YOU REST, SECURELY CUDDLED at my breast, as I begin to process your birth. I have wanted to write it down for the past three months, ever since you entered my life, but I haven't found the perfect moment... until now.

Your father, Amichai, and I returned home after spending the weekend with my parents. We joined them at a barbecue with friends before heading out on our two-and-a-half-hour drive back to Philadelphia. Although I am not much of a meat eater, that day I seemed to have consumed enough steak and hot dogs to feed a small army. Unbeknownst to me at the time, my body was storing energy for your labor, just hours away. The barbecue was fun and I laughed a lot, deep penetrating laughs. At one point, I thought I felt a muscle pull from a particularly long belly laugh. In retrospect, it was my labor starting. Your aba (father) and I believe that you were created with laughter, and therefore it was only appropriate that your birth began with laughter.

After we arrived home and settled in, I began my nightly ritual of yoga stretches. Without this thirty-minute practice, I was unable to sleep. At around 2:00 in the morning, I was still stretching! I realized that these "tight muscles" were probably contractions!

This was it! I'd finally get to meet you! I woke up Amichai to tell him and he went into shock. He told me to try to sleep, or relax and to try to do my birth project. Yet the contractions were getting closer together and more intense. All I could focus on was you.

At this point, your aba had fully awakened and called in our support—the midwife Barbara, and Yiscah, my soul sister. When I called your grandfather, instead of passing the phone over to my mother, he hung up on me! It was 2:30 in the morning! I had to wait for the next contraction to wash over me before calling again.

Your aba was in rare form—filling up the birthing pool, clearing an area for the midwife to place her equipment, lighting candles and putting on the music we had chosen to welcome you into the world.

The world was so dark and still; your aba and I submerged together in the birthing pool—alone and intimate before the cavalry began to arrive. You had been created with love and light, and we wanted a private moment to complete that circle of life, your creation and your birth.

As people began to arrive, they respected the quiet atmosphere we had created. We wanted your entrance into this world to be as peaceful and serene as possible. Yiscah arrived first, relaxed and aglow. She and Amichai took turns massaging my back and hips for 11 hours. They offered words of encouragement as they escorted me to and from the bathroom.

I remember being in the warm water and surrendering to the contractions. They were the intense energy that was bringing you forth into the world. I loved every second of it! It wasn't painful; it was intense. It was an experience I had never had before and one that I would never forget. This was something only you and I felt. It created a truly spiritual bond between us, a bond that I will always cherish. I know that there were other people in the room, a halo of support and love, yet I was hardly aware of them. I was cognizant of your aba's loving touch and Yiscah's soothing hands, but that's it. I too was encased in a womb—waters that brought me back to the Garden of Eden, where the universe began. I was in touch with all women from all time who had given birth and who will give birth. It was such a feeling of empowerment!

At one point, I was asked by the midwife to get out of the pool to encourage my cervix to open. I had been pushing prematurely and as a result my cervix had begun to swell. I guess I was just really eager to meet you! That was an incredibly intense time—the room was dark and very still. I could hear the candles flicker and the incense smoke waft through our intimate home. I lay incredibly still, in my deepest meditation. I don't think I had ever achieved such a level of spiritual focus, except at your aba's and my wedding. Suddenly I felt a shift in the room, and sensed Sara Imeinu's (Sara, the matriarch's) presence. She represented all women to me and guided me through this most challenging part of my labor. "Open up. You are a vessel," she kept softly repeating in my ear. It worked. I tapped into resiliency that I had stored in my soul and made it through—bright, glistening and glowing.

Barbara, my midwife, wanted to check my dilation while I was on our bed to make sure the cervix was completely dilated before I got back into the pool for the water birth we had planned. But higher powers were at work and this was not meant to be. Your heart rate began to drop and Barbara felt you should be birthed on the bed, on my back. It was the VERY position I was so adamantly against. This was the birthing position that used to be enforced (and sometimes still is) in hospitals for the convenience of the doctor, and often to the disservice of the laboring mother. Yet, did I hesitate? Did I protest? NOT FOR A SECOND! Your well-being was of utmost importance, not my birthing plan. I was becoming a mother. You taught me the precious lesson that every mother needs to know—the practice of surrender. I had to let go of the "perfect" birth to make space for *your* birth, which was the true birth. Once I had learned this invaluable lesson, you entered my life.

I had told the midwife that I wanted to catch you when you were born. However, at the time of your birth, it was not a passive act. It was active and primal. I claimed you. You were mine. I placed you, slippery and precious, on my naked skin and embraced you.

You slowly crept your way to my breast to receive your hard-earned nourishment. Thank you for entering my life and choosing me to be your mommy.

I love you, Yakir Daniel.

Your ima (mommy)

A Mother's Guidance: I recall so eagerly anticipating the birth of my first child, and I was told more "horror" stories than "beauty" stories; yet I was determined to create my own story, my own memory. Our home birth was the most empowering experience I have ever had. Since his birth two years ago, I have given birth to his sister, Ma'ayan Neomi, in a home water birth. Suggested reading to support a natural birth: *Birthing from Within* by Pam England and Rob Horowitz, and *Mothering* magazine.

Yael Solomon, her husband Amichai, and their two children live in Elkins Park, Pennsylvania. Yael is originally an American, but moved to Israel eight years ago, where she met and married her husband. They returned to the States for a few years but plan to move back to Israel in the future. Professionally, Yael is a psychologist and has worked in Israel as a crisis-intervention and trauma counselor. She was part of a team that responded to terrorist attacks, treated the victims and their families, and helped the communities heal. Here in America, Yael is a full-time mom. She works in her son's Montessori school, teaching Hebrew.

VISUALIZATIONS AND AFFIRMATIONS

VISUALIZATIONS AND AFFIRMATIONS are powerful ways to program the subconscious mind to allow for an easier, empowered experience. The following visualizations were composed by Gloria Lemay. Say and visualize these affirmations several times a day throughout pregnancy:

• My baby's birth is a calm, joyous experience.

• Each part of my body is completely relaxed, allowing the easy passage of my baby.

• I relax through each stretching sensation, allowing my uterus to work effectively.

• I am safe and my baby is safe when the sensations are strong.

• The stretching sensations appear to last only a short time, but are efficient, and quickly open the cervix... opening... so my baby can be born.

• I focus my attention on my breathing, bringing in oxygen which surrounds my muscles; bringing in nourishment, and washing out fatigue.

- I am never alone... I have sisters throughout my city, my province, my country and around the world who will be having their babies at the same time as me. I tune in to them and send them my love and reassurance.

- I direct my energy from my head, down through my body and out through my vagina. This energy assists my muscles to work efficiently, and helps my baby come out... easily... effortlessly... comfortably.

- I now completely forgive the hospital staff and my parents for any mistakes they made at my own birth. It is now safe for me to let go completely.

- My uterus is working well to bring the baby down and out of the pelvis... there is plenty of room for my baby to pass through... easily, effortlessly, and comfortably.

- It is safe for me to verbalize my feelings and desires. I am willing to allow others the pleasure of serving me.

- My baby is being massaged and stimulated through the sensations of birth.

- As I feel my vagina being pressed open by my baby's head, I surrender completely, and open like a beautiful rose in full bloom.

from www.birthlove.com

Glossary of Terms

active labor a stage of labor when contractions are approximately three to five minutes apart and lasting approximately one minute. The cervix is dilating to eight centimeters during this phase of labor.

affirmations positive statements that program the subconscious mind. Examples include: "I trust my body to ease my baby into the world," or "I love and approve of myself," or "I deserve to have a great birth."

amniotic fluid the fluid that surrounds the baby in the womb. When the "water breaks," the amniotic sac has ruptured, releasing amniotic fluid.

artificial induction starting labor through the use of drugs. Pitocin is the most commonly used drug to start labor.

back labor a specific type of labor pain caused when the baby is positioned with its spine against the mother's, instead of against the front wall of the uterus. There are methods to reduce back labor by moving the baby into an easier position.

bag of waters the amniotic sac, or membranes that surround the baby and contain the amniotic fluid.

birth ball an inflatable ball used for labor that is useful for opening up the pelvic region. It is also called an exercise ball or physical therapy ball. These can be purchased at sporting goods stores or online.

birth center (free standing) a maternity center that is based on the midwifery model of care. While they are equipped to handle some emergencies, they accept only low-risk clients and do not offer pain medication. They are family- and client-centered and not associated with a hospital.

birth center (hospital affiliated) a maternity center that is associated with, and often located within, a hospital. Supportive of natural birth, limited intervention and low-technology care during labor. Usually they will only accept expectant women that fit within the guidelines for a low-risk pregnancy.

birth plan a detailed description of birth preferences, including type of monitoring, intervention guidelines and procedures for newborn care. They are especially helpful in a hospital. There are many sample birth plans online at www.birthplan.com.

birth stool a device used in birthing that allows a mother to sit while still allowing a care provider access to the vaginal area.

blessing ceremony a non-denominational tradition that nurtures, honors and celebrates a woman's transition into motherhood.

bloody show a blood-tinged mucus discharge that indicates that the cervix is dilating or softening.

Braxton-Hicks mild, painless contractions that may occur throughout pregnancy. These serve to tone the uterus and prepare it for labor, but do not indicate true labor.

breathing down a method of expelling the baby where you literally breathe down to release the baby. It is a very gentle and effective technique taught in HypnoBirthing classes.

Brewer diet a specific diet, developed by Dr. Tom Brewer, that can lower the risk of pre-eclampsia, toxemia and preterm labor. This diet is very well known with midwives, as well as the Bradley Method and HypnoBirthing communities. Getting enough protein, salt and water are important components of this diet. For more information, go to www.blueribbonbaby.org.

cervix entrance to the womb. Usually 1.75 centimeters to three centimeters long and closed, it shortens and thins out (effaces) as it dilates to ten centimeters to allow a child to pass though.

CNM stands for Certified Nurse Midwife. A registered nurse with additional training as a midwife who delivers infants and provides ante-partum and postpartum care.

counter pressure pressure put on the back to relieve back pain.

crowning the point when the widest part of the baby's head is visible, just before the baby's head passes over the perineum.

doula a woman experienced in childbirth who provides continuous physical, emotional and informational support to the mother before, during and just after birth. There are birth/labor doulas as well as postpartum doulas. For more information please visit www. dona.org or www.alace.org.

due date a projected date on which the baby will be born, calculated from the first day of the woman's last menstrual period, and based on a 40-week gestation period. In reality, only 2-5% of babies are born on this date.

effacement the softening and thinning of the cervix. The cervix needs to be soft, like an earlobe, before the baby can pass through it.

episiotomy surgical incision in the perineum to allow easier passage of a baby's head.

Heparin lock device that allows access to veins for fluids and medication.

midwife trained professional who assists a woman before, during and after birth and delivers babies. Some midwives work within hospital environments, offering an alternative model of care, while other midwives work at freestanding birth centers, private offices and/or clients' homes.

mucous plug mucous that seals the cervix during pregnancy. Sometimes women will notice the mucous plug discharge before or during labor.

oxytocin a hormone that is involved in the onset of labor and contraction of the uterus, as well as many other things. It is also released during nipple stimulation. Anxiety or severe distraction can inhibit its production and release.

pelvic rocking rolling or swaying your hips to bring the baby down.

perineum the tissue and between the anus and the vagina. It can be massaged and supported to stretch around the baby's head while staying intact. The site of episiotomies.

perineal massage the act of slowly stretching and working the tissues of and around the perineum so that it will stretch during the birth and remain intact.

Pitocin a synthetic form of oxytocin used to initiate or augment contractions. It is also used to control postpartum bleeding.

placenta an organ that connects the mother to the baby via the umbilical cord, providing nourishment to the baby and removing byproducts of the baby's system from its environment.

surge a gentle word for contraction, often used in HypnoBirthing.

transition the phase after active labor in which the cervix finishes opening to 10 centimeters.

VBAC acronym for vaginal birth after cesarean.

vernix the whitish coating on the skin of newborns.

water birth birthing in water. Many women claim that warm water is "nature's epidural."

Childbirth Preparation Classes

Birthing from Within®   Information on classes and instructors is available at www.birthingfromwithin.com or by calling (505) 254-4884. These classes are based on the book *Birthing from Within* by Pam England and Rob Horowitz. The premise of the classes and book is that birth is a rite of passage and not a medical event. Classes emphasize self-knowledge instead of assimilation of OB knowledge. They help parents to embrace whatever outcome happens instead of being outcome focused. They recognize that pain is a natural part of childbirth, but stress that much can be done to ease the pain. This is a parent-led class, and each class is unique. Takes into account the perspectives of the mothers, babies, dads, birth companions and cultures. Classes range in length from intensive one-day to seven-week classes because all educators are independent. Most classes are a minimum of 12 hours.

Birth Works®   Information is available by calling (888) 862-4784, or visiting www.birthworks.com. Embodies the philosophy of developing a woman's self confidence, trust and faith in her ability to give birth. The goal is to promote safe and loving birth experiences through education, introspection and confident action. Classes are traditionally 10 weeks for 2 hours each class. Some instructors offer private, individualized sessions.

Bradley Method® Information is available on the website at www.bradleybirth.com or by calling (800) 4-A-BIRTH. The Bradley Method is a 12-week course that teaches natural childbirth and views birth as a natural process. They encourage mothers to trust their bodies using natural breathing, relaxation, nutrition, exercise and education. They also teach couples how to stay low risk.

Lamaze® Information is available at www.lamaze.org, or by calling (800) 368-4404. Each class is a minimum of 12 hours. Lamaze-certified childbirth educators must have strong knowledge of normal birth. Sometimes the information that is taught in a hospital-sponsored class may be restricted by physicians who practice there. If you can find an independent class, information will be less biased. Lamaze International encourages expectant parents to read more about normal birth at www.normalbirth.lamaze.org.

HypnoBirthing® Information is available on the website at www.hypnobirthing.com or by calling (877) 798-3286. According to the website, "HypnoBirthing—The Mongan Method is as much a philosophy as it is a technique. The concept of HypnoBirthing is not new, but rather a "rebirth" of the philosophy of birthing as it existed thousands of years ago and as it was recaptured in the work of Dr. Grantly Dick-Read, an English obstetrician who first forwarded the concept of natural birthing in the 1920s. The method teaches you that in the absence of fear and tension, severe pain does not have to be an accompaniment of labor." Classes are five weeks long, one class per week. For referral to a certified HypnoBirthing practitioner in your area, e-mail distribution@hypnobirthing.com or call (877) 798-3286.

Hypnobabies Information is available on the website at www.hypnobabies.com or by calling (714) 898-BABY. A complete childbirth education course using Gerald Kein's Painless Childbirth techniques to eliminate pain and fear from childbirth. Includes nutrition and exercise, comfort in pregnancy, consumer issues, birth plans, optimal fetal positioning and much more. Materials for each

Hypnobabies student are: the Hypnobabies Workbook, five hypnosis scripts, six CDs (or audio tapes), the book *Back Labor No More*, the *Birth Partner's Guide* and the *Hypnobabies Quick Reference Guide*. Self-study courses are also available. It is a five-week course, with one three-hour class each week.

Prenatal yoga classes can help during birth because yoga increases breath and body awareness. The gentle and safe movements of yoga help the body to strengthen and stay limber. It releases and opens the pelvic opening in preparation for birth, and it allows for a more controlled birth by toning the pelvic floor.

RECOMMENDED RESOURCES

Magazines

The Compleat Mother, www.compleatmother.com
The Mother Magazine, www.themothermagazine.co.uk
Mothering, www.mothering.com
Pandora's Box, www.pandorasboxmagazine.com

Websites

www.amazingpregnancy.com
www.alace.org
www.birthingfromwithin.com
www.birthlove.com
www.birthnetwork.org
www.blueribbonbaby.org
www.bradleybirth.com
www.dona.org
www.freebirth.com
www.freestone.com
www.hypnobabies.com
www.hypnobirthing.com
www.journeyintomotherhood.com
www.lalecheleague.org
www.maternitywise.org
www.motherfriendly.org

www.mothering.com
www.normalbirth.lamaze.org
www.spinningbabies.com
www.waterbirth.org
www.waterbirthinfo.com

Audios

Journeying Through Pregnancy and Birth by Jennifer Houston

Videos/DVDs

Baby and Mom Prenatal Yoga with Gurmukh Kaur Khalsa

Birth Day

Birth into Being: The Russian Waterbirth Experience
by Barbara Harper

A Clear Road to Birth by Judy Seaman

Prenatal Yoga with Shiva Rea

*The Method—Baby & Mom Pre-Natal Yoga
with Gurmukh Kaur Khalsa*

WATER BABY: Experiences of Water Birth

Books

Active Birth: The New Approach to Giving Birth Naturally
by Janet Balaskas

*After the Baby's Birth: A Woman's Way to Wellness:
A Complete Guide for Postpartum Women* by Robin Lim

The American Way of Birth by Jessica Mitford

*The Attachment Parenting Book: A Commonsense Guide to
Understanding and Nurturing Your Baby*
by William and Martha Sears

Baby Catcher by William J. Weise

The Baby Catcher: Chronicles of a Modern Midwife by Peggy Vincent

The Birth Book: Everything You Need to Know to Have a Safe and Satisfying Birth by William and Martha Sears

The Birth Partner by Penny Simkin

Birth Reborn by Michel Odent

Birth without Violence by Frederick Leboyer

Birthing from Within: An Extra-Ordinary Guide to Childbirth Preparation by Pam England and Rob Horowitz

The Breastfeeding Book: Everything You Need to Know About Nursing Your Child from Birth Through Weaning by William and Martha Sears

A Child is Born by Lennart Nilsson

Childbirth without Fear by Grantly Dick-Read

The Complete Book of Pregnancy and Childbirth by Sheila Kitzinger

Easing Labor Pain: The Complete Guide to a More Comfortable and Rewarding Birth by Adrienne Lieberman

Fit & Pregnant: The Pregnant Woman's Guide to Exercise by Joan Marie Butler

Five Standards for Safe Childbearing by David Stewart

Gentle Birth Choices: A Guide to Making Informed Decisions About Birthing Centers, Birth Attendants, Water Birth, Home Birth, Hospital Birth by Barbara Harper

A Good Birth, A Safe Birth: Choosing and Having the Childbirth Experience You Want by Diane Korte and Roberta Scaer

Healing Wise by Susun Weed

Heart & Hands: A Midwife's Guide to Pregnancy & Birth
by Elizabeth Davis

Home Birth Advantage by Dr. Mayer Eisenstein

Husband Coached Childbirth: The Bradley Method of Natural Childbirth by Robert Bradley

HypnoBirthing: A Celebration of Life by Marie Mongan

Immaculate Deception: A New Look at Women and Childbirth by Suzanne Arms

Immaculate Deception 2, Myth, Magic and Birth by Suzanne Arms

Ina May's Guide to Natural Childbirth by Ina May Gaskin

The Mask of Motherhood: How Becoming a Mother Changes Our Lives and Why We Never Talk About It by Susan Maushart

Mind Over Labor by Carl Jones

Misconceptions: Truth, Lies, and the Unexpected on the Journey to Motherhood by Naomi Wolf

Mother's Intention: How Belief Shapes Birth by Kim Wildner

Natural Childbirth the Bradley Way by Susan McCutcheon

Nurturing the Unborn Child by Thomas Verney and Pamela Weintraub

Open Season: A Survival Guide for Natural Childbirth and VBAC in the 90s by Nancy Wainer Cohen

Our Babies, Ourselves: How Biology and Culture Shape the Way We Parent by Meredith Small

The Power of Pleasurable Childbirth: Safety, Simplicity, and Satisfaction Are All Within Our Reach! by Laurie Annis Morgan

The Pregnancy Book: Month-by-Month by William and Martha Sears

Pregnancy, Childbirth and the Newborn: Revised and Updated: The Complete Guide by Penny Simkin

Pregnant Feelings
by Rahima Baldwin and Terra Palmarini Richardson

Prenatal Yoga and Natural Childbirth by Jeannine Parvati Baker

Primal Mothering in a Modern World by Hygeia Halfmoon

The Thinking Woman's Guide to a Better Birth by Henci Goer

Seasons of Change: Growing through Pregnancy and Birth by Suzanne Arms

Silent Knife by Nancy Wainer Cohen and Lois Estner

Special Delivery by Rahima Baldwin

Spiritual Midwifery by Ina May Gaskin

The Tao of Motherhood by Vimala McClure

Unassisted Childbirth by Laura Kaplan Shanley

Unassisted Homebirth: An Act of Love by Lynn Griesemer

The VBAC Companion: The Expectant Mother's Guide to Vaginal Birth After Cesarean by Diana Korte

Water Birth: A Midwife's Perspective by Susanna Napierala

What Every Pregnant Woman Should Know: The Truth about Diet and Drugs in Pregnancy by Gail Brewer

Wise Woman Herbal for the Childbearing Year by Susun Weed

Your Pregnancy Week by Week by Glade Curtis and Judith Schuler

HAVING A BABY?
TEN QUESTIONS TO ASK

HAVE YOU DECIDED how to have your baby? The choice is yours!

First, you should learn as much as you can about all your choices. There are many different ways of caring for a mother and her baby during labor and birth.

Birthing care that is better and healthier for mothers and babies is called "mother-friendly." Some birth places or settings are more mother-friendly than others.

A group of experts in birthing care came up with this list of 10 things to look for and ask about. Medical research supports all of these things. These are also the best ways to be mother-friendly.

When you are deciding where to have your baby, you'll probably be choosing from different places such as:

• birth center,

• hospital, or

• home birth service.

Here's what you should expect, and ask for, in your birth experience. Be sure to find out how the people you talk with handle these ten issues about caring for you and your baby. You may want to ask the questions below to help you learn more.

1. *"Who can be with me during labor and birth?"*
    Mother-friendly birth centers, hospitals and home birth
    services will let a birthing mother decide whom she wants
    to have with her during the birth. This includes fathers,
    partners, children, other family members or friends.

    They will also let a birthing mother have with her a person
    who has special training in helping women cope with labor
    and birth. This person is called a doula or labor support
    person. She never leaves the birthing mother alone. She
    encourages her, comforts her and helps her understand
    what's happening to her.

    They will have midwives as part of their staff so that a
    birthing mother can have a midwife with her if she wants to.

2. *"What happens during a normal labor and birth in your setting?"*
    If they give mother-friendly care, they will tell you how they
    handle every part of the birthing process. For example, how
    often do they give the mother a drug to speed up the birth? Or
    do they let labor and birth usually happen on its own timing?

    They will also tell you how often they do certain procedures.
    For example, they will have a record of the percentage of
    C-sections (Cesarean births) they do every year. If the number
    is too high, you'll want to consider having your baby in
    another place or with another doctor or midwife.

    Here are some numbers we recommend you ask about.

    • They should *not* use oxytocin (a drug) to start labor for
      more than 1 in 10 women (10%).

    • They should *not* do an episiotomy (ee-pee-zee-AH-tummy)
      on more than 1 in 5 women (20%). They should be trying
      to bring that number down. (An episiotomy is a cut in the
      opening to the vagina to make it larger for birth. It is not
      necessary most of the time.)

- They should *not* do C-sections on more than 1 in 10 women (10%) if it's a community hospital. The rate should be 15% or less in hospitals which care for many high-risk mothers and babies.

A C-section is a major operation in which a doctor cuts through the mother's stomach into her womb and removes the baby through the opening. Mothers who have had a C-section can often have future babies normally. Look for a birth place in which 6 out of 10 women (60%) or more of the mothers who have had C-sections go on to have their other babies through the birth canal.

3. *"How do you allow for differences in culture and beliefs?"*
   Mother-friendly birth centers, hospitals and home birth services are sensitive to the mother's culture. They know that mothers and families have differing beliefs, values and customs.

   For example, you may have a custom that only women may be with you during labor and birth. Or perhaps your beliefs include a religious ritual to be done after birth. There are many other examples that may be very important to you. If the place and the people are mother-friendly, they will support you in doing what you want to do. Before labor starts tell your doctor or midwife special things you want.

4. *"Can I walk and move around during labor? What position do you suggest for birth?"*
   In mother-friendly settings, you can walk around and move about as you choose during labor. You can choose the positions that are most comfortable and work best for you during labor and birth. (There may be a medical reason for you to be in a certain position.) Mother-friendly settings almost never put a woman flat on her back with her legs up in stirrups for the birth.

5. *"How do you make sure everything goes smoothly when my nurse, doctor, midwife, or agency need to work with each other?"*
   Ask, "Can my doctor or midwife come with me if I have to be moved to another place during labor? Can you help me find people or agencies in my community who can help me before and after the baby is born?"

   Mother-friendly places and people will have a specific plan for keeping in touch with the other people who are caring for you. They will talk to others who give you birth care. They will help you find people or agencies in your community to help you. For example, they may put you in touch with someone who can help you with breastfeeding.

6. *"What things do you normally do to a woman in labor?"*
   Experts say some methods of care during labor and birth are better and healthier for mothers and babies. Medical research shows us which methods of care are better and healthier. Mother-friendly settings only use methods that have been proven to be best by scientific evidence.

   Sometimes birth centers, hospitals and home birth services use methods that are not proven to be best for the mother or the baby. For example, research has shown it's usually not helpful to break the bag of waters.

   Here is a list of things we recommend you ask about. They do not help and may hurt healthy mothers and babies. They are not proven to be best for the mother or baby and are not mother-friendly.

   - They should *not* keep track of the baby's heart rate all the time with a machine (called an electronic fetal monitor). Instead it is best to have your nurse or midwife listen to the baby's heart from time to time.

   - They should *not* break your bag of waters early in labor.

- They should *not* use an IV (a needle put into your vein to give you fluids).

- They should *not* tell you that you can't eat or drink during labor.

- They should *not* shave you.

- They should *not* give you an enema.

A birth center, hospital or home birth service that does these things for most of the mothers is not mother-friendly. Remember, these should not be used without a special medical reason.

7. *"How do you help mothers stay as comfortable as they can be? Besides drugs, how do you help mothers relieve the pain of labor?"* The people who care for you should know how to help you cope with labor. They should know about ways of dealing with your pain that don't use drugs. They should suggest such things as changing your position, relaxing in a warm bath, having a massage and using music. These are called comfort measures.

   Comfort measures help you handle your labor more easily and help you feel more in control. The people who care for you will not try to persuade you to use a drug for pain unless you need it to take care of a special medical problem. All drugs affect the baby.

8. *"What if my baby is born early or has special problems?"* Mother-friendly places and people will encourage mothers and families to touch, hold, breastfeed and care for their babies as much as they can. They will encourage this even if your baby is born early or has a medical problem at birth. (However, there may be a special medical reason you shouldn't hold and care for your baby.)

9. *"Do you circumcise baby boys?"*

Medical research does not show a need to circumcise baby boys. It is painful and risky. Mother-friendly birth places discourage circumcision unless it is for religious reasons.

10. *"How do you help mothers who want to breastfeed?"*

The World Health Organization made this list of ways birth services support breastfeeding.

- They tell all pregnant mothers why and how to breastfeed.

- They help you start breastfeeding within 1 hour after your baby is born.

- They show you how to breastfeed. And they show you how to keep your milk coming in even if you have to be away from your baby for work or other reasons.

- Newborns should have only breast milk. (However, there may be a medical reason they cannot have it right away.)

- They encourage you and the baby to stay together all day and all night. This is called "rooming-in."

- They encourage you to feed your baby whenever he or she wants to nurse, rather than at certain times.

- They should not give pacifiers ("dummies" or "soothers") to breastfed babies.

- They encourage you to join a group of mothers who breastfeed. They tell you how to contact a group near you.

- They have a written policy on breastfeeding. All the employees know about and use the ideas in the policy.

- They teach employees the skills they need to carry out these steps.

Would you like to give this information (and more) to your doctor, midwife or nurse?

This information was taken from *The Mother-Friendly Childbirth Initiative* written for health care providers. You can get a copy of the Initiative for your doctor, midwife, or nurse by mail, e-mail, or on the World Wide Web at www.motherfriendly.org.

©2000 by the Coalition for Improving Maternity Services

Permissions

Like Thunder Rumbling Through, printed by permission of Kelly Camden. Copyright 2002 Kelly Camden

A Love Letter, printed by permission of Anna Stewart. Copyright 2004 Anna Stewart

Cherishing Every Sensation, printed by permission of Susan McClutchey. Copyright 2004 Susan McClutchey

From Denial to Ecstasy, printed by permission of Michele Zeck. Copyright 2004 Michele Zeck

In Her Own Time, printed by permission of Catherine Amador-Locher. Copyright 2003 Catherine Amador-Locher

A Secret Home Birth, printed by permission of Gina Kennedy. Copyright 2004 Gina Kennedy

Bornfree!, reprinted by permission of Laura Shanley. Copyright 2000 Laura Shanley

Heavenly Scent, printed by permission of Leanne Mitchell. Copyright 2004 Leanne Mitchell

A Pivotal Moment, printed by permission of Nancy McInerney. Copyright 2004 Nancy McInerney

CALL FOR MORE BIRTH STORIES

WE ARE ALWAYS on the lookout for inspiring birth stories, as the next book is already in the womb!

If you had a birth that is unusual, inspirational and helpful to expectant mothers, we would love to include your story in our next book. I know that there are many more methods, tools and birth classes that weren't covered in this book, so please feel free to send us stories that represent those pieces as well.

Your story can be a few short pages or many pages long. It can start from before you conceived or even the moment you went into labor. Perhaps you are a doctor, nurse, midwife, doula or family member who wants to share a beautiful birth memory. As long as the family you are writing about approves, we would love to see your story.

For submission guidelines, please refer to our website at www. JourneyIntoMotherhood.com. You can also send an e-mail to stories@whiteheartpublishing.com, or write to:

White Heart Publishing
PO Box 235705
Encintas, CA 92023-5705

In addition to new stories, we want to know: Did this book change the way you think about or experienced birth? Did it open up new ways of seeing things, show you new possibilities, or help you shift someone else's point of view? Please share these things with us! Your comments help direct our next steps in the quest to improve America's birthing culture.

A Message from the Author

THIS BOOK WAS INSPIRED by and born from the passionate commitment to improving women's experience of birth, both individually and collectively. It is a commitment shared by so many, and is growing by the day. The horror stories are fewer, and empowered births are much more common than they were even last year. The culture of birth in America is changing.

But not by chance. Every professional that encourages and/or facilitates natural, normal birth was educated by someone who is passionate about women's right to birth in ways that align with and support her instinctual and innate feminine wisdom. Every facility that supports natural birth is part of a network of institutions that set standards, uphold integrity, establish legality and ensure safety.

These institutions exist because people care and are willing to take action, willing to step forward and say, "This matters!"

As one of these people, I highly encourage you to join us. Some way, somehow, lend your voice in support of mother- and baby-friendly hospitals.

Write to your local hospitals to express your position. Encourage the addition of birthing tubs and birthing balls to labor-and-delivery rooms. Ask that labor-and-delivery staff be educated in the many natural birthing modalities, so at the very least they are familiar with Bradley techniques, the language of HypnoBirthing, the philosophy behind Leboyer techniques, and the principles of active labor, to name just a few. Ask that the dangers and side effects of using drugs be included in hospital-sponsored childbirth preparation classes. There is so much that hospitals could be doing to encourage satisfying birth experiences, but only your voices will inspire movement in this direction.

You can also join one (or more!) of the many organizations that support and advocate the rights and options of birthing women. I encourage you to consider and explore the following:

International Cesarean Awareness Network (ICAN): a nonprofit organization that works to improve maternal-child health by preventing unnecessary cesareans through education, providing support for cesarean recovery and promoting Vaginal Birth After Cesarean.   www.ican-online.org

Coalition for Improving Maternity Services (CIMS): a collaborative effort of individuals and more than 50 organizations representing over 90,000 members. It promotes a wellness model of maternity care that improves birth outcomes and substantially reduces costs.
www.motherfriendly.org

Citizens for Midwifery (CfM): the only national consumer-based group promoting the midwives model of care. CfM works to provide information and resources that promote and encourage midwifery care across the country.   www.cfmidwifery.org

Even if you don't intend to birth in hospital, contact your local hospitals and let them know exactly what it is about their policies and procedures that turn you off. A hospital is a business, and when hospitals come to realize how much money they lose through their current standards, they consider changing the policies, procedures and options available to women and their families. Your letters support positive birth experiences for all the women who will birth there in the years to come.

About the Author

SHERI MENELLI HAS DEDICATED her career to the education and empowerment of pregnant woman, focusing on techniques for easing labor, birth options, tools and resources for positive birth experiences, and breastfeeding. She taught Hypno-Birthing classes for several years and has assisted many women through labor and birth. Sheri produced and co-hosted a radio show, *The Real Side of Birth*, interviewing dozens of moms, doulas, midwives, doctors, nurses and childbirth authors to uncover the secrets to a powerful and positive birth experience. She also authored and produced two guided meditation CDs: *Light Meditation* and *Breastfeeding Meditation*.

Her experience as a childbirth educator revealed the impact of birth stories on the birth experiences of the expectant women who heard them. In her work she also found that most pregnant women weren't aware of their rights and the options that could make birth such a natural, intuitive experience. This led to Sheri's obsession with finding and sharing positive, empowering birth stories, and her devotion to teaching women how to empower themselves during labor.

Sheri is the mother of three daughters, Allison, and twins Lauren and Caitlin.

**If you have comments or questions about the book,
please call 760-431-2228, or write to:**
P.O. Box 235705
Encinitas, CA 92023-5705
comments@journeyintomotherhood.com

In addition to authoring books, articles, and guided meditation CDs, Sheri is also a talented public speaker. If you are interested in booking Sheri for a speaking engagement, please contact her directly at: *sheri@journeyintomotherhood.com*.

Sheri also offers birth- and baby-related tele-classes, including:
Secrets to a Better Birth
Caring for Your Newborn
Baby Sleep Magic

For the current schedule, please check our website:
www.JourneyIntoMotherhood.com.